Towards a Global Polity

'This collection of essays on the evolution of a "global polity" is an exciting and important contribution to the scholarly literature on globalisation.'

Kim Richard Nossal, *Queen's University, Canada*

'Essential reading for faculty preparing to teach courses on global governance, globalisation and the many other courses which need to incorporate these ideas.'

Richard Langhorne, *Director, Center for Global Change and Governance, Rutgers University-Newark*

Globalisation is also a political phenomenon. While 'one world government' is not on the cards, the globalisation of political life has progressed significantly over the last decades. Rather than adding on to existing theoretical frameworks such as the realist picture of international anarchy or the English School's 'international society', this volume starts out from the idea of the world as one interconnected political system and explores ways and perspectives to analyse it as such.

The contributors examine central aspects of this emerging global polity such as the role of law, of networks and of civil society. They discuss key theoretical and meta-theoretical questions on how to analyse and theorise the global polity, what drives it forward, and whether it can be democratised.

Morten Ougaard is a Reader in International Political Economy at Copenhagen Business School. His research interests include international political economy, global governance, the international regulation of business and US foreign policy.

Richard Higgott is Director of the Centre for the Study of Globalisation and Regionalisation and Professor of International Political Economy at the University of Warwick. His recent publications include two edited volumes, *Non State Actors and Authority in the International System* and *The Political Economy of Globalisation*.

Routledge/Warwick Studies in Globalisation

Edited by Richard Higgott and published in association with the Centre for the Study of Globalisation and Regionalisation, University of Warwick.

What is globalisation and does it matter? How can we measure it? What are its policy implications? The Centre for the Study of Globalisation and Regionalisation at the University of Warwick is an international site for the study of key questions such as these in the theory and practice of globalisation and regionalisation. Its agenda is avowedly interdisciplinary. The work of the Centre will be showcased in this new series.

This series comprises two strands:

Warwick Studies in Globalisation addresses the needs of students and teachers, and the titles will be published in hardback and paperback. Titles include:

Globalisation and the Asia-Pacific
Contested territories
Edited by Kris Olds, Peter Dicken, Philip F. Kelly, Lily Kong and Henry Wai-chung Yeung

Regulating the Global Information Society
Edited by Christopher Marsden

Banking on Knowledge
The genesis of the global development network
Edited by Diane Stone

Historical Materialism and Globalisation
Essays on continuity and change
Edited by Hazel Smith and Mark Rupert

Civil Society and Global Finance
Edited by Jan Aart Scholte with Albrecht Schnabel

Towards a Global Polity
Edited by Morten Ougaard and Richard Higgott

Routledge/Warwick Studies in Globalisation is a forum for innovative new research intended for a high-level specialist readership, and the titles will be available in hardback only. Titles include:

1. Non-State Actors and Authority in the Global System
Edited by Richard Higgott, Geoffrey Underhill and Andreas Bieler

2. Globalisation and Enlargement of the European Union
Austrian and Swedish social forces in the struggle over membership
Andreas Bieler

3. Rethinking Empowerment
Gender and development in a global/local world
Edited by Jane L. Parpart, Shirin M. Rai and Kathleen A. Staudt

Towards a Global Polity

**Edited by Morten Ougaard and
Richard Higgott**

London and New York

First published 2002 by Routledge
11 New Fetter Lane, London EC4P 4EE

Simultaneously published in the USA and Canada
by Routledge
29 West 35th Street, New York, NY 10001

Routledge is an imprint of the Taylor & Francis Group

© 2002 Morten Ougaard and Richard Higgott

Typeset in Baskerville by Wearset Ltd, Boldon, Tyne and Wear
Printed and bound in Great Britain by TJ International, Padstow,
Cornwall

British Library Cataloguing in Publication Data
A catalogue record for this book is available from the British Library

Library of Congress Cataloging in Publication Data
A catalog record for this book has been requested

ISBN 0-415-27770-1 (hbk)
ISBN 0-415-27771-X (pbk)

Contents

Illustrations

Figures

Tables

Boxes

Illustrations

Contributors

Sven Bislev is Associate Professor of Political Science and Head of the Department of Intercultural Communication and Management, Copenhagen Business School.

A. Claire Cutler is Associate Professor, Department of Political Science, University of Victoria, Canada.

Hans Krause Hansen is Associate Professor in Latin American Studies, Department of Intercultural Communication and Management, Copenhagen Business School.

Richard Higgott is Professor of International Political Economy and Director, Centre for the Study of Globalisation and Regionalisation, University of Warwick.

Knud Erik Jørgensen is Associate Professor of International Politics, Department of Political Science, University of Aarhus, Denmark.

Anthony McGrew is Professor of International Politics, Department of Politics, University of Southampton.

Craig N. Murphy is Margaret E. Ball Professor of International Relations, Wellesley College, USA.

Morten Ougaard is Reader in International Political Economy, Department of Intercultural Communication and Management, Copenhagen Business School.

Ben Rosamond is Senior Lecturer in Politics and International Studies and Principal Research Fellow, Centre for the Study of Globalisation and Regionalisation, University of Warwick.

Dorte Salskov-Iversen is Associate Professor in British Studies and Vice Dean, Department of Intercultural Communication and Management, Copenhagen Business School.

Jan Aart Scholte is Professor of Politics and International Studies and Senior Associate, Centre for the Study of Globalisation and Regionalisation, University of Warwick.

Diane Stone is Reader in Politics and International Studies and Senior Associate, Centre for the Study of Globalisation and Regionalisation, University of Warwick.

Georg Sørensen is Professor of International Politics, Department of Political Science, University of Aarhus, Denmark.

Michael Zürn is Professor of International Politics and Transnational Relations, Institute of Political Science and Co-Director of the Institute for Intercultural and International Studies, University of Bremen, Germany.

Series editor's preface

Warwick Studies in Globalisation are books arising out of the activities of the ESRC Centre for the Study of Globalisation and Regionalisation at the University of Warwick (CSGR). Founded in October 1997 as a result of its success in the ESRC's Thematic Priorities Competition to establish a research centre in the area of globalisation studies, CSGR has rapidly become an international site for the study of key issues in the theory and practice of globalisation and regionalisation. The Centre's agenda is avowedly inter-disciplinary. Research staff are drawn from international relations, political science, economics, law and sociology. While the Centre is committed first and foremost to scholarly excellence, it also strives to be problem solving in its methodological orientation and outlook.

Cognisant of the now ubiquitous and problematic nature of the notion of 'globalisation', three broad categories of activity inform and underwrite the research agenda of the Centre: (i) how do we understand the notion of globalisation?; (ii) can, and if so how, do we measure its impacts across a range of issue areas?; and (iii) what are the policy implications of the changes arising from globalisation as both theory and fact? Globalisation is seen as multi-dimensional – economic, political, cultural, ideological. Thus work in CSGR sees globalisation in at least two ways. First, as the emergence of a set of sequences and processes that are increasingly unhindered by territorial and jurisdictional barriers and that enhance the spread of trans-border practices in economic, political and socio-cultural domains. Second, as a discourse of political and economic knowledge offering multiple views of how to make the postmodern world manageable. Centre research and publications attempt to ask what kinds of constraints and opportunities globalisation poses for independent policy initiatives on the part of policy-makers in both public and private domains, and under what conditions these constraints are enhanced or mitigated by globalising tendencies.

Within these broad contexts, empirical work at CSGR focuses on three principal areas of research: (i) on how particular regional projects in Asia, Europe and the Americas relate to wider globalising pressures and initiatives; (ii) on the development of international institutions, rules and policy competencies on questions of trade, competition and international finance and investment; and (iii) normative questions about governance, sovereignty, democratisation, accountability and policy-making under conditions of globalisation. Indeed, CSGR research has placed a particular emphasis on the wider normative nature of many of the questions arising from the continued progression of globalisation and the accompanying emergence of counter-tendencies and sites of resistance to globalisation at regional and local levels and that give rise to different understandings of the importance of space and territoriality. *Routledge/Warwick Studies in Globalisation* provide an avenue for the publication of scholarly research monographs, policy-oriented studies and collections of original themed essays in the area of the research agenda of CSGR.

This current volume on the *global polity* perfectly represents the research agenda of CSGR. It is both a theoretically inquisitive and policy-relevant investigation into the question of the degree to which the international system of governance beyond the borders of the territorial state might be developing polity-like characteristics. It reflects the fruits of a collaborative endeavour by some of the key researchers at CSGR with several scholars from the Copenhagen Business School. Coordinated by Morten Ougaard and Richard Higgott, the contributors in this volume met for two days in May 2000 at Toruplund, outside Copenhagen, to present and discuss the initial drafts of their chapters. Attempts were made to hammer out an understanding of what constitutes the notion of a 'global polity', indeed, to ask whether the notion of the global polity is a meaningful concept. It was never the intention of the group to attempt to secure a common definition of a global polity, but it did become clear to all involved in the project that there was something different about the contemporary global era that required us to think about it in a different way to much contemporary, disciplinary-based, or indeed sub-disciplinary-based literature. This volume represents the fruits of this endeavour. In my judgement, it makes a valuable contribution to an increasingly important debate about the nature of global governance in the contemporary global era.

Richard Higgott
Centre for the
Study of Globalisation
and Regionalisation
University of Warwick

Acknowledgements

This volume could not have been produced without the help of a number of people. In addition to people acknowledged by the individual authors, the editors of the volume would like to thank the following people for their help and support. At the Copenhagen Business School we would like to thank Jane Mølgaard Rossen for organising the initial workshop, Jette Steen Knudsen and Kevin McGovern for participating in the workshop and their comments on several chapters. At the University of Warwick thanks for their support in the organisation of the workshop go to Jill Pavey and Denise Hewlett and also to Denise and Kevin for their assistance in the production of the manuscript. We would also like to thank Liliana Pop for her editorial input. The workshop was funded by a grant from the Danish Social Science Research Council and the Economic and Social Science Research Council of the UK.

Abbreviations

AFL-CIO	American Federation of Labor-Central Industrial Organization
AIDS	acquired immune deficiency syndrome
ANZCERTA	Australia New Zealand Closer Economic Relations Trade Agreement
APEC	Asia-Pacific Economic Council
ASEAN	Association of South East Asian Nations
BIS	Bank for International Settlements
CEOs	Chief Executive Officers
CEPS	Centre for European Policy Studies
CFSP	Common Foreign and Security Policy
CITES	Convention on International Trade in Endangered Species of Wild Fauna and Flora
CLAD	Latin American Center for Development Administration
CSCE	Commission on Security and Cooperation in Europe
CSGR	Centre for the Study of Globalisation and Regionalisation
CUSTA	Canada–United States Free Trade Agreement
EC	European Community
ECOSOC	United Nations Economic and Social Council
EEU	Environment and Economics Unit
EINIRAS	European Information Network on International Relations and Area Studies
EMU	Economic and Monetary Union
ESRC	Economic and Social Research Council
EU	European Union
FAO	Food and Agriculture Organization
FDI	foreign direct investment
FRG	Federal Republic of Germany
FTA	free trade agreement
G3	Group of three
G7	Group of seven
G7(8)	Group of seven (eight)
GATT	General Agreement on Tariffs and Trade

GCC	Global Climate Coalition
GDN	Global Development Network
GDR	German Democratic Republic
GNP	gross national product
GPA	Global Programme on AIDS
GSM	Global Social Movement
HIPC	Heavily Indebted Poor Countries
HIV	Human Immuno-Virus
IAEA	International Atomic Energy Agency
IAEN	International AIDS Economic Network
IAPAC	International Association of Physicians in AIDS Care
IAS	International AIDS Society
ICASO	International Council of AIDS Service Organizations
ICSID	International Center for the Settlement of Investment Disputes
IGO	international governmental organization
ILO	International Labour Organization
IMF	International Monetary Fund
IO	international organization
IPE	international political economy
IR	international relations
ISO	International Organization for Standardization
ITL	International Trade Law
JHA	Justice and Home Affairs
MAI	Multilateral Agreement on Investment
MERCOSUR	Southern Cone Common Market
MLG	multi-level governance
MNC	multinational corporation
MOSOP	Movement for the Survival of the Ogoni People
MTN	Multilateral Trade Negotiations
NAALC	North American Agreement on Labor Cooperation
NAFTA	North American Free Trade Agreement
NATO	North Atlantic Treaty Organization
NED	National Endowment for Democracy
NGO	non-governmental organization
NIEO	New International Economic Order
NPM	New Public Management
OECD	Organization for Economic Cooperation and Development
OPEC	Organization of Petrol-Exporting Countries
OSCE	Organization for Security Cooperation in Europe
PD	Prisoners' Dilemma
PUMA	Public Management Programme (of OECD)
SALT	Strategic Arms Limitation Talks

SIGMA	Support for Improvement in Government and Management in Central and Eastern European countries
SIPRI	Stockholm International Peace Research Institute
START	US–Russian Strategic Arms Reduction Treaty
TDC	transnational discourse community
TEU	Treaty of European Union
TNGO	transnational non-governmental organization
TNO	Institute of Environmental and Energy Technology (The Netherlands)
TREVI	Text Retrieval and Enrichment for Vital Information
TRIPS	Trade-Related Aspects of International Property Rights
UIA	Union of International Associations
UK	United Kingdom
UN	United Nations
UNAIDS	United Nations Programme on HIV/AIDS
UNDP	United Nations Development Programme
UNEP	United Nations Environment Programme
USA	United States of America
USAID	United States Agency for International Development
WB	World Bank
WBI	World Bank Institute
WEF	World Economic Forum
WHO	World Health Organization
WMO	World Meteorological Organization
WTO	World Trade Organization

Introduction

Beyond system and society – towards a global polity?

Richard Higgott and Morten Ougaard

Beyond the internationalization of the state – the globalization of political life

Historical continuities notwithstanding, there is something new afoot. Globalization, that most over-used expression after the end of the Cold War is, despite the hype, different from previous historical eras.[1] Moreover, in addition to its now more commonly understood economic and cultural dimensions, the parameters of a concomitant process of political evolution, we suggest, can also be discerned. This we choose to call the emerging *global polity*. We recognize this is a contentious claim, likely to provoke resistance in a range of differing scholar communities of thought in international relations. Some scholars, with good cause, would argue that they have been talking about the institutionalization of world politics for more than twenty years (Keohane and Nye 1997). Quite so, but this is not the agenda of the essays in this volume which rather aspire to clarify a range of conceptual ways of thinking about what we call the 'globalization of political life'. The argument to be advanced in this volume is not, we hasten to add at the outset, simply an exercise in academic or scholarly introspection. Strong connections between the emerging discourse on the global polity and contemporary political practice across the borders of the nation-state already exist. Theorizing about the nature of politics in the abstract casts massive policy shadows in the opening stages of the twenty-first century, and, we should add, vice versa.

Once upon a time, claims to the existence of a nascent global polity would have appeared to be grand, courageous, or naively idealistic. We hope to persuade the readers of this volume that this is no longer the case. While recognizing the complexity of modern life and particularly the continued role of nation-states as formal sovereign actors, we wish to transcend traditional state-centric understandings of international politics by offering a series of insights and perspectives on non-state processes that are now generating changes which, until now, have been primarily handled by theoretical *supplementation* rather than radical theoretical restructuring. We mean we wish to progress beyond a process in which neo-liberal institutionalism, to give but one example at this stage, has gradually added a series of non-state and transnational dimensions to traditional state-centred realist understandings of international relations. Our aim, rather than use a theoretical strategy of 'additionality', is to start from a different place. We propose, as a theoretical starting point, a view of the world as a much more inter-connected whole than much contemporary academic literature, and policy practice, would concede.

This claim is not as radical as it might at first seem. There is already a substantial body of empirical evidence of actors and activities that constitutes the 'stuff' of the emerging global polity. Similarly, there is now a large body of well-known secondary scholarly material on the topic, even if the word 'polity' is not the common descriptor used by all writers (see *inter alia*, McGrew 1992a and 1992b; Zacher 1992; Waters 1995; Zürn 1998; Reinecke 1998; Held *et al.* 1999 and Higgott and Payne 2000). The essence of the concept of 'the polity' exists in a range of different guises. Concepts like international or global governance (Rosenau 1992; Murphy 1994; Commission on Global Governance 1995; Young 1997; Hewson and Sinclair 1999 to name but a few), geo-governance (McGrew 1997), the post-national constellation (Habermas 1998; Zürn 1999), the world polity (Brown 1992; Ruggie 1998), the global polity (McGrew 1992b; Ougaard 1999b), or even the world political system (Luard 1990) or the global state (Albrow 1996; Shaw 2000) if not interchangeable, at least point in the direction of a system with 'polity'-like qualities. Even the more focused policy-oriented work such as that on global public policy undertaken at the World Bank (Reinecke 1998) and global public goods undertaken at UNDP (Kaul *et al.* 1999) emphasize the *global* nature of these processes.

Towards 'polityness'

Polityness is in a state of evolution and is, very often, contested. Nevertheless we believe it is possible to identify at least five principal characteristics. First, most obviously, there is a growing political inter-connectedness. This is a phenomenon recognized several decades ago (Keohane and Nye 1977), but inter-connectedness in a global polity, as opposed to a more traditional understanding of an international system, is not only between states, but also supra-, sub- and non-state actors. It is nicely illustrated by the way in which sub-national systems of government increasingly interact with their counterparts and other non-state actors beyond the borders of the nation-state.

Second, more concretely, as scholars such as Reinecke (1998) and many others (e.g. McGrew 1992a and 1992b; Zacher 1992; Zürn 1998; Held *et al.* 1999; Braithwaite and Drahos 2000) have identified, there is a vast and interlocking network of global regulation and sites of decision-making where policies of a (quasi-) global nature are made. The obvious examples of such activity are to be found in the international organizations (especially in the trade, financial and environmental domains) that have developed throughout the second half of the twentieth century. But also in the last quarter of the century, organizations of private and non-state regulation have stretched out across the public–private divide in international life (see Cutler *et al.* 1999). Similarly, regulatory agencies operate at both regional and inter-regional levels (see Coleman and Underhill 1998; Barry and Keith 1999). For the purpose of defining the global polity, the often limited efficacy of some of these organizations is of less salience than their existence.

Third, perhaps a more difficult dimension of this process to capture, but no less important for that, is the growing sense of 'community' that appears to be developing beyond the confines of the state. As Robertson (1992: 132) would have it, globality is defined in the context of a consciousness 'of the world as a single place'. This is not to suggest the emergence of a common set of global values rather than to indicate the growth of thinking about 'the world' as an identifiable sense of place or space where different values can legitimately contest one another. While the consensus may be minimal, there nevertheless exists a recognition of the appropriateness of global discourse in the emerging global public space. A quintessential fact of international political life has been the multiplication of global gatherings. These can range from meetings of small non-governmental organizations (NGOs) and Global Social Movements (GSMs), through to the UN conference system. Gatherings at the global level cover issues as diverse as gender, development, environment, welfare, cities, security to the Davos gatherings of the rich and powerful of the private (and public) sector policy-making world and their counterpart gatherings such as the Porto Allegro World Social Forum – that argue over the validity of a multiple array of global principles and practices. Again, while there may not be agreement arising from these global public discourses, the fact that they take place is, we would argue, testament to the existence of 'global polity-like behaviour'. The frequent absence of consensus in most of these global discourses does not rule out the recognition of 'community' present in that strand of activity that constitutes the emerging global polity.

In short, while there is no agreement over the legitimacy of many global processes, there would appear to be a shared understanding of the emergence of these processes. In contrast to what is accepted practice within the confines of the developed nation-state, the global polity does not yet exhibit a unified set of settled constitutions, institutions and practices. This is not a reaffirmation of the traditional realist or systems theorists' understanding of international anarchy where the best that can be hoped for is the existence of a set of weak norms and principles to which traditional state actors may or may not adhere. Rather, we are advancing an understanding of the global polity in which the existence of norms and principles that guide states are also joined by an ever-thickening web of institutions and regulatory activities at the global level that approximate to some extent the developments that have occurred throughout the nineteenth and twentieth centuries within the borders of the sovereign state. Evidence of this process is to be found in Murphy's chapter in this volume and in his discussion of the development of international organization throughout the twentieth century (see Murphy 1994). Even if states and non-state actors are in disagreement about the norms and principles that are emerging, in practice by the very fact they are contesting the nature of these principles and practices in global assemblies and other instances of global public space, it has the consequence (unintended as it may be) of furthering the development of a global polity.

Fourth, the significance of the global polity as a category is enhanced by the weakening effect that globalization has on the domestic polity. Richard Devetak and Richard Higgott have argued that one of the major impacts of the consolidation of globalization in OECD countries is the manner in which it has begun to weaken the social bond between citizens and the state that had been developed since the consolidation of the Westphalian system. This argument is an extension of an earlier argument about the relativization of individual reference from national societies (Robertson 1992: 26–27). In this context, the language of democracy and justice takes on a more important rhetorical role in a global context at the same time as globalization attenuates the hold of democratic communities within the confines of the territorial state. Indeed, as the role of the nation-state as a vehicle for democratic engagement becomes more problematic, the clamour for democratic engagement at the global level may become stronger.

The final characteristic we would wish to emphasize is that we are at the beginning, not the end of this process. This is not to suggest that such processes do not have historical parallels nor suffer setbacks and reversals, but rather that from the time of ancient Rome through that of medieval Western Europe to today, the secular trend has been in the direction of more complex, more all-embracing institutional organization (Murphy 1994; Braithwaite and Drahos 2000). Were Marx alive today, he would be anticipating the globalizing of the political superstructure to accompany the globalization of the economy. Similarly, were Weber with us today, we feel sure he would see the appropriateness of attempting to theorize the global polity. Of course, nor are we suggesting that the form of this evolution is predetermined. No teleology is implied. It is for this reason that global life is a political issue. It is politics (not just dramatic economic and technological change) that will constitute the shape and evolution of the global polity over the coming decades.

Moreover, with the events of the last decade, as economic globalization (especially the deregulation of the global financial markets) has exacerbated financial volatility, these questions have taken on a greater sense of urgency. The Asian financial crisis, its extension to other erstwhile emerging markets, the Battle of Seattle, and many other manifestations of the desire for 'voice' by traditionally less influential actors in global policy-making are but empirical indicators and motivators of a new global 'meta'-politics, a politics that is not only concerned with the substance of policy output from global institutions, but where also the 'regime architecture' has been politicized by state and non-state actors. This meta-politics emphasizes questions of legitimacy and accountability not present during the tighter disciplinary era of Cold War politics when order and stability were the more salient questions.

The Cold War veil over international relations scholarship

The Cold War veiled the emerging global polity from intellectual attention. It did so to such an extent that the study of its incipient forms seemed permanently relegated to secondary status as a research topic pursued mainly by idealist and radical scholars. The most obvious reason for this situation was the dominant presence for almost fifty years of a deep global divide in world politics which inevitably overshadowed the real, albeit weak, development of a sense of global community. But the Cold War had the added effect of screening the magnitude of change that was taking place in the global economy outside the communist countries, the effect of which was to stifle the concomitant understanding of the organizational and political impact that globalization was having beyond the borders of the nation-state.

In short, and notably in the USA, scholars and analysts were so strongly focused on the security dynamic of the Cold War, especially with the emergence of the neo-realist challenge in the late 1970s (cf. Waltz 1979) to the interdependence theory that had developed in the previous decade, that they did not see what was happening around them. Indeed, the study of international organization and political integration became marginalized in mainstream international relations scholarship as it went in search of an over-arching rationalist science of international politics (see Katzenstein *et al.* 1988 and Breslin and Higgott 2000). Other important innovations, in both theory and practice, such as the development of the European Union (EU) and the emergence of sophisticated theorizing about the evolution of regional integration in Europe went off the mainstream screen. North–South issues, an important dimension of the international discussion in the first decades after the decolonization process, similarly disappeared from discussion with the hardening of the North towards Southern requests for a New International Economic Order (NIEO) in the early 1970s (see Cox 1981; Higgott 1983; Ougaard 1984; Krasner 1985) and as we entered the era of global free market liberalism of the 1980s.

The effect of these movements were, we suggest, to turn analysts' attention away from the manner in which the nascent characteristics of the global polity were slowly forming. The 1990s, however, have reversed these trends, the theory and practice of integration have now re-emerged as a central scholarly priority and the South (although no longer referred to as such) has been incorporated into the discussion and concerns of the multilateral agendas. This is not to suggest that the conflict between the North and South over how the global economic order is to be managed is resolved. Indeed, the contrary situation is the case. It is quite clear that some key battles of the early twenty-first century are going to be precisely over distributive and justice questions in North–South relations (Woods 1999a). Rather, to return to our theme, it is to insist that these agenda items and the manner in which they will be addressed – that is, in global fora – reinforce our argument about the emergence of a global polity.

Pre-empting our critics

We do, of course, anticipate some resistance to the argument advanced above. At this stage we see at least five responses from those who would resist a suggestion of the emergence of a global polity. The first pertains to the question of constitutionality. How is it possible, critics would argue, to talk about the existence of a polity in the absence of constitutional arrangements or formally codified norms? This, we would argue, is an important question in some contexts, but not the relevant question here. Formal constitutional arrangements are more the essence of statehood than they are of politics. Constitutionalism is an element of a polity, but not the defining one. Moreover, constitutional arrangements can emerge over time through custom and practice. It is not always the case that they are formally codified. At the risk of seeming frivolous, were constitutional codification the essential prerequisite, it would be possible to argue that the United Kingdom was not a polity.

A second objection to the identification of a global polity would, no doubt, point to the absence of universalism and the unevenness of, indeed, in some cases, total lack of inclusion of large sections of the world in these processes. The argument would be that this renders unacceptable any notion of full globality. Again, as important as this issue is, it is not the central question here. We fully recognize the reality of unevenness and the lack of universalism in the emerging global polity. That the processes may be partial does not make them any the less real. This unevenness should only be expected. As Robert Cox (1987: 258) has noted, what he calls the 'international political structure . . . appears to be more evolved, more definitive in some of its parts, less formed, more fluid, in others, and connections between the parts are more stable in some cases and more tenuous in others'. Indeed, it is clearly most developed in the northern world and especially at the regional level (cf. the EU and North American Free Trade Agreement (NAFTA)), and in the USA's inter-regional relations across the Atlantic and, albeit to a lesser extent, across the Pacific. These linkages are clearly least developed between the North and the South (where the relationship is one of asymmetric integration of the South into the global economy) and between states and non-state actors in the South where the linkages are more often simply undeveloped.

The third objection we would wish to anticipate is that we might simply be equating the global polity with the emerging international institutional architecture of global governance. This too we would resist. We see the architecture of global governance as but a component, although a central one, of a wider global polity. To date, understandings of global governance that have emerged principally in the policy-oriented literature have focused on the concept of governance as one of effectiveness and efficiency. While this is important, it is, we think, limited and precludes from the agenda the widening discussion on questions of accountability, legitimization and democracy that have been developing, with less impact to this stage it must be stressed, in the academic literature. There is an explanation for the disjuncture between the policy-oriented analysis of governance and the scholarly analysis. The narrower understanding of global governance is very much reflective of that era that came to be known as the Washington Consensus (see Higgott 2001).

Global governance was about how best to implement the kinds of economic policies that had underwritten the rapid expansion of the global economy during the 1980s and 1990s and how to extend these systems of management to the developing world. A new understanding of global governance has gained currency over the last few years as the articulation of a counter-globalization view has developed among a range of serious non-state actors and global social movements formerly outside the mainstream of international policy-making. Significant milestones in the development of these counter positions on globalization are to be found with the response to the Multilateral Agreement on Investment (MAI), the Asian financial crisis and the challenges to a new MTN round at the Seattle World Trade Organization (WTO) Ministerial Meeting that closed the twentieth century and the creation of the World Social Forum at the beginning of the new century. There is now a much stronger normative agenda that cannot be contained within the existing structures of global institutional governance.

This is not to suggest that a normative agenda for a more just and humane global order did not exist prior to the signal effects of the late 1990s. Rather, the point is that the scholarly contributions of authors such as Richard Falk (1999), David Held (1991) and work by international commissions such as *Our Common Future* (World Commission on Environment and Development 1987) and *Our Global Neighbourhood* (Commission on Global Governance 1995) did not make much impact on the corridors of the international institutions and Treasuries of the major world powers until there was a recognition that without a stronger normative reform agenda the prospects of continued global economic liberalization might be much more problematic than had previously been assumed.

Moreover, the discussion of the global polity extends beyond the question of global governance (even when it is writ large to consider normative questions as well as questions of effectiveness and efficiency.) There are two sub-issues that need to be addressed here. First, the policy-oriented literature is not, of its own accord, sufficient to assist in the explanation of what is happening in the larger context. In order to explain the evolution of the governance system it needs to be located within the context of a wider understanding, what we have chosen to call the global polity. Logically, for instance, the discussion of global public goods, ways to provide them, and reasons for their underprovision, requires a definition of the 'global public' as a 'publicum' that is entitled to such goods. According to Kaul *et al.* (1999: 9–11) this 'publicum' ideally should consist of humanity as a whole, including future generations. Thus the scholarly discourse on global public goods presupposes a notion of humanity as not only the total sum of individuals in the world but also as a collectivity, a community, to which public goods should be provided. Without wishing to seem excessively scholarly, the emergence of the global governance system can only be understood within wider epistemological and ontological contexts. For obvious reasons, this is the domain of the scholar, not the practitioner.

Second, global governance has traditionally been thought of as a top-down phenomenon driven by inter-governmental organizations. It is nowadays quite clear that a major impetus for the organization of global political life is coming from the bottom up, driven by non-state and sub-state actors as well as the more traditional actors in international relations. If private actors coordinate their political claims to national government policy across borders, this is not an instance of global governance in the sense it has been traditionally understood, but rather an instance of what we would call the globalization of political life. Indeed, at a lesser formal level, it is sufficient for national actors merely to inspire each other through processes of cross-border socialization and policy learning for it to be meaningful to talk of internationalization of political life. Thus we would argue, the emerging global polity is more than global governance in the traditional, narrower sense (Lynch 1999; Keck and Sikkink 1998; Hansen *et al.* 2001; Stone and Scholte in this volume for examples of different types of transnational networks and activities).

A fourth objection, and the one that those of a realist persuasion would find the most significant, pertains to the issue of security in contemporary international relations. A realist line of argument might suggest that talking about the emergence of 'polityness' in the economic and social domain might be acceptable in an era of increased interdependence but such a line of argument would not be acceptable in the security context. We would wish to resist this critique by insisting that the empirical evidence on the response of major actors to security questions over the last several decades, and especially since the end of the Cold War, allows for an alternative reading. Key events such as the building of coalitions during the Gulf War; and following the attack on the World Trade Center on 11 September 2001 and the humanitarian interventions in Kosovo and East Timor, for example, can be interpreted as merely repetitions of traditional great power politics. However, a 'global polity'-style argument of the kind advanced in this book could also see them as normatively progressive moves towards what we might call the joint policing of the global neighbourhood. Drawing domestic historical analogies, such events could be seen to have a correspondence with the establishment of domestic social orders in the early stages of state- and nation-building.

A fifth and final objection is essentially a methodological-cum-theoretical one. We need to confront the question of whether the topic of the global polity is actually too vast for meaningful scholarly inquiry. There are several responses that can be made to this suggestion that in no way attempt to minimize the seriousness of the point. First, there is already a range of theoretical work, across time and the intellectual and ideological spectrum, that attempts to grasp global totalities. Even ignoring Marx, notably here is that intellectual tradition of world systems theory that dates from Braudel to Wallerstein and Samir Amin or in the tradition of Marx scholars such as Robert Cox (1987), other historians such as Charles Tilly, more specifically within mainstream traditions in international relations scholars such as Modelski (1990), Waltz (1979) and Gilpin (1981) attempt to establish broad theories of international politics; also Keohane and Nye in *Power and Interdependence* (1989[1977]) made significant statements about world politics as a whole.

A further point to be noted here is that, in contrast to the suggestions of some (see Viotti and Kauppi 1983), attempts to totalize are not *ipso facto* attempts to produce radical explanations of change on a global scale but they do have a common theme in their approach. All of them demonstrate that in order to grasp the totality of the global structure, several core, simplified assumptions and abstract concepts are required to make the process manageable. The crucial issue is to secure the most appropriate concept. Here we think that the concept of the global polity is one that is appropriate for its time.

We think it is much more appropriate than either a neo-realist understanding of international system (Waltz 1979), on the one hand, or, for example, a so-called English School concept of an international society. This is not to demean the significance of the notion of international society as developed by Bull and earlier exponents of the English School such as Carr and Wight (Carr 1946; Wight 1977; Bull 1977). They were attempting to create a seriously historically informed understanding of international relations. This we think is the correct approach rather than attempt to create ahistorical theoretical generalization (*pace* Waltz) or to privilege a situation where the world is seen as an ever-maturing anarchy with the state still as the paradigm defining theoretical variable *pace* Buzan's (1993) recent reformulations of the English School. Rather, it is to suggest the now limited utility of the concepts of both system and society in an era of globalization precisely because, continuities notwithstanding, we are in a new historical phase that has evolved in the twenty-five years since *The Anarchical Society* was first published. The key point is to develop a notion of the totality that transcends the state-centred perspective in a conscious theoretical fashion rather than (*pace* Kenichi Ohmae 1990 and 1995 or even Susan Strange 1996) in a populist dismissal of the state as a serious political actor under conditions of globalization.

Thus, our response to the methodological concern with the vastness of the concept of the global polity is not only are we in good historical and intellectual company, but that without an attempt to generalize – given that abstraction is the hallmark of good theory – theoretical advance is unlikely. The dual approach adopted in this volume is essential. The study of the constituent dimension of the global polity requires the larger conceptual context. Conversely, attempts to develop a theory of the global polity merely by adding new concepts and metaphors without grounding them in empirical analysis of the constituent parts would prove equally sterile. Theoretical problem-solving is not achieved by throwing metaphors at it.

Defining the global polity

The preceding discussion represents an attempt to establish some ground on which to move towards a tentative definition of the global polity. We have attempted to suggest that there are certain characteristics developing that are constitutive of a global polity. We have also recognized that there are legitimate questions that need to be addressed if we are to progress to definition stage. Resisting the obvious critiques and identifying the constituent elements of a global polity does not, however, represent a definition *per se*.

Let us start by considering some previous attempt to define something akin to the global polity. For example, Seyom Brown (1992: 7) provided a definition of the 'world polity' as 'the worldwide configuration of systems of enforceable societal relationships'. At face value this includes the totality of socio-political relations in the world. This we think is too broad to be informative. There are several reasons for this. First, with this definition it would be meaningful to talk about the existence of a world polity throughout the ages. Configurations of systems have always existed. This definition misses the heightened political interconnectedness that makes the current global age distinct.

Second, it misses a sense of global community (albeit 'thin' community) that in the previous section we tried to suggest is emerging in the contemporary era. Third, when applying Brown's definition to the contemporary age it makes no provision for the fact that some of his 'enforceable societal relationships' are actually more relevant in a global context than others. To give a fictitious example, imagine a meeting of council elders in Irian Jaya. When they are discussing the organization of a local festival or hunt, they are not participating in, or receptors of, influences from the global polity. However, when that same group meets with the field officer from the World Bank, or some non-governmental aid-giving organization such as Oxfam or Community Aid Abroad to discuss the provision of support for the drilling of a well they are clearly participants in, and receptors of, influences from the global polity.

Thus any meaningful definition must have this added level of specificity that is missing from Brown's definition. The criterion will of necessity be 'fuzzy' but they will pertain in all circumstances to the global, as opposed to purely local, nature of these societal relations. By global here, we do not mean 'in its entirety', rather than that the relationship has some trans-border quality. This, as in the case of our Council of Elders, can be of a minimalist kind. Alternatively, if we were to examine the interaction of the Chief Executive Officers (CEOs) of the world's top twenty finance houses and their participation in the Joint Annual Meetings of the World Bank and the International Monetary Fund (IMF), then we are talking about involvement in the global polity of a different order of magnitude. These two examples demonstrate the uneven quality and asymmetries in the process of forming the global polity we identified in the previous section. The further scholarly or theoretical consequences of this asymmetry is that attention invariably focuses on what is the more salient of the two relationships for the student and practitioner of international politics. Thus the outlines of a definition of the global polity are in large part determined by what scholars and practitioners observe and what they do. This, we would argue, is legitimate. It is inevitable that, as in all activities, observers and participants privilege the core of their interests. In so doing, however, the continuing salience of what happens at the peripheral must be acknowledged.

If one wanted to elaborate on Brown's definitional emphasis on societal relationships, alternative perspectives are on offer. Susan Strange, for example, sets much greater store on the importance of structures. In her now justifiably famous definition of structural power in the global system, she identifies structures of production, knowledge, finance and security (Strange 1988). At the time, this was clearly a major intellectual advance in our understanding of how power operated in the global system. With the passage of time, however, the limitations of this definition also have become apparent. It is now not sufficient to privilege structures at the expense of agency. Thus we need some kind of definition that makes provision for the presence of both structures and agents. In this regard, our understanding of the global polity makes room for both. Strong global structures, of the kind identified by Strange and others, have consolidated over the last several decades while at the same time the role and indeed number of actors capable of intervening in the international process have augmented considerably. To this extent they are the players in the polity. Agents that would have once focused most of their attention on attempting to influence the policy process within national polities now channel more energy than in the past towards securing influence beyond the boundaries of the state. We recognize that this is an assertion in need of testing and empirical support, albeit that the argument advanced here is based on commonsensical observation. However, serious empirical research is now in train (Zürn *et al.* 2000). Thus, we think this gives the 'global' its 'polity'-like qualities. Our definition would include structures, agents and process. Thus we consider the global polity to be: 'that totality of political structures, agents and processes, with transnational properties, that in the current historical context have developed a high level of *thick* interconnectedness and an element of *thin* community that transcends the territorial state'.

The strength of the definition we would argue is fourfold: (i) it is an historicized definition that takes account of the specificities of the global age; (ii) while it identifies a structuralist logic to the global order, it at the same time takes account of the important dimension of agency missing from structuralist definitions of the kind advanced by Strange; (iii) it provides a tighter articulation of societal relationships by focusing only on those that have transnational properties in contrast to Brown, for example, who has a more embracing definition of societal relationships in his 'world polity'; and (iv) perhaps most importantly, it exhibits an element of realistic 'thin' community absent from all, but cosmopolitan, understandings of the global order. Our definition thus has the added benefit, we would argue, of recognizing the growing presence of 'thin' community in what we have called the 'globalization of political life' without recourse to the often overly optimistic position to be found in many contemporary cosmopolitan understandings.

What do we mean by 'thin community'? In 1992, in an important original insight McGrew wrote of the signal emergence of a 'fragile global polity', but we think that the element of community is more robust than that and that clearly the most probable scenario for the future is that it will continue to grow. We do so because the driving forces behind it (economic growth, technology, communications, etc.) are most unlikely to stop, and because the forces that over the last half millennium have hindered or destroyed the element of community – religious wars, wars of great power rivalry, colonialism and imperialism, fascism/nazism, and Stalinist totalitarianism – are not likely to reappear in a world clearly dominated by stable 'market democracies' as the Americans call it. When talking about 'thin community' we are taking up Roland Robertson's notions of 'the scope and depth of consciousness of the world as a single place' (1992: 183) and 'the concretization of the sense of humankind' (ibid.: 104). Along this line we are suggesting that there is a robust community although still vague and general and with only few concrete manifestations, and that the most probable prediction is that concrete manifestations of the recognition of the 'community of fate' of all humankind will continue to multiply and strengthen. The element of community suggested by the word polity is robust but little developed and with relatively few concrete manifestations.

In developing a definition of the global polity we recognize, as in all things, there is more than one way to proceed. What we have attempted to do is to combine the elements of McGrew's broad understanding of global governance with a tighter understanding of the global polity. This, we suspect, probably reflects our more circumspect view of cosmopolitanism than that of McGrew. The difference is, however, essentially one of degree rather than kind and reflects what is developing as an important debate about the global polity and that this volume aims to advance, namely, the degree to which the concept of community may, or may not, move from what we have described as its currently 'thin' status to a 'thicker', or stronger role in the global order to which those of a stronger cosmopolitan persuasion aspire. Moreover, without the input into this debate by scholars such as McGrew (and others such as his erstwhile collaborator Held 1995) and Linklater (1998) over the past ten years, any understanding of the global polity could not be as informed as it is today.

Outline of the book

The preceding discussion has elaborated an understanding of the nature of what we have called the emerging global polity. We have concluded by offering a tentative definition. In this section we say something about the structure of the book and the manner in which the chapters in this volume contribute to our overall understanding of it. We should say that the authors were not asked to write their chapters with our definition in mind. Rather, the definition has emerged out of the original and innovative, but diverse 'takes' on the questions of a global polity to be found in the contributions of a singular set of scholars to be found in this volume. This, we think, is the strength of the preceding discussion. It has been able to draw on their work to identify a series of themes and commonalities present in an emerging global polity as identified from their wide-ranging and different perspectives and analyses.

The contributions to the book are grouped into three Parts. Part I represents an attempt to address those various elements that would be central to any *theoretical* understanding of the global polity – particularly questions of epistemology and method, the role of the state, the role of international institutions and the role of international law. Without trying to shoe-horn the chapters into a tight formation it is possible nevertheless to identify a common core theme. Central to all chapters in Part I is an implicit (sometimes explicit) understanding of the manner in which globalization (sometimes intentionally, sometimes unintentionally) is bringing about a transformation of our traditional understandings of international relations. Further, all chapters accept that this transformation, inevitably, must have implications for what we understand by the concepts of 'governance' and 'polity' beyond the level of the territorial state.

Part II examines some of the increasingly important non-state actors and processes that are joining with traditional actors (states) and processes, to give the global level some of its 'polity-like' characteristics. The art of the new global politics in the global polity is not like the traditional diplomacy of the inter-state system. Developments at the global level now exhibit the characteristics of 'politics' in the widest sense of the word. Thus, the focus of Part II is not simply on the nature of the 'new actors'. The chapters also say something important about the manner in which these actors are reshaping knowledge and politics in the global polity. Part III develops logically from Parts I and II by taking a more forward-looking and normative approach to the analysis of the global polity. The chapters in Part III ask a series of questions about the nature of the global governance agenda as the twenty-first century proceeds apace. The understanding of global governance moves beyond the one that pertained in the last decade of the twentieth century – an agenda driven by managerial notions of effectiveness and efficiency – to an agenda that addresses the increasingly important questions of democracy, accountability and legitimacy under conditions of globalization.

In the first chapter of Part I Morten Ougaard engages in an important methodological deck-clearing exercise. In it he outlines those elements of research into the global polity that make this a new and challenging field of investigation. He identifies epistemological and methodological questions that need to be addressed in this emerging field. While highlighting the diversity in what he calls global polity research, Ougaard nevertheless demonstrates the existence of some important common characteristics in the literature. Primarily, these commonalities have to do with the nature of the topic: it is both an *emerging* and a *singular* phenomenon. These are not trivial findings. Among their consequences is the fact that it invites, indeed Ougaard implicitly suggests it demands, the application of theories and concepts from comparative political analysis and indeed social inquiry in general. This amounts to a significant reversal of the research strategy that has prevailed in the vast majority of state-centred research activity that prevailed in the field of international relations since its birth as a discipline in the early twentieth century. Ougaard's chapter also demonstrates the degree to which global polity research varies along several dimensions; the consequence of which is that it is neither possible nor helpful to group the research into a few neatly labelled categories. Traditional taxonomies of the realism, liberalism, globalism variety are far too simplistic.

What is needed is a higher level of abstraction that allows specification of the dimensions on which these approaches might differ. A way of tackling this need for specification is suggested in the chapter.

In Chapter 2, Georg Sørensen investigates the changes in statehood that have occurred in a rapidly globalizing world. In contrast to much earlier literature that talks about the end of the state, Sørensen makes the compelling case that they remain central in world politics, but they are *transformed* by globalization. Growing political interconnectedness has led to a new *modality* of 'domestic' and 'international' in the constitution of statehood. This new modality entails a change in the core aspect of the 'sovereignty game', that is the way that the two basic norms of non-intervention and reciprocity are played out in the context of different types of substantial statehood. Sørensen traces this change with respect to two main types of states: the postmodern and the postcolonial, and concludes that the continued development of a global polity will sharpen the conflict between the principle of integration and the principle of autonomy.

In Chapter 3, Claire Cutler focuses on the increasingly important role of law in the global polity. Specifically, she addresses the question of the sources and subjects of international law and its subsequent efficacy under conditions of globalization. In a very comprehensive review of the contemporary literature, the chapter summarizes how these issues are dealt with by conventional and unconventional approaches in legal studies and international relations respectively. For Cutler, globalization is bringing about fundamental changes for source, subjects and effects of international law alike. Particularly salient is the appearance of new non-state sources and subjects in international law alongside those already in existence. Cutler further argues that conventional approaches – notably legal positivism and neo-realism – that share a state-centred perspective, generate different answers to the questions of these relationships under conditions of globalization than do the unconventional approaches emanating from the critical legal, feminist and critical international relations communities. The implications for the global polity of these alternative approaches to international law lead Cutler to conclude with an analysis of the emancipatory potential of law in the global polity. A central message to be drawn from Cutler's chapter is the fertility of research in international law for the advancement of our understanding of, and the enhancement of the practices in, the global polity.

In Chapter 4, Michael Zürn, preferring the term 'societal denationalization' to globalization shows us how the impact of societal denationalization on governance at the state level and on the role of international institutions at the international level has for too long been studied and analysed in a seriously disconnected manner. Zürn's chapter then proceeds to offer a new insight into how to end this unfortunate dichotomy. Using a mix of innovative conceptualization and hard quantitative and qualitative data from the OECD world, Zürn shows us how governance beyond the level of the state is already much better established than many of a more sceptical persuasion would have us believe. More importantly, Zürn shows us that the nature of this governance is not monolithic. Drawing on a distinction between 'negative' and 'positive' international institutions, he demonstrates that negative international governance – governance that locks in states to international institutional commitments – is extensive and, albeit with a lagged effect, has in no small way kept pace with societal denationalization. On the other hand, the development of positive international governance – purposive, action-oriented, governance – presents us with a more complex picture. Only in the security domain, in contrast to, say, social welfare beyond the level of the nation-state, has it been possible to meet some of the demand for positive international institutions.

The theoretical discussions of states and inter-governmental actors in Part I are essential introductions to any discussion of an emerging global polity, but they are only part of the story. Many of the activities and political interconnections occur across other domains nowadays. No state actors have taken on an increasingly important role in world affairs in the past several decades. As we argued earlier in this Introduction it is their behaviour as agents of change that gives the international arena some of its 'polity'-like characteristics. In Part II Hansen *et al.*, Stone and Scholte look at a range of different types of political interconnections and partial processes in one integrated world society.

Chapter 5, by Hans Krause Hansen, Dorte Salskov-Iversen and Sven Bislev focuses on a topic that is rarely studied by international relations scholars, namely, that of local government. By demonstrating how local governments in several countries are enmeshed in transnational networks, they underscore how the political interconnectivity of the global polity reaches into domestic society below the level of central government. The authors approach this phenomenon by means of the conceptual tool of *transnational discourse communities* – a term they prefer to the much over-worked concept of epistemic communities. Through the lens of transnational discourse communities they empirically investigate three such networks, one centred on the UN, one on the OECD's Public Management Committee, and a cluster of networks represented here by the private Bertelsmann Network for Better Local Government. Drawing on fieldwork in eleven municipalities in five countries, they show how new discourses – and the discourse on New Public Management in particular – have been received, adapted and modified constructively across borders. In doing this they show that this kind of political globalization is not a uniform top-down process, but rather a process of dialogical discourse development. Moreover, it is a process in which transnational connections increasingly matter. The salience of this investigation for this volume is evident and important. It reveals a mode of activity among actors not traditionally thought of as participants in international relations who are quite explicitly contributing to the polityness of the global polity.

Diane Stone picks up a similar topic in Chapter 6, namely, that of knowledge networks. Her analysis addresses the theme of the book at two levels. At one level, she shows how knowledge networks, in which expert discourses are treated as sources of authority in global debates about health and welfare, market reforms, human rights or democratic development, are a manifestation of and contribution to the globalization of political life. Such networks are instances of what we identify in our definition of the global polity as 'thick connectedness', i.e. concentrations of policy practices and understandings of 'the world as a single place' that contribute to the development of community. At second level, Stone contributes to the analysis of another important aspect of the global polity, namely, that of the relations between knowledge and power within it. Stone first describes major sources of knowledge in the global polity – universities, think tanks, foundations, and the consultancy industry. She then considers the way in which knowledge is infused into international policymaking. She does this by the introduction of the concept of knowledge networks and empirically examines three such networks. From her cases she argues that knowledge influences policy and as such is a power resource, but one that is mainly available to well-organized and well-financed actors. Thus, the power relations of the wider global polity are clearly reflected within these knowledge networks. However, the hegemony of established interests is incomplete, uneven and contested. Thus, knowledge networks can also represent a medium through which alternative world-views and new policy thinking can be articulated.

There is now a vast body of literature on the growing influence of civil society NGOs. Indeed, they may be the best-researched aspect of the emerging global polity. This volume is thus not the place to replicate what is now an extensive body of analytical literature on civil society. Thus Jan Aart Scholte, in Chapter 7, takes the debate about the role of NGOs as actors in the global polity one stage further than much of the earlier literature. The chapter, in the minds of the editors at least, represents one of the first systematic attempts to assess the actual impact of civil society NGOs on global governance across a number of issue areas. In so doing, it identifies the range of diversity that marks civil society activism on global governance issues. An important implication of Scholte's analysis is the need to address the issue of impact and legitimacy for civil society involvement in global governance raised by this activism. On the former question – of impact – it is becoming increasingly clear that civil society has had a recognizable impact on global governance, but this impact can be both beneficial and negative. Either way, it is, we would argue, evidence of what we have defined as polityness. On the latter question – of legitimacy – it is clear from Scholte's chapter that there is much to be done to ensure that civil society actors might approximate the standards of legitimacy that they are frequently wont to demand of other actors in the emerging global polity.

Moving from the discussion of the increasing salience of new actors and new knowledge, the chapters in Part III address the theory and practice of a governance agenda in the global polity for the twenty-first century. In Chapter 8, Craig N. Murphy ponders the current prospects for a more substantively democratic global polity in the light of the history of international institutions since the Industrial Revolution. Murphy's Gramscian analysis identifies a stepwise dynamic in the relationship between the development of international institutions and the advance of globalization. The key to this dynamic is the changes in lead industries with growing geographical reach, and the struggles between new and old social forces for the shaping of social orders with a similarly expanding geographical scope. If we were to use history as our guide, then we would expect that, at a certain point in this process, reformist social forces would find the opportunity to shape the social order in a more democratic direction. Murphy argues that although some productive strategies are open to today's egalitarian social movements, a point at which a more democratic order might emerge has yet to be reached in the current 'information age'.

In Chapter 9, Knud Erik Jørgensen and Ben Rosamond offer an insight into the development of the European Union as a laboratory for asking a series of questions about the prospects for a global polity. They are, of course, not unaware of the risky nature of such an enterprise and the methodological differences entailed in this kind of jump between different levels of analysis. But implicit in their study is the need to recognize that any understanding of governance beyond the level of the nation-state is going to be an exercise in multi-level analysis. The logic of their argument is that in any study of an *emerging* phenomenon (one of Ougaard's key characteristics of the global polity), it makes good sense to go to the most developed example. Controlling for the unique institutional features of European integration and the similarly unique historical circumstances under which these institutions were created, Jørgensen and Rosamond utilize Helen Wallace's analysis of multiple layers of integration with different dynamics. This is clearly a valid exercise. Some of the dynamics found in the European context are also to be found in the context of the global polity. For example, the European regulatory model of 'negative market' integration finds echoes at the global level in Zürn's understanding of negative institutionalism. Again, as Zürn demonstrated, the global polity also exhibits elements of supra-nationalism and trans-governmentalism. That it is not at the level to be found in the European Union is not the point. The point is that the European experience, in either a negative or positive sense, may tell us something about where the rest of the world may be heading in the long term. Moreover, as Jørgensen and Rosamond note, we have to talk about the EU *and* the global polity in one way or another.

In the final chapter, Anthony McGrew, a leading cosmopolitan theorist of international relations analyses the prospects for democratizing the global polity. In the context of globalization – for McGrew an era in which public and private power is manifested and exercised on a transnational, or even a global scale – a serious reappraisal of the prospects for democracy is overdue. Summarizing recent scholarly debates on the issue, McGrew outlines the arguments against transnational democracy and the counter-arguments as to why it cannot be so easily dismissed. In the burgeoning literature on transnational democracy, four distinctive normative theories can be identified: liberal-internationalism, radical pluralist democracy, cosmopolitan democracy and deliberative democracy. Reviewing their respective strengths and weaknesses, McGrew on balance favours cosmopolitan and deliberative democracy as the most promising ways of re-imagining democracy. That McGrew's chapter is the last chapter of the volume is apposite. For there to be conclusion beyond it would be superfluous. McGrew's chapter is theoretically informed, normatively speculative and forward-looking. Global polity research, we have suggested, is an emerging phenomenon at the beginning of its career rather than the end of it. It is a domain of research that casts massive policy shadows. For it to develop in a meaningful way, future research following McGrew must also be theoretically informed, normatively speculative and forward-looking.

Note

1 The discussion over whether the late twentieth and early twenty-first century is similar or not to the late nineteenth and early twentieth century is effectively over. The balance of evidence would now confirm that we are in a different era. The various processes gathered under the generic heading of globalization do represent a significant societal transformation. Of the voluminous literature see by way of example, Held *et al.* (1999) and Scholte (2000a).

Part I

Theorising the global polity

1 Global polity research

Characteristics and challenges

Morten Ougaard

Introduction

There is no clearly distinct group or school of research that identifies itself as 'global polity research'. Yet a number of scholarly contributions in international relations share some common characteristics that allow us to group them under this label. Most importantly, they share a focus on global politics as a much more interconnected and institutionalized whole than is recognized by more traditional state-centred perspectives. Most agree that even an embryonic world government or global state is still only a distant and uncertain, if not impossible and undesirable prospect, including those who introduce terminology to that effect (e.g. Luard 1990; Albrow 1996; Shaw 2000). Nevertheless, a seemingly growing number of researchers recognize that decisions are made and policies carried out with consequences for all or many countries through international and transnational structures and processes, and increasingly so. Consequently, researchers have begun to develop perspectives, concepts and theories that transcend the traditional distinction between domestic and international politics and direct attention to international and transnational political structures and processes in new ways. In this sense I would argue that a new research agenda has emerged. 'Global polity research' is used here to label these research efforts, whether or not the scholars in question would accept being pigeonholed as such.

This new agenda can and has been tackled in a variety of ways. Indeed, it is argued below that the global polity can be approached from a range of different paradigmatic positions and theoretical perspectives. Yet at a meta-theoretical level there is an agenda that poses common challenges, and in consequence all such perspectives have shared characteristics that set them apart from other approaches to international relations and world politics. This chapter will elaborate these points. First, two characteristics of the research topic that have important consequences for research strategy are pointed out, namely, that the global polity is both an emerging and singular phenomenon. It is argued that this has invited the application of concepts from comparative political analysis, and indeed general social inquiry to world politics, not simply concepts specific to the tradition of international politics alone. This reflects a significant reversal of research strategy which has further consequence. Differences of paradigm and theoretical approach derived from these fields are necessarily reflected in approaches to the global polity.

An emerging phenomenon

The global polity is an emerging phenomenon in two senses. First, it is a fairly recent phenomenon. While it can be shown that its roots are old (Murphy 1994; Boli and Thomas 1999) and indeed traceable back to early modern developments in international law (Braithwaite and Drahos 2000), there is much evidence to support the claim that it was not until the 1970s that the movement towards much denser political integration at the global level accelerated (Braithwaite and Zürn 1998; Held *et al.* 1999; Drahos 2000). Second, the global polity is also emerging in the sense that the transformative trends with which it is associated are likely to continue in the future. This was argued in the Introduction to this volume, but what deserves attention here is the sense of attempting to 'capture something new', of identifying new institutional forms, new political practices, new modes of interaction between well-known types of institutions and actors. It is this research orientation that is shared by many global polity researchers.

In this kind of research there is, in other words, a heightened sensitivity to new forms of politics, an urge to try to capture central features of a development that is still unfolding. It tries to identify transformations that are under way, to specify theoretical and empirical reasons why they should be expected to continue, and to theorize their possible and likely consequences for the entire international system. In the words of Michael Zürn and Gregor Walter (1999), there is an element of 'transformation consequences research' involved in much work on the global polity.

For example, Keck and Sikkink (1998) argued that the *transnational advocacy networks* they studied are important not only because they had a demonstrable impact on the specific issues they targeted (human rights in Argentina and Mexico, rainforests in Brazil and Malaysia, violence against women), but also because they exemplify a phenomenon whose significance is expected (for specified reasons) to grow in the future. In consequence, Keck and Sikkink argue that 'scholars of international relations should pay more attention to network forms of organization', and 'we expect the role of networks in international politics to grow' (ibid.: 200). This leads them to consider a 'vision of the global potential and limitations of a cosmopolitan community of individuals' (ibid.: 213) and to the claim that understanding transnational advocacy networks is 'an important element in conceptualizing the changing nature of the international polity' (ibid.: 216). This type of argumentation is often encountered in global polity research, precisely because of the emerging nature of the topic. Its central elements are the identification of new or hitherto neglected forms and practices, the claim that they are important and for specified reasons likely to become more prevalent in the future, and an attempt to theorize the possible future consequences of these developments, in this case 'a cosmopolitan community of individuals'.

Other examples of global polity research drawing attention to new international political phenomena are not hard to come by. The emergence of transnational classes or a transnational ruling class (e.g. Van der Pijl 1998; Sklair 2001), the internationalization of law (e.g. Held *et al.* 1999), the rise of private authority in international relations (e.g. Cutler *et al.* 1999), and the legalization of world politics (Goldstein *et al.* 2000) are but a few.

The obvious danger inherent in the orientation towards all things new is the risk of overstating the case and exaggerating the extent and significance of new phenomena. Claims about the existence of a transnational ruling class, to be discussed below, or a world state, are strong candidates for the list of victims to fall into this particular trap, as indeed is much of the 'hyperglobalist' literature. The challenge facing all scholars, of course, is to get the balance right, neither overstating nor ignoring or underestimating new phenomena and their significance. In the final analysis, however, getting the balance right is a matter of judgement, and what perhaps distinguishes global polity researchers in this regard is that they would rather risk erring on the side of overstating than underrating transformations. The bias is forward-looking, not conservative and there is a reason for this. To quote Andrew Linklater, 'identifying the seeds of future change in existing social orders is a key feature of sociological inquiry' (1998: 3), and therefore it is often worthwhile identifying and analysing new phenomena where they are most developed, ascertaining their characteristics and potential for further development, even if they are not yet widespread or significant in their consequences. Having analysed industrial capitalism in England, where it was most developed, Marx told his readers in Germany, where this mode of production was still in its infancy, that he was showing them an image of their future ([1867]1996: 9). An example of a cautious application of this principle is found in Chapter 9 in this volume in Jørgensen and Rosamond's discussion of European integration as a laboratory for the global polity. In a similar vein, political integration in the entire OECD area, and in particular the Atlantic relationship, arguably the most developed case of transregional integration, can be examined for indicators of institutional forms and modes of interaction that increasingly will characterize the entire global polity.

Finally, the emergence of phenomena studied by global polity research has consequences for the balance between inductive and deductive research. All theory-building depends on both types of research, and their inherent complementarity is well known: existing concepts and theories guide the search for empirical data, and the facts in turn provoke refinement and development of new theories and concepts. Thus, theories cannot be developed without a foundation in factual knowledge (and the broader and better the knowledge, the better the theories), but when dealing with emerging phenomena attempts to theorize depend on information on matters to which existing theories only randomly or unsystematically draw attention. David Easton has suggested that there may be a cyclical movement between facts and theory:

> It could be demonstrated that in the short history of social science there is a tendency for the pendulum of research to swing from commitment to empirical research – discovery of the 'facts' – to theoretical attempts to make sense of them. Each new theoretical commitment raises the need for new kinds of 'facts', given the problems that the theories raise, which in due course leads to the return to theory as a way of trying to understand the new facts, and so on in an endless cycle.
>
> (1990: 320, n 23)

Concerning global polity research, this pendulum image is too schematic, but clearly in recent research there has been a concern to ascertain 'facts', to compile empirical descriptions and indicators of aspects of political globalization as a basis for attempts to theorize more adequately contemporary international politics (e.g. Zürn 1998; Held *et al.* 1999; Braithwaite and Drahos 2000; Balanyá *et al.* 2000; Sklair 2001). The study of global business regulation by Braithwaite and Drahos in particular illustrates this. Although initial theoretical concepts and concerns guided their study, the main effort was to inductively arrive at empirical generalizations (resulting in forty-four empirical conclusions) based on a vast amount of collected facts, not to test hypotheses derived from existing theoretical models. Braithwaite and Drahos actually develop many promising theoretical insights although there are reasons to be critical of several of their conclusions. More importantly, by bringing together so much information about the global regulation of economic activity across so many issue areas, they have vastly improved the factual basis for future discussions. What this illustrates is the value of this kind of empirically rich research that leans more towards the inductive end of the spectrum when discussing emerging phenomena.

A singular phenomenon

The global polity is also a singular phenomenon – there is only one. Diachronic comparisons with earlier 'world polities' are possible, of course, and can be illuminating (Murphy 1994). But such historical 'global polities' can also be seen as earlier stages in the evolution of a single global political entity, and from a methodological point of view the salient fact is that there can be only one contemporary *global* polity. Thus the nomothetic research strategy that has dominated much research on international institutions and regimes, while providing indispensable insights, has limits when analysing the global polity. It is necessary to supplement such efforts with historical, idiographic strategies that take a holistic perspective (Ougaard 1999b). This point has important implications and requires some elaboration.

The distinction between idiographic and nomothetic research was introduced by the German philosopher Wilhelm Windelband (1848–1915) (Riedel 1973). The word id*i*ographic is not to be confused with id*æ*ographic. The latter stems from the Greek *ideo* and refers to human concepts and, to be precise, ideas. *Ideography* thus normally means the representation of ideas by signs, hence Chinese characters are called ideograms. *Idio*graphic derives from the Greek prefix *idio*, referring to that which belongs in particular to, or is a unique property of something, as in *idiosyncratic*. Nomothetic research seeks common properties and general laws covering a class of phenomena; it is a generalizing research strategy. Idiographic studies, in contrast, seek to develop concepts and theories that capture the uniqueness of a single phenomenon and the particular configuration of cause–effect relationships that has shaped it.

Studies of the global polity call for an idiographic research strategy for the simple reason that it is a unique phenomenon. It is incidentally not the only phenomenon of a singular nature that is of great interest to international relations research. As noted by Barry Eichengreen, 'It is hard to imagine a field of international relations in which unique situations . . . were excluded because of the lack of an adequate, comparable group of situations' (1998: 1012). Examples such as the Cold War spring easily to mind.

Idiographic research purposes have often been associated with hermeneutic methodologies and epistemologies, but this link is not axiomatic. Idiographic research is not bound to focus on 'ideational factors' as the only or primary source of explanation; nor does it exclude assumptions about rational behaviour. For instance, idiographic analysis could explain a unique agricultural system as the result of rational adaptation to a particular physical environment. The core of the distinction between idiographic and nomothetic research is one of research purposes, not necessarily one of epistemology or ontology (Ougaard 1995). It should be noted that the antinomy between idiographic and nomothetic employed here differs from the one between ideographic and nomothetic introduced by Katzenstein *et al.* (1998: 682).

The two types of research are complementary. Often the identification of what is unique requires as a matter of logic an understanding of what is common, and vice versa. Furthermore, idiographic analysis of a unique phenomenon will often require generalizations about its constituent parts. Thus, analysing the global polity is an idiographic venture, but it can draw heavily on input from nomothetic studies into its constituent parts – types of states, groups of institutions, classes of actors, etc. It can also use general insights into human behaviour and societal development generated by nomothetic research efforts and theories. However, when fitting the pieces together, overarching concepts that capture central features of the 'whole' are needed. For this reason the impressive body of institutionalist theory on international institutionalization is at the same time both indispensable and insufficient for the exploration of the global polity.

A note on nomothetic institutionalist theory

The impressive research effort that has been devoted to the analysis of international regimes and institutions has played a major role in the fields of international relations and international political economy (Krasner 1983a; Keohane 1989a; Efinger *et al.* 1993; Levy *et al.* 1995; Hasenclever *et al.* 1996; Martin and Simmons 1998). The theoretical debates and empirical studies generated by such research have clarified important issues, and in a sense an emerging consensus is identifiable. Institutionalist theory has made a convincing case that institutions do matter, and it has identified a set of key explanatory factors: shared interests, the power of states, knowledge and ideas, domestic politics, and learning (see Hasenclever *et al.* 1996 for a synthesis of regime theory). Thanks to this effort, we now know much about the conditions under which institutions are created and become effective.

This impressive body of research, however, also has limitations. One is that a wider perspective has been downplayed. After all, in Keohane and Nye's seminal book from 1977 the analysis of regimes was only one component – albeit a major one – in a larger inquiry. The 'first major question' on their agenda was 'what are the characteristics of world politics under conditions of extensive interdependence?' (Keohane and Nye 1977: 19). The central focus was regimes, but the purpose was a wider one: to understand the nature of the changes in world politics resulting from increased interdependence, a research agenda that has clear parallels to the one addressed here. In ensuing years, however, the main body of regime theory has not systematically addressed questions about patterns in regime formation and the nature of the resulting overall 'regime architecture'. One reason, probably, is the strong focus on proving that *institutions matter*, necessitated by the neo-realist challenge (Martin and Simmons 1998: 757 make a similar point). However, another and equally important reason seems to be that the goal has been to produce *nomothetic theory*, that is, general statements about regimes, not about the resulting totality of international institutions. The result is a body of 'micro-theory' of international institutions, whereas 'macro-theory' of global institutionalization is underdeveloped. This is, by the way, not only a problem from the perspective of the global polity. It also calls into question the very possibility of a strong nomothetic general theory of regimes because, as argued by Vinod Aggarwal, regimes are often 'nested' in 'meta-regimes' (Aggarwal 1998; also Ougaard 1999b). In other words, the formation and roles of regimes can only be understood if their situation in the wider institutional set-up is considered, and it will probably be very difficult to develop a strong explanatory theory of regime formation without taking this into account. When approaching the global polity, the insights from nomothetic institutionalist theory are indispensable, but they are not sufficient because the cumulative results of regime formation are little explored.

Breaking with state-centred perspectives

Understanding the global polity, as pointed out frequently (e.g. Milner and Keohane 1996; Strange 1996; Cutler *et al.* 1999), necessitates a break with state-centred perspectives and an attempt to transcend the distinction between the national and the international, between comparative and international politics. It calls for a break with 'methodological nationalism' to use a provocative formulation (Scholte 1993; Zürn 2002). Clearly and emphatically this is not a claim that states have lost relevance, but an argument that state-centred perspectives are insufficient to understand the global polity, and indeed that states themselves must be seen in a global context if their roles are to be adequately theorized, as also argued by Sørensen in this volume. The question is how to effect this break. In this case there are also common denominators across paradigmatic differences of the way in which global polity research tries to achieve this.

First of all, it is considered inadequate to conceive of the global polity as a system of states. It is *also* a system of states, but it is more than that, because it includes non-state actors and a variety of international and transnational processes, and because the institutionalized interactions between states have reached a new level. On the other hand, while it is not a unified political system or an emerging global state, it still has *state-like qualities* or some of the features of political systems: interests are articulated and aggregated, decisions are made, values allocated and policies conducted through international or transnational political processes. Consequently the analysis of the global polity invites the application of approaches and concepts that are used in the analysis of *domestic political systems* and *political analysis in general.*

Examples abound. Susan Strange, for instance, chose to make Easton's (1953) definition of politics a central tenet of her analysis of the diffusion of power in the world economy (Strange 1996). Clive Archer (1992) discussed the *functions* of international organizations in terms derived from Almond and Powell's (1966) contribution to comparative politics; Martin

Shaw (2000) posed the question of the *theory of the global state*; Braithwaite and Drahos (2000) directly addressed *global business regulation*; while other scholars have focused on *global policy analysis* (Soroos 1991), *global public policies* (Reinicke 1998), *global public goods* (Kaul *et al.* 1999), *global social policy* (Deacon *et al.* 1997), or have applied Marxian or Gramscian concepts of *class, power and hegemony* (e.g. Van der Pijl 1984, 1998; Cox 1987; Murphy 1994; Gill 1995; Sklair 2001), or the Habermasian concept of *communicative action* (Risse 2000a) to international politics and international political economy.

This presents a seemingly straightforward solution to the question of how to transcend state-centred perspectives. It contrasts with attempts to theorize the new pattern of world politics through the invention of entirely new concepts, neologisms, and creative metaphors, a strategy that at times seems to have been quite faddish. Of course, new concepts should be added when truly justified, but obviously many researchers have found it more productive to turn to long-established concepts and theoretical perspectives from comparative politics, general political analysis and political economy, and apply them to the global context. This in turn *also* contrasts with attempts by state-centred theorists to face the theoretical challenge by restating and adding on to the state-based model of the international political system. Indeed, what it implies is in a sense a *reversal of strategy* for theory-building.

Efforts towards systematic theory-building often begin from the most abstract and fundamental concepts and propositions, and then proceed to add specifications to bring theoretical statements closer to reality, removing simplifying assumptions along the way. The traditional approach to building theories of the global polity can be described as one of beginning from the anarchical state system and then adding on the complications of cooperative behaviour, institutions, norms, domestic politics, transnational politics, etc.

The opposite tack, taken by a growing number of researchers, is to begin with a conception of one world political system, or an aspect of world politics, and then add the complications arising from the persistent reality that this system lacks a unified authority structure and has formally sovereign states among its fundamental building blocks. An example of this second, encompassing strategy is Susan Strange's definition of politics as the 'processes and structures through which the mix of values in the system as a whole, and their distribution among social groups and individuals [is] determined' (1996: 34), whereas Bob Deacon's analysis of global social policy exemplifies the exploration of one selected aspect of world politics as a whole. In both cases, as well as in numerous other examples, the point is not that states have become irrelevant or insignificant, but that the intellectual starting point is the system as a whole. This reversal of strategy does not of necessity imply that reality is fundamentally different from what is suggested by a modified state-centred perspective. It is instead a different way of looking at the same reality, a perspective that is chosen because it enables a sharper focus on important new features of contemporary world politics.

Effecting this reversal, in turn, by applying concepts from general political analysis and political economy to world politics, brings to the forefront basic theoretical and methodological issues and disagreements about notions of politics, of the state, the political system and society. As argued by Jan Aart Scholte, 'globalization is a new subject of study around which long-running debates about methodology can be played out' (2000a: 197). Liberal, statist, historical-materialist, Coxian critical, discourse-based and other theoretical approaches to political phenomena are all possible starting points for the analysis of the global polity (see also Moravcsik 1997). This observation is offered not only to argue the case for theoretical pluralism, but also to argue that the time has come to pay more attention to the ways in which such basic questions from political analysis are present in debates about the global polity, and for that matter, about international relations in general. Much theory-building in international relations (IR) has seemingly pursued an exclusive strategy of developing its own theories of politics and society, its own concepts of the state and relevant actors as if, for instance, the state in international politics is entirely different from the state in its domestic context. Perhaps this is an exaggeration, but it is remarkable for a research tradition in which 'the state' figures so prominently, that there has been so little attention to theories of the state, political system, and politics and the debates they have engendered in comparative politics and general political analysis. Barry Buzan's discussion of the state in the international system is a case in point (1991). Alexander Wendt's 'Social theory of international politics' (1999) is a recent and welcome departure from this, although it remains firmly within a state-centred perspective. Wendt opens the state system to society, but not to international society, and thus remains confined by methodological nationalism. To reiterate, the international realm is different, not least because it lacks one unified centre of authority, and the application of concepts from general political analysis cannot be expected to solve all problems emanating from this. Still, a heightened attention to the basic political concepts employed in IR research is brought to the forefront by the reversal of theory-building strategy effected by global polity research; similar arguments are made by Strange (1996), and in a different context Moravcsik (1997). Some of the promises and pitfalls involved in this reversal of strategy will now be illustrated by discussing two examples.

Two examples: power and class

First, consider the concept of *power*, a key concept in all political analysis. In comparative politics, depending on the theoretical framework applied, the referent object of the concept of power can be individuals, interest groups, political parties, social classes or social forces, discursively constructed communities, or a variety of combinations thereof. In domestically oriented political analysis the referent object is rarely the state, which is rather seen as an embodiment of the power of social forces or citizens, a place where power is represented, or an arena where power struggles are fought out. In some statist approaches, the state, or specific institutions of the state, can be ascribed power in their own right ('the ministry of finance is very powerful'), but then always as only one actor in a societal configuration of relations of power. In traditional state-centred approaches to *international* relations, on the other hand, the state is invariably the sole referent object of power, and often the distinctions between the state as a centralized authority structure and the state as the totality of government machinery, territory and population is not spelled out. But when approaching the global polity as a societal entity with state and non-state actors, the question of the referent object of power becomes more intricate. Simply to let power refer to all kinds of actors – state, non-state and inter-governmental organizations – is not a wholly satisfactory solution, because non-state actors appear on both sides of the equation. It is not meaningful to discuss the power of states *vis-à-vis* the power of non-state actors if states represent or embody the power of citizens or social forces. Is American power in the global context identical to the power of the American people, the power of the American government, the power of the dominant political coalitions in the USA, or the power of an American ruling class? The answers to such questions determine whether it is meaningful to discuss American power as something separate from, for instance, the power of US transnational corporations. In a similar vein, if we claim that the IMF is a powerful institution, does this mean that it has the capability to secure outcomes in accordance with its own preferences, or that it represents the interests and power of certain states or social forces?

This example illustrates two things. First, the importance of fundamental theoretical assumptions about society, the state and politics in approaching such questions. In other words, answers depend very much on the basic theoretical framework of political analysis employed, whether explicitly or implicitly. In liberal approaches, ultimately the power of a state is tantamount to the power of the ruling domestic coalition represented by the state, or the power of the entire citizenry in relation to citizens of other countries. In realist notions, power accrues to the undifferentiated unity of state and nation in relation to other nation-states, whereas some statist and critical or Marxist approaches that recognize the relative autonomy of politics and state will accept power as referring to both states and citizens/interest groups, or classes and social forces.

The second point illustrated by the example is that the application of the concept of power – or any other concept from general political analysis – to the global polity presents problems that are specific to the international realm. It brings added complexity because of the more composite nature of the societal entity being studied. Such problems cannot be defined away, but must be dealt with explicitly in the international context. However, a viable solution hinges upon a clarification of the basic assumptions about society and politics involved.

While clarification along these lines is necessary, it would be wrong to suggest that it is always sufficient, and there is moreover an inherent pitfall in this strategy: that of bringing concepts too readily and thereby in an unmodified form from the domestic into the international realm. Good examples are the concepts of class and social forces, and especially claims forwarded by several writers that in the global polity there is now an identifiable dominant transnational class, labelled, for instance, the 'transnational managerial class', the 'Atlantic ruling class', or the 'transnational capitalist class'. Obviously these claims are made within specific theoretical contexts in which concepts of class or social forces are constitutive elements, and the purpose here is not to discuss the merits of such approaches in general, but to illustrate that concepts from the domestic context should be applied cautiously at the global level, and preferably in their most abstract form. This requires a discussion of the notion of a transnational class in some detail.

For Robert Cox the 'transnational managerial class' consists mainly of 'those who control the big corporations operating on a world scale', plus public officials in national and international agencies, and a whole range of experts. Although this group does not identify itself as a class, it has 'attained a clearly distinctive class consciousness' with an 'awareness of a common concern to maintain the system that enables the class to remain dominant' (Cox 1987: 358–359). Kees van der Pijl's case for the existence of an 'Atlantic ruling class' rested on somewhat similar arguments (Van der Pijl 1984, 1998). In both cases, fora such as the Trilateral Commission and the World Economic Forum at Davos, along with inter-governmental institutions like the G7, the OECD, and the World Bank Group, are identified as evidence of, as well as venues for, the development of a shared world-view that holds the class together (see also Gill 1990: 48–50, 217).

These claims are, however, open to criticism, even within the theoretical tradition from which they are made. There is, in the tradition inspired by Marx, more to the concept of class than empirically observable behaviour. A classic starting point for discussing this theme is the distinction between class 'an sich' and class 'für sich', the point being that a class can exist 'of itself', as a group of individuals sharing the same position in the division of labour, without being a class 'for itself' which requires a shared understanding of the interests to be articulated on this basis, as well as the capacity for joint political action. Modern class theory is much more sophisticated than this simple dichotomy (Jessop 1985; Wright 1997). It is, however, useful in the present context where it infers that in order to sustain the notion of a transnational ruling class there must be evidence of both a shared structural position in the global division of labour and a shared world-view.

To substantiate the existence of a class *of itself* is an act of theoretical inference from analyses of production structures, property relations, etc., which is entirely different from the search for observable instances of actor participation in and impact on decision-making processes. However, when we look to the *for itself* aspects of class, the latter kind of evidence becomes crucial. The existence of organized mechanisms for the articulation of interests, and especially for political action to pursue those interests as they are constructed, are central and empirically verifiable indicators of the existence of classes for themselves.

The question, then, is whether the existence of a transnational ruling class has been substantiated in both respects, and this in turn depends on how restrictively one chooses the criteria. Clearly one can argue that the owners and controllers of international businesses, at least from the industrialized capitalist economies, are situated in similar structural positions in the global economy and consequently have common interests in important respects. On the other hand, scholarly debates about the convergence of 'business systems' and domestic institutions strongly suggest that, even for companies with a global presence, the home country base still matters very much, and the resilience of national systems against pressures for convergence indicates that there are important structurally based conflicts between variants of national capitalism.

It probably can be shown that there is, in the transnational business community, widespread consensus on some basic issues, centred on the desirability of a growing and open international market economy, and it is possible to identify observable institutional mechanisms through which this consensus is maintained, developed and disseminated. Nevertheless, in light of the density of interest organizations, think tanks, political parties, etc. operating at the domestic level, and the intensity of their contacts to national governments, it seems doubtful that the existence of a transnational class has been substantiated, at least if one wants to apply the same criteria in both contexts. The Trilateral and the Davos fora do not appear to qualify in terms of a more restrictive conception of class, even when taken together with examples of contacts between business leaders and policy-makers from national governments and international institutions. Not even in Europe, where economic and political integration is most advanced, has a decisive move occurred to a situation where international interest organizations are dominant in relation to national ones (Streeck and Schmitter 1991; Sidenius 1999). Perhaps research into organizations like the International Chambers of Commerce, the World Business Council for Sustainable Development, the International Organization of Employers, and the European Roundtable of Industrialists may lead to a different conclusion, but so far claims of the existence of one transnational ruling class in a more restrictive sense of the concept seem premature.

On the other hand, when approaching the global polity from a class perspective, it clearly no longer suffices to conceive of social classes and social forces in purely domestic terms (if it ever did). The real problem is to investigate how class formation is affected by internationalization. In the 1970s Nicos Poulantzas tried to answer this question. He concluded that internationalization had rendered the traditional concept of 'the national bourgeoisie' obsolete, since all domestic capitalist classes in the developed countries were by then firmly dependent on the internationalized economy under US hegemony. To capture the essence of this new situation he coined the term 'the internal bourgeoisie', which was still constituted within the confines of nation-states (Poulantzas 1978: 72). In other words, the bourgeoisies 'of themselves' were internationalized, while as classes 'for themselves' they were strictly national. Today what is interesting to investigate is the extent to which transnational classes 'for themselves' are under formation and how.

Theoretically, it is a highly plausible hypothesis that movement in the direction of transnational class formation is happening, and not only concerning dominant classes. Several reasons can be specified for this. One is that economic internationalization affects the interests, bargaining strength and patterns of potential coalition-building of domestic interest groups (Milner and Keohane 1996: 244–245). In particular, it has been argued that the negative economic effects of internationalization on 'trade losers' can undermine the support for economic openness (ibid., Frieden and Rogowski 1996), but the idea has wider applicability. Economic internationalization presents new opportunities as well as new challenges for interest groupings rooted in domestic business systems, 'trade winners' and 'trade losers' alike, and regime formation and international institutionalization bring new issues onto political agendas, around which interests are articulated and coalitions built. Keohane, partly arguing in parallel with Robert Cox, suggested that 'evidence seems plentiful that in contemporary pluralist democracies, state interests reflect the views of dominant domestic coalitions, which are constituted increasingly on the basis of common interests with respect to the world political economy' (Keohane 1995: 174). To the extent that dominant coalitions in several countries share some interests in the world political economy, this amounts to the emergence of transnational classes 'an sich'. A similar argument can be made concerning 'trade losers', who can also acquire parallel interests in relation to the world political economy. Combined with the internationalization of politics, and the ensuing need to transfer political activity to the international level, this supports the expectation that transnational class formation will occur as a long-term trend. Furthermore, it is possible to find examples that support the plausibility of this hypothesis. Just two illustrations: the International Chamber of Commerce is evidently trying to position itself as *the* leading global business organization, and it was called upon to present a business point of view to the leaders of the G7 at the 1997 Denver Summit (International Chamber of Commerce 1997). In the same vein, the International Confederation of Free Trade Unions is developing a global agenda and trying to strengthen its voice in several international fora (International Confederation of Free Trade Unions 1996). Yet the evidence suggests that movement towards transnational class formation is still fairly limited, and we should not expect a speedy process in that direction for the entire global political economy, not even for the most integrated core of industrialized capitalist countries. However, between the two extremes of strictly national class formation and fully-fledged transnational classes there might be a growing field of shared interests and concerns that are articulated and organized transnationally. If the class perspective is to contribute more to the understanding of 'the global polity', it must move beyond simplified notions of either one transnational ruling class or separate 'national bourgeoisies', and look at the concrete organization of transnational business interests, as well as emerging organizations of workers, farmers, consumers and even political parties, to ascertain to what extent and how such organizations organize and pursue their interests transnationally and internationally.

In the present context, then, the lesson to be learned from the discussion of a 'transnational ruling class' is that the concept of class is highly relevant for the analysis of the global polity, since it provokes constructive questions. But the notion that there is *one* dominant or hegemonic class cannot readily be transferred from the national to the international realm. The fruitful employment of the concept of class in the global context should instead take the road of applying the more abstract class problematic, that is, the question of class formation, to the global polity. In more general terms, the application of concepts and theories from the analysis of single societies is highly productive, but the inherent pitfall is to do so at too high a level of specification. In general, concepts like power, interest aggregation, corporatism, systems persistence, class formation, or any other concept derived from the study of domestic politics or general political and social analysis, should as a starting point be employed in their most abstract forms.

No neat labels

The categorizing and labelling of scholarly work in international relations have been an often repeated activity over the last decades, and also a useful one since a sensible grouping of theoretical approaches can serve as a guide for newcomers to major debates in the field. But more often than not, it implies a certain reductionism in which quite diverse contributions are subsumed under a small number of headings defined by a few key principles. If labels then become hypostatized as if they define the field, much is lost in terms of precision and adequate representation of the rich variety of contributions. When characterizing global polity research it seems particularly important to avoid this danger because it is an area that varies along too many dimensions to allow a meaningful grouping into a few neat categories. As an alternative, I will sketch three main dimensions along which global polity research varies.

First of all, as argued in the preceding sections, important variations derive from basic theoretical assumptions and conceptualizations of the state, society and politics employed in global polity inquiries. The global polity can be and is approached from the whole panoply of theoretical perspectives available to political and social science – liberal, marxist, statist, critical, pragmatic, new political economy approaches that combine a measure of theoretical pragmatism with a keen eye for the 'who-gets-what-when-where-and-how' of international relations, etc. There is no need to elaborate this point further.

Another dimension derives from the balance between normative concerns and explanatory questions. Most inquiries contain both elements, and as in all social science, value-free research is a chimera. But there are distinct differences in emphasis between work that is oriented towards the discussion, elaboration and propagation of certain values, and work that emphasizes description, analysis and explanation, even when it also leads onto discussions of policy implications and normative issues. Keck and Sikkink (1998) are a case in point. Furthermore, among global polity researchers that emphasize normative or policy-oriented concerns, there are clear differences between those who are interested in improving the efficiency of the global governance system, i.e. tend to take a global manager perspective or policy studies approach (Nagel 1991; Kahler 1995; Reinicke 1998), and those who are more concerned with issues of equity, justice, development or democracy (Rosenau and Czempiel 1992; Deacon 1997; Falk 1999; Jones 1999). In spite of such differences, these contributions have the shared characteristic of a normative emphasis, which sets them apart from analyses with an explanatory emphasis.

Finally, a set of differences derives from the empirical focus, also among researchers who take a global perspective. Some are mainly interested in international economic issues, some more concerned with environmental affairs, human rights or development issues; some focus on institutions and formal agreements, others on norms and soft law emanating from multiple sources; some focus on non-state actors; and some highlight North–South dimensions, while others focus more on relations within the developed world. They all, however, share the characteristic of locating the particular aspect being studied in a wider global economic, political and cultural context.

Hence, in a broader and more basic sense, setting aside the different societal theories involved, a global polity research agenda is discernible:

that of analysing global political structures and processes – (rephrase according to preferred theoretical perspective on society, the state, structure and agency) – in a way that includes state and non-state actors and processes and attempts to maintain the focus on the larger picture, the global holistic perspective.

One may ask, then, which challenges this research agenda is facing if it is to move forward. Naturally there are many and in a sense they are no different from the challenges faced by all IR research. But some are of particular importance for global polity research in its present stage and deserve special attention.

One such challenge is further conceptual clarification. The appreciation of theoretical pluralism notwithstanding, there still is a need for further elaboration of concepts of the global polity (the definition offered in the Introduction to this volume included). An upshot of the discussion in the present chapter is that it will help remedy this if more attention is given to the explicit elaboration of the basic concepts of society, politics and the state involved in any effort to theorize the subject, and perhaps also if the inclination to add neologisms and rely on fancy metaphors is tempered.

Maintaining a systemic perspective presents a challenge in itself. The need to explore the global polity through manageable research efforts, and consequently to focus on selected and limited aspects, militates against the effort to maintain a systemic perspective and tends to dissolve it into a myriad of case studies of limited scope. On the other hand, the insistence on a strictly holistic perspective entails a high risk of over-simplification and one can argue with some justification that some attempts have fallen into this trap. In facing this challenge it is probably chimerical to search for the perfect balance in a single piece of research, and global polity research is likely to oscillate between striving for holistic theoretical perspectives and accurate empirical representation.

A third challenge is posed by questions of causation and explanation. A hyper-complex entity, the global polity invites multi-factor explanatory models, and due to the idiographic nature of the research effort and the singularity of the object under investigation, as well as the frequent lack of comparable cases, the problem of over-determination will often be encountered. Too many independent variables impact plausibly on the dependent ones, and hard tests will often be virtually impossible to design. This problem is compounded by the possibility of systemic causation, i.e. the notion that in a complex interconnected system, the whole impacts upon the parts while at the same time the whole only exists as the product of the parts and their interaction. In such a situation the relative significance of each explanatory factor and the interaction between factors can only be ascertained through theoretical reasoning, often with the assistance of counter-factual arguments: what it is likely would have happened if factor X had not been present in the situation in which a given outcome occurred. Employing this kind of reasoning brings global polity research closer to historical interpretation than to those social science disciplines that can rely on statistical and comparative methods (although such methods should be employed where possible), but the challenge is to build such interpretations on precise and explicit theoretical foundations.

A further challenge is of a different nature. Although much work on the global polity, or of relevance to it, has been done, there also seems to be a need for more 'facts': there is still a great deal of room for further empirical mapping of aspects of the global system of political structures and processes. There are aspects which on theoretical grounds or based on lay observation of current events could be expected to be quite significant, but about which we have very little systematic information. Much has been done in recent years on transnational activities of social movements and civil society NGOs, but the transnational political activities of business and labour seem to be greatly under-researched. Some institutions in the global polity have long been subject to much scholarly attention (the GATT/WTO, the World Bank/IMF, parts of the UN system and a host of other institutions and regimes on which case studies have been made. But other institutions that quite plausibly are important have received little attention, in particular the institutionalized cooperation between the leading industrialized nations – the G7(8) – which has taken on a broad and seemingly growing agenda outside of its traditional core purpose of macro-economic coordination.

Finally, global polity research faces normative challenges of paramount importance. It was previously argued that in analytical work, global polity research employs theoretical perspectives derived from general societal theory and then adds the significant complications arising from the multi-state nature of the topic. In parallel fashion, the normative issues at stake in the interconnected world political system are basically the same as in all discussions of political theory: freedom, justice, equity, democracy and the rule of law. However, they take on a certain urgency in the global polity because of the glaring global inequalities which exist and because the differences between national cultures and domestic institutions are much greater than in any single society. They also acquire greater complexity because such universal norms that basically accrue to all individuals, even if they were universally accepted which is by no means certain, co-exist with equally strong norms that derive from the state system, the norms of national sovereignty and non-interference. The current configuration of the world political system is built upon but increasingly transcends a system of sovereign states. This being the case, the question of how universal norms, with due respect to difference, can be converted into building blocks for the future is a central normative challenge on the agenda of global polity research.

2 The global polity and changes in statehood

Georg Sørensen

Introduction

This is an essay reflecting on the notion of globalization (defined as the expansion of social relations across borders) and a global polity (as defined in the Introduction to this volume) and its relation to sovereign statehood. A standard way of approaching the expansion of social and political interconnectedness across borders is the 'state-plus-approach'. It takes the conventional realist model of the sovereign state as its starting point and then adds on other actors, from individuals and NGOs to all kinds of international, transnational and global organizations. This view is not entirely wrong – there are an increased and more diverse number of actors on the international stage today compared to previously – but it is misleading in the sense that it indicates that the sovereign state is the same as it always was. Globalization and the emergence of political structures with transnational properties both affect and are in some ways part of a process of fundamental change of the sovereign state in ways that the 'state-plus-approach' tends to downplay or even fails to notice. The most important of these changes are the subject of this chapter. I outline how substantial statehood has changed in the post-1945 period. A postmodern type of state in the advanced part of the capitalist world and a postcolonial type of state in the periphery is identified. I also summarize the main changes in sovereignty. Overall, I hope these notes can help launch a discussion about the central questions in a research programme on changes in statehood and their relationship to globalization and a global polity.[1]

Globalization, global polity and statehood

The concept of a global polity suffers from some of the same problems as its broader sister concept, that of globalization. Globalization is, in the broadest sense, the expansion of social relations across borders. As a starting point for research, there are at least two problems with this concept: first, it is misleading in that most globalization is not really global in scope; second, the notion of social relations is too broad and imprecise.

As regards the scope of globalization, it is clear that far from all processes considered parts of globalization are of truly global reach. Many take place on primarily regional or even less extended levels. The concept of a global polity has a similar problem: it speaks of something global, but many or even most of the 'political structures, agents and processes, with transnational properties' (Higgott and Ougaard, Introduction to this volume) are less than global.

Second, the concept of globalization speaks of 'social relations' which is supposed to signify the range of processes for which an analysis of globalization is relevant. The problem with this is, of course, that 'social relations' is basically everything and as such it is difficult to delimit and to use with analytical clarity. Similarly, the concept of a global polity speaks of a 'totality' of structures, agents and processes; this leads to the problem of what to focus on and what not in a potentially huge and disparate research agenda. Social activity does not lend itself to one big theory about it all; fortunately there is a way around this, as indicated in the editors' Introduction to this volume. It is to single out core aspects of the potentially huge research territory, and frame more analytically distinct questions about them. My proposition for such a question in this chapter concerns the impact of and relationship between increased political interconnectedness and changes in sovereign statehood.

What happened to the sovereign state? This is the central question in the debate about effects of globalization. Held and McGrew *et al.* (1999a) make a distinction between 'hyperglobalists', 'sceptics' and 'transformationalists'. The 'hyperglobalists' believe that globalization spells 'the end of the nation-state'; the 'sceptics' find that states retain their central role ('internationalization depends on state acquiescence and support'), whereas 'transformationalists' find that globalization is 'transforming state power and world politics' (ibid.: 10). It seems clear that all sensible participants in the current debate are 'transformationalists' nowadays. It might even be claimed that the two other positions are opposite extremes, difficult to support in full: who will seriously argue that we live in a world where the nation-state has 'ended'? Who will seriously argue that we live in a world where the nation-state remains unchanged and where everything about globalization is a myth? Consequently, the real issue is this: sovereign states have changed as a result of many factors; globalization and increasing political interconnectedness are important elements among those factors. These changes have made the sovereign state stronger in some respects and weaker in others.

The fact that sovereign statehood changes over time seems self-evident. But many scholars, especially in the discipline of international relations, have tended to work on the assumption that the modern, sovereign statehood has a set of fixed and stable common characteristics which pertains to (almost) all sovereign states in the international system. That is not the case, of course; sovereign states have changed constantly since their early inception some four or five hundred years ago (cf. Sørensen 1997). The modern, liberal-democratic states did not emerge in large numbers until the present century.[2] Globalization, the growth of political interconnectedness and other factors have changed sovereign statehood in decisive respects since the end of World War II.

These are complex issues to sort out. Instead of identifying and explaining causal relationships, I will be basically descriptive and employ ideal types.[3] The first ideal type identified is that of the modern state. The argument is that when we look at advanced states during the early decades after World War II, they basically conformed to this type. Against this background, then, we have a model of 'what was' which can be used as basis for identifying changes. Statehood never stands still, and qualitative changes have taken place; they concern both the advanced states in the North and the less developed states in the South. In making that description, statehood will be assumed to consist of three basic elements: government (the institutions of the state); economy (the material basis of the state); and nationhood (the idea of the state) (cf. Buzan 1991). Furthermore, all types of state rest on a common foundation of a population within a defined territory, with the government enjoying juridical sovereignty (constitutional independence).

Modern, postmodern and postcolonial statehood

The major substantial features of the modern state are shown in Box 2.1. For quite some time, the modern state has been considered the final stage of the development of statehood: this was the kind of statehood the premodern or less developed states in the South were striving for; this was the kind of statehood that the advanced states in the North had already achieved. It has already been indicated that this is a profoundly misleading standpoint. It is so partly because it assumes that there is some

---

Box 2.1 Major substantial features of the modern state

Government	A centralized system of rule, based on a set of administrative, policing and military organizations, sanctioned by a legal order, claiming monopoly of the legitimate use of force.
Nationhood	A people within a territory making up a community in the 'Gesellschaft' and the 'Gemeinschaft'* sense, involving a high level of cohesion, binding nation and state together.
Economy	Segregated national economy, self-sustained in the sense that comprises the main sectors needed for its reproduction; major part of economic activity takes place at home.

Note: *The 'Gemeinschaft' component is the cultural–ethnic idea of a community of people defined by the nation. The 'Gesellschaft' component is the duties and obligations of individuals to the state and the rights and privileges (including material ones) that they receive in return.

uniform end stage of state development to which all states aspire, and partly because it assumes that states will suddenly stand still and not develop or change any further when this stage has been reached. Both views are wrong; statehood does not develop towards some uniform end stage; and the development of statehood does not stand still for those that have reached the level of modern statehood.

This means that we have to theorize a world of sovereign states which is much more complex and diverse than has often been assumed. To make some sense of this situation, the notion of ideal types is helpful, because it helps us look for common patterns while respecting diversity. In addition to the modern state ideal type, two additional main types of state have emerged in the post-World War II international system. They are the postmodern and the postcolonial state.

Let me focus on the postmodern state first. The postmodern state can be considered the preliminary result of the development of advanced states beyond modern statehood, pushed by globalization and other factors. In contrast to many sociologists I make no clear distinction between 'late modern' and postmodern. Both labels indicate changes going beyond modern statehood. The postmodern state can be characterized as shown in Box 2.2.

The development of these traits of postmodern statehood is uneven across countries. The relevant 'inner circle' in this regard is the EU where multi-level governance has developed most. The relevant 'outer circle' are the members of the OECD.

Qualitative changes in statehood pertain not only to the North. In the South, a new type of weak player has emerged, in part as the result of the changes in the international system of norms connected with decolonization. Decolonization set up a new framework for the formation of sovereign states. In Europe and elsewhere, modern statehood had emerged out of a long process of violent struggle where stronger rulers swallowed weaker competitors (see Box 2.3). The normative framework around decolonization, by contrast, gave the right of independence to ex-colonies, no matter what level of actual weakness that they displayed. The

---

Box 2.2 Postmodern statehood

Government	Multi-level governance, based on supra-national, international and sub-national institutions (in various combinations).
Nationhood	Supra-national and international institutions are sources of citizenship rights. Collective identity also tied to levels above and below the nation.
Economy	Major part of economic activity embedded in cross-border networks. 'National' economy much less self-sustained.

Box 2.3 Postcolonial statehood

Government	'Captured autonomy',* based on weak administrative and institutional structures. Rule based on coercion rather than the rule of law. Monopoly of the use of legitimate violence not established.
Nationhood	Predominance of local/ethnic community. Low level of state/nation cohesion. Low level of state legitimacy.
Economy	World market dependence and structural heterogeneity. Coherent national economy not developed.

Note: *The state is autonomous in the way that it is not significantly constrained by forces outside of the state apparatus; yet the state is captured in the sense that the elite controlling the state is exploiting that control for the benefit of its own narrow interests.

---

universalization of the institution of sovereignty therefore helped create a new, weak player in the international system.[4]

My assumption is that these three ideal types identify the main current modalities of present substantial statehood in the international system, although in some concrete cases (Russia, China) there will be elements of all three in combination. But these remarks have been focused on the substance of states, not on sovereignty. What happened to sovereignty in context of the substantial changes depicted here? The next section offers an answer to that question.

Sovereignty and types of state

The discussion of sovereignty and statehood concerns three different aspects that should not be mixed up:[5] (i) the constitutive rules of sovereignty; (ii) the regulative rules of sovereignty; and (iii) the features of substantial statehood as they have developed over time, cf. the previous section.[6] Constitutive rules are foundational (Philpott 1999); they define the core features of what sovereignty is. Sovereignty in this fundamental sense is constitutional independence which, according to Alan James, is 'a legal, an absolute and a unitary condition' (1999: 462). That it is a legal condition means that sovereignty is a juridical arrangement under international law. The sovereign state stands apart from all other sovereign entities, it is 'constitutionally apart' (ibid.). That means that the sovereign state is legally equal to all other sovereign states. Constitutional independence is also an absolute condition; it is either present or absent. Other juridical categories share that quality; an individual may be a German citizen or not, for example. There is no legal status of being 75 per cent German. Finally, sovereignty as constitutional independence is a unitary condition. That means that the sovereign state is of one piece; there is one supreme authority deciding over internal as well as external affairs.

My claim is that constitutional independence is the stable element in

sovereignty which marks the continuity of that institution. The comprehensive talk about changes in sovereignty should not ignore this vital
element of continuity. This is not to say that there have been no changes
in the institution of sovereignty. There have been very substantial changes
in sovereignty; they pertain to the regulative rules, the rules that the sovereignty game is played by.

The regulative rules of sovereignty regulate interaction between the
'antecedently existing' (Searle 1995: 27) entities that are constitutionally
independent states. How states go about dealing with each other in war
and peace, who gets to be a member of the society of states on what quali-
fications, are examples of areas of regulative rule. The regulative rules of
the sovereignty game have changed in several ways over time. One important area of change concerns the rules of admission. The precise criteria
for recognition have always been a subject of debate in the society of states
and for a very long period there were no clear criteria supported by all
states (Østerud 1997). After the Congress of Vienna in 1815 rules of
recognition became clearer, but were still subject to exemptions which
reflected the specific interests of the European great powers. The emergence of nationalism and ideas about the nation were also reflected in
recognition practices, but clear guidelines applying the principle of self-
determination were not formulated (cf. Mayall 1999). Human rights
emerged as a possible condition of recognition after the end of the Cold
War, but it has not been consistently applied. In any case, it ought to be
clear that the rules of admission to the society of states have changed in
several ways over time. Once the membership issue is decided, by what
rules is the game played? Robert Jackson identifies a number of playing
rules, among them 'non-intervention, making and honouring of treaties,
diplomacy conducted in accordance with accepted practices ... the rules
include every convention and practice of international life' (1993: 35). It
is immediately clear that these regulative rules of the sovereignty game
have changed substantially overtime.

Against this background it should be clear that the debate about
whether sovereignty has changed in every respect – as some scholars claim
– or it remains wholly unchanged – as other scholars claim – is not very
helpful. There is a stable element of continuity in sovereignty, embodied
in the constitutive rule of constitutional independence. And there is a
dynamic element of change in sovereignty, embodied in the institution's
regulative rules. Furthermore, there is a third element of dynamic change
which is substantial, empirical statehood, that is, the concrete features of
statehood (government, economy, nationhood) as they have developed
over time. These substantial developments are summarized in the above
ideal types of modern, postmodern and postcolonial state. If we consider
these three elements to be different aspects of sovereign statehood, then it
is very often the case that those talking about continuity of sovereignty
and those talking about change of sovereignty are addressing different

aspects and in that sense, talking past each other. The 'change people' talk about the development and change of substantial statehood, or the development and change of sovereignty's regulative rules, or some mix of the two (e.g. Camilleri and Falk 1992; Weber 1995). The 'continuity people' (e.g. James 1999) emphasize the stability of constitutional independence. Both have a point; but each view addresses different aspects of the complex phenomenon that is sovereign statehood.

A better way of getting a grip on what has happened to sovereign statehood is via the notion of sovereignty games. Each of the three types of state described above plays a distinct game of sovereignty. The common element of the three games is that of the constitutive rules: all types of state possess constitutional independence. At the level of regulative rules, it is relevant to focus on the two *Grundnorms* or 'golden rules' (Jackson 1993: 6) of sovereignty: non-intervention and reciprocity. Non-intervention is the prohibition against foreign interference in the domestic affairs of other states; reciprocity is the principle of quid pro quo, the 'exchange of roughly equivalent values' (Keohane 1986: 8) between the legally equal partners of the sovereignty game. The point is that these two *Grundnorms* are played out in different ways in the context of different types of substantial statehood.

The modern sovereignty game

The substantial features of modern statehood were described earlier. The modern sovereignty game is based on non-intervention and reciprocity. For modern states, non-intervention is the right of states to conduct their affairs without outside interference. That also implies that the modern sovereignty game is one of self-help; states are individually responsible for looking after their own security and welfare: the state decides for itself

> how it will cope with its internal and external problems, including whether or not to seek assistance from others ... States develop their own strategies, chart their own courses, make their own decisions about how to meet whatever needs they experience and whatever desires they develop.
>
> (Waltz 1979: 96)

That situation is of course not only one of opportunity, but also of constraint: 'Statesmen are free within the situation they find themselves which consists externally of other states and internally of their subjects. That is obviously a circumstance of constrained choice' (Jackson 1993: 6).

The dealings with other states are based on reciprocity, that is, they involve a notion of symmetry, of giving and taking for mutual benefit. In the present context, reciprocity should be seen less as a bargaining strategy employed by single actors and more as a systemic norm according to which bargains between parties are made. A game based on reciprocity is a symmetric game where the players enjoy equal opportunity to benefit from bi- and multilateral transactions. Reciprocity in this sense is expressed, for example, in the 1947 adoption of the General Agreement of Tariffs and Trade (the GATT). That organization is based on rules which are basically liberal in character. The basic norm is the 'most favoured nation' rule which stipulates equal treatment in commercial relations between states, regardless of size, power, location and any further particulars about them.

The correspondence between the substantial features of statehood and the rules of the modern sovereignty game should be emphasized: the game can only be one of self-help, as expressed in the principle of non-intervention, because modern states are capable entities that are able to take care of themselves. They are able to take care of themselves because of the healthy and productive resource base made up by their national economies, their efficient political institutions, and the strength and support of a population which is a community that provides cohesion and legitimacy to the state. Similarly, the game is one of reciprocity, because modern states do not expect special treatment, or assistance, from others. Nor do they, as a principle, offer it in return.

The modern sovereignty game is based on a clear distinction between what is domestic and what is international. Again, there is correspondence between substantial features of statehood and the rules of the game. In substantial terms, modern states can make very clear distinctions between inside and outside. The sovereign border is not a mere juridical construction; it expresses in real terms that the national polity, the national economy, and the national community exist within the territory demarcated by that border. Non-intervention is the recognition in formal rule terms that there is a clearly defined domestic realm; reciprocity is the defining condition on which relations between inside and outside can be established.

The postmodern sovereignty game

The substantial features of postmodern statehood were described earlier. The sovereignty game played by postmodern states differs in basic respects from the 'modern' sovereignty game. The following clarification of this will focus on the EU, because this is where multi-level governance has advanced most.[7] In that context, the rule of non-intervention is seriously modified in that a set of formal and informal channels have been created for legitimate outside intervention by member states in national affairs. In formal rule terms, this is most clearly evident in the Single Market Treaty where a majority of member states may define rules applicable to all members. This 'First Pillar' of cooperation as defined by the Maastricht Treaty (ratified in 1993) was set to expand to cover additional areas in coming years. By the late 1990s, the current dominant project is the European Monetary Union and the introduction of the common currency. During the past decade, institutions at the European level have gained considerable influence over areas that were traditionally considered to be prerogatives of national politics: currency, social policies, border controls, law and order.[8] An important player in this context is the European Court of Justice which has helped push supra-national governance by establishing the supremacy of Union law in important areas.[9] This is clearly not a system of non-intervention. It is rather a system of regulated intervention which is continuously being developed. Because the political compromises made in context of the treaties (Maastricht, Amsterdam) are often unclear, it is left to future bargaining processes to determine the exact scope and content of European level governance in specific areas.

As regards reciprocity, the classical system has been modified as well. Whereas in the modern game, the rule of reciprocity is basically that of competition, in the postmodern game it is cooperation rather than competition. For example, poor regions get special, preferential treatment. In other words, there is some redistribution of economic resources across national boundaries which is not based strictly on member countries, but also on regions within countries. This resembles the aid regime described in the postcolonial game below, but there is a decisive difference. In the EU context, there is an institutional structure with overseeing powers. That is, EU institutions have the legal possibility of controlling whether aid for poor regions is actually used according to intentions and take corrective measures if this is not the case. A similar combination of cooperation and control is absent from the postcolonial sovereignty game.[10]

The modifications of the regulative rules of the sovereignty game described here imply that postmodern states have become integrated in the sense that they have developed systematic procedures for the intervention in their respective 'domestic' domains. These procedures correspond in basic ways to the way in which the substantial features of postmodern statehood have developed. Their polities, economies and societies are increasingly integrated as well. Instead of border controls which have largely been removed, there are several cases of development of intensive forms of local cross-border cooperation (Brock and Albert 1995; Christensen and Jørgensen 1995).[11] The development of transnational elites, it has recently been suggested, has undercut the possibility for governments to play two-level games, because 'the two audiences overlap, swap information, form transgovernmental coalitions, respond to transnational lobbies. European governance is above all governance by committee: through multilateral negotiation, mutual accommodation, intensive and extensive consultations and exchanges of information' (Wallace 2000: 347).[12] European level 'international' politics has become so thoroughly integrated with 'domestic' politics that it is increasingly difficult to make a clear distinction between the two.

Postmodern states, then, have also developed a specific modality of 'domestic' and 'international'. Constitutional independence remains in place; in that basic sense also postmodern states stand apart from all other sovereign states. But in terms of substantial statehood, postmodern states by no means stand apart; they are increasingly integrated with other states. That substantial integration has developed in interplay with significant modifications of the regulative rules of the sovereignty game where a similar integration between 'domestic' and 'international' has taken place.

The postcolonial sovereignty game

The distinctive features of postcolonial statehood were outlined above. The *Grundnorms* of non-intervention and reciprocity both create problems for postcolonial states; they cannot fully play by these 'golden rules' because their deficiencies in substantial statehood do not allow that. As concerns reciprocity, postcolonial states cannot systematically base their relations with developed countries on reciprocity. They are too weak to reciprocate in a quid pro quo manner; they need special, preferential treatment from the developed world. That is the basis for the emergence of development assistance regimes, where economic aid flows from rich, developed countries to poor, under-developed countries. This is a sharp deviation from the liberal, equal opportunity principle in relations between states; what has emerged instead is a principle of special, preferential treatment for the weak party. Postcolonial states have attempted to make the most of these principles, as reflected in the demands for a New International Economic Order and numerous other, more recent declarations, including calls for debt relief, preferential treatment of technology transfer, special subsidies for export items, and, in general, higher levels of economic aid.

The aid regimes and the existence of special treatment in an additional number of areas, such as, for example, the GATT/WTO regime which has special provisions for weak, postcolonial states,[13] reflect a difference between a classical principle of reciprocity among equals to a new principle of non-reciprocity among unequals. The system is not supposed to be permanent, but temporary. When the weak players have gained strength (i.e. development), they are supposed to graduate from the special treatment of non-reciprocity to the standard treatment of reciprocity. This is an indication that there are sharp limits to the scope and depth of non-reciprocity. A comprehensive regime of global redistribution from rich to poor has by no means replaced the classical liberal regime of equal opportunity.[14]

Even if reciprocity has not been fully replaced by non-reciprocity, it is clear that the international system is not one of self-help for postcolonial states. Nor is it purely non-self-help, because the international society has not assumed full responsibility for the development and security of postcolonial states. It is rather a self-help plus: in basic ways, postcolonial states are required to take care of themselves, but this takes place within a context where there is no severe external security threat and where donors provide some socio-economic safety nets in terms of various systems of preferential treatment.

Economic and other aid gives the donors an amount of influence over the domestic affairs of recipients. The attitude of donors has been chang-ing, from one of refraining from comprehensive interference in postcolo-nial states in the 1960s and 1970s, to one of increasingly demanding specific changes and reforms as a condition for providing economic and other assistance. Such changes clearly put pressure on the principle on non-intervention. The clearest example of setting aside the principle of non-intervention is the case of humanitarian intervention. Such inter-vention is explicitly defined as 'dictatorial or coercive interference in the sphere of jurisdiction of a sovereign state' (Bull 1984: 1). Political or eco-nomic conditionalities are not accompanied by similar dictatorial interfer-ence, but they may be difficult for weak, postcolonial states to reject anyway. If this is neither intervention, nor classical non-intervention, what is it? This new regime could be called 'negotiated intervention'. The term 'intervention' emphasizes the element of outside interference in the 'domestic' affairs of postcolonial states; the term 'negotiated' emphasizes that postcolonial state elites, because of constitutional independence, retain a significant measure of bargaining power over the concrete terms of such interference.[15]

Some will argue that this relationship is not at all exceptional, because in international society weak states have always had to deal with strong states from a disadvantaged position. Three elements suggest, however, that 'negotiated intervention' can be seen as a peculiar feature connected to weak, postcolonial states. The first is the scope of such intervention; it has developed to encompass every sphere of society, from regime forms and political institutions, over economic strategy and structure, to the con-struction of major aspects of civil society. The second element is the depth of intervention; election systems are set up; constitutions are rewritten, economic policies are overhauled, civil associations are set up, etc. Finally, negotiated intervention takes place against the backdrop of aid regimes. Donors are in a special position because they supply the necessary funding. Yet state elites continue to be able to influence the terms and, perhaps more significantly, the implementation of the bargains made with outsiders.

In sum, the regulative rules of reciprocity and non-intervention have been significantly modified in the postcolonial sovereignty game. The co-existence of reciprocity and non-reciprocity creates a situation of 'self-help plus'. Similarly, non-intervention and intervention have been combined in a regime of negotiated intervention.

The weak, postcolonial states are in major ways non-capable entities, unable to take care of themselves. Therefore, their deficiencies in terms of substantial statehood do not allow them to play a sovereignty game of complete self-help; they would be comprehensively unable to survive in a highly competitive state system. Because non-intervention and reciprocity are golden rules connected with the institution of sovereignty, they have not been completely abandoned in the case of these states. Instead, they have been modified so as to compensate for the weaknesses in substantial statehood. But 'self-help-plus' and 'negotiated intervention' are unstable compromises,[16] because they encompass elements of qualitative different systems: the classical liberal system of self-help and equal opportunity, and a very different system of non-self-help and global redistribution.

It is against this background that weak, postcolonial states display a distinct modality of 'domestic' and 'international'. On the one hand, postcolonial states have constitutional independence just as any other sovereign state; therefore, the sovereign postcolonial state stands apart from all other sovereign states. In terms of legal, political authority, constitutional dependence therefore creates a clear distinction between inside (the territorial realm of the sovereign state) and outside.

On the other hand, this clear distinction between inside and outside does not correspond to the substantial features of postcolonial statehood. Behind the sovereign border are not entities that are able to take care of themselves; they are substantially dependent on the international system. The weakest states are placed under direct care of the international system, as happens in the case of humanitarian intervention. The less weak, but still highly dependent ones, must accept a very high degree of outside interference in their political, economic and social affairs. This peculiar combination of 'domestic' and 'international' at the level of substantial statehood is reflected at the level of the regulative rules of the postcolonial sovereignty game. 'Self-help-plus' and 'negotiated intervention' are an expression in formal rule terms of a similarly peculiar combination of 'domestic' and 'international'.

Statehood, sovereignty and the global polity

I have identified the major changes in sovereign statehood since World War II. These changes especially concern the three basic elements of substantial statehood (government, economy and nationhood) and the regulative rules of sovereignty. They are the result of a large and complex set of factors, among them ideological (e.g. the view on colonial possessions, changing from 'the white man's burden' to the unacceptability of any form of colonialism; the new emphasis on human rights); institutional (e.g. the admission of a new type of weak player in the society of states; the new forms of supra-national cooperation; the changed role of international organizations such as the World Bank and the IMF); economic

and technological (e.g. the new technological possibilities for design, production and distribution on a world scale; the enhanced role of finance capital on a world scale); and security factors (e.g. US hegemony in the Western sphere in the context of bipolar confrontation, the success of embedded liberalism in the West and the failure of planned economies in the East). These are just a few of the relevant elements, of course.

In sum, a host of factors push the transformation of state power and world politics. It remains in this brief overview to better connect these changes in sovereign statehood with the overall concern of this volume, the global polity. I cannot fully exhaust this large issue, but it is relevant to comment upon three themes. The first theme concerns the political integration of postmodern states in the context of multi-level governance and their integration in other domains as well. International political integration is precisely the most salient feature of the global polity when defined by 'thick political interconnectedness', as suggested in the Introduction. It was argued above that this led to a new, specific modality of 'domestic' and 'international', because the strict separation between the two that characterized the modern state can no longer be upheld. The political integration of postmodern states as exemplified by the EU helps provide a clearer understanding of what 'thick interconnectedness' can mean. It means a situation where states are no longer in full control of political developments. Core aspects of rule-making and rule adjudication are in the hands of actors such as the European Court of Justice by the rulings of which even the largest and strongest states in the EU have to abide.[17]

'Thick interconnectedness', in other words, contains significant elements of international collaboration which has gone beyond purely inter-governmental cooperation where states remain decisively in the driver's seat, to various forms of supra-national governance where new, supra-national actors take the lead. Ironically, the more demanding forms of international cooperation have in most cases been created by states themselves. States have obviously found that they need very high levels of mutual commitment in order to regulate a number of areas where purely 'national' control is now out of the question because of the economic, social and other integration which has taken place in context of processes of globalization. Once such supra-national organs have been created, they can stipulate rules that states do not always like, but which they have to accept anyway.

This opens up an important research question which must be taken up in context of future analysis of an emerging global polity: to what extent does this emerging global polity display such features of 'thick interconnectedness' that go beyond inter-governmental cooperation where states remain in basic control of developments? I have focused my remarks on the EU, because here is a case where states have relinquished formal powers to supra-national organs. But there are many areas where regulative patterns have changed even if this is not the case. In other words, even if formal control has not been surrendered to supra-national organs, patterns of policy-making have changed, away from the traditional picture of states as unitary actors that operate coherently. That is to say, traditional inter-state relations are increasingly supplemented by transgovernmental and transnational relations, a development first emphasized in Keohane and Nye's analysis of complex interdependence more than twenty years ago (1989[1977]). Today, transgovernmentalism 'is rapidly becoming the most widespread and effective mode of international governance' (Slaughter 1997: 185). In sum, both at the formal level, as exemplified by the EU, and to an even larger extent in daily regulatory practice, the traditional picture of modern, autonomous, self-help states no longer applies. The growing political interconnectedness, as depicted in the notion of a global polity, is a significant aspect of the development and change of sovereign statehood.

The second theme I want to address concerns the relationship between the advanced, postmodern states in the North and the weak, postcolonial states in the South. The issue is relevant for evaluating the extent to which an emerging global polity might be defined by asymmetry and unevenness of integration. In short, is there an uneven hierarchy, a centre–periphery structure, built into the global polity? Yes there is, because of the vast inequalities in power, influence and resources between the advanced states and the weak, postcolonial states. The latter are subject to dependence rather than to interdependence; in economic terms they continue to depend on exports of a very limited number of primary goods and raw materials to the world market. At the same time, they try to get hold of whatever economic and other development aid that they can get. In socio-political terms, they largely have to accept the international rules of the game stipulated by the stronger players in the North.

But this is not the whole story; while weak postcolonial states are dependent on the international system, they also in decisive respects draw strengths from the emerging global polity and normative framework which sustains it. In a pure self-help system, the weak, postcolonial states would be swallowed by stronger competitors. This is exactly what happened to the weak states in the context of European state formation. Successful state building in Europe after Westphalia required demonstrating the ability to defend the realm and to create domestic order without which military power could not be freed to be projected externally. No such demands were visited upon the postcolonial elites in context of decolonization. Instead, international society accepted a new set of norms that gave ex-colonies a right to independence irrespective of their substantial weaknesses (Jackson 1993). In other words, weak, postcolonial states depend on international norms for their survival; they would not be able to survive in a self-help system.

Immediately after independence, the postcolonial states enjoyed a high moral standing in the international society; they were also able to play on the East–West confrontation in the context of the Cold War. The UN Charter on the Economic Rights and Duties of States, which was passed in the mid-1970s, reflected the strong international voice of the weak states. The Charter emphasized that all states are 'juridically equal' and that all entertain the 'right to participate fully and effectively in the international decision-making process' (quoted from Jackson 1993). Unfortunately, this favourable standing of the weak states did not lead to socio-economic development, primarily because of self-seeking state elites in the periphery.

With the end of the Cold War, and with a marginalized position in economic globalization, the weak states are much less influential. There is no risk that they will be wiped out, but the international norms protecting their continued existence have tended to benefit predatory state elites rather than benefit their populations. Recent attempts to remedy the situation through political and economic conditionalities have not brought encouraging results. So even if there is an emerging global polity, successful processes of development continue to depend heavily on domestic forces, in particular state elites that are seriously interested in promoting development rather than merely looking after themselves.

That takes me to the third and final theme connecting sovereign statehood and the emerging global polity. It has to do with the institution of sovereignty; what will happen to it if and when the political interconnectedness implied by the global polity continues to develop and intensify? The question is best approached by taking a closer look at the postmodern and the postcolonial sovereignty games as they were described earlier.

In the case of postmodern states in the EU, it was noted how, on the one hand, they continue to be constitutionally independent while, on the other hand, they have become increasingly integrated with each other as concerns substantial statehood. Furthermore, this substantial integration is also reflected in the regulative rules of their sovereignty game, in that postmodern states have created standard operating procedures for intervention in their respective 'domestic' domains. In other words, the formal sovereignty of postmodern states is simultaneously characterized by a high level of autonomy (i.e. constitutional independence) and by a high level of integration (expressed in the regulative rules).

How can this tension be resolved? There are two possibilities; first, the EU might integrate even further and create a federation. In that case, constitutional independence would be abandoned and replaced by a legal framework of integration which corresponds to the integration on the levels of substantial statehood and the regulative rules of the sovereignty game. Second, the level of cooperation can be scaled back to the conventional, inter-governmental level. In this case, the regulative rules would be changed to conform with the existing constitutive rules, i.e. there would be much more autonomy and much less integration at the levels of substantial statehood and regulative rules.

None of these possibilities appear likely in the short to medium run, so the tension will remain. It is reflected every day in the debates about the EU's future development. A similar tension will have to come to characterize the global polity provided that 'thick interconnectedness' further develops in the direction of more supra-national governance, cf. above. One cannot simultaneously integrate and remain autonomous. Sooner or later, the development of a global polity will be challenged by the constraint that is constitutional independence as it was developed in an earlier age and for a different kind of player, the modern state.

In the case of weak, postcolonial states, it was emphasized how the regulative rules of their sovereignty game are characterized by 'self-help plus' and by 'negotiated intervention'. The terms indicate that these weak entities are unable to take care of themselves. Dependence must lead to external interference; the weak states are therefore by no means autonomous; they are fundamentally dependent on the international system. At the same time, like every other sovereign state, they have the fundamental autonomy of constitutional independence.

How can this tension be resolved? Again, there are two possibilities. The first is that the weak states can enjoy a successful process of development and thereby graduate to become capable entities that can take care of themselves. In other words, the autonomy expressed in constitutional independence could apply to substantial statehood as well and thus there would be no need for 'self-help plus' and 'negotiated intervention'. Instead of postcolonial states, they would become modern states. The second possibility is that constitutional independence is taken away from several postcolonial states, because they remain so very weak. In that case they would probably come under UN supervision in some sort of post-sovereign arrangement.

It is not likely that successful development will happen in many weak, postcolonial states sometime soon, at least not if the experience of the past forty years in Sub-Saharan Africa is anything to go by. But because it invokes memories of colonialism, and because nobody is willing to shoulder the expenses, a post-sovereign arrangement under UN supervision is not likely either. The tension will therefore remain and it seems inescapable that the emerging global polity will continue to be characterized by a particular form of hierarchy.

Conclusion

I have briefly explained the development and change of sovereign statehood in an era of globalization and an emerging global polity. It is clear that the transformation of sovereign statehood is a crucially important element of a research programme aiming at exploring the global polity.

Both in postmodern and in postcolonial states, the conditions for the 'good life' of their populations are increasingly dependent on the international context in which they are integrated. The autonomous 'self-help' model of the modern state is more and more a thing of the past. At the same time, successful development continues to depend heavily on domestic forces. In this complex situation, further development of the global polity will be challenged by the continued existence of that core of the institution of sovereignty that is constitutional independence. The world of sovereign states is based on the fundamental principle of auto-nomy. The emerging global polity is based on the fundamental principle of integration. Continued development of a global polity will sharpen the conflict between these principles.

Notes

1 Helpful comments on an earlier version of this chapter, from the participants at the Toruplund seminar and especially from the editors of this volume, are gratefully acknowledged.
2 As usefully emphasized by Held, McGrew *et al.* (1999a) and many others.
3 The ideal types are discussed much more in my forthcoming book on changes in statehood. Some of what follows draws on that manuscript.
4 Decolonization was not the single, effective cause; not all ex-colonies conform to the postcolonial ideal type described below (and some countries that were not colonies do conform to it).
5 The following argument draws on Sørensen (1999).
6 The distinction between constitutive and regulative rules draws on Searle (1995).
7 As noted by Keohane (1995) and Zürn (1998), other countries are increasingly involved in multi-level governance as well; this is especially the case for the OECD countries.
8 Cf. Wallace (2000).
9   The Court itself has aggressively molded the various treaties and laws of the Union into a constitutional charter. . . . It has not only established the supremacy of Union law but also simultaneously augmented the power of the national courts by giving them the authority to invalidate national legislation on the basis of Union law.

(Caldeira *et al.* 1995: 4)

10 While classical reciprocity has been modified, it has not disappeared. To some extent, redistribution to poor regions are parts of larger compromises where this is part of a compensation to poorer countries for accepting other measures of integration; yet this remains more a cooperation game than a competition game.
11 It has been suggested that such cooperation is emerging not only in context of the EU, but also in the larger postmodern realm (see Brock and Albert (1995)).
12 'States have ceased to act as gatekeepers between domestic and international politics in intra-European relations.' (Wallace 2000: 345).
13 The most favoured nation principle is the expression of classical reciprocity: equal treatment of all parties. The generalized scheme of preferences is the expression of non-reciprocity: special treatment for the weak party.

14 A similar conclusion is set forth by Robert Jackson:

> The reality is not that the law of welfare – nonreciprocity – has replaced
> the law of liberty – reciprocity ... Nor is it likely. Rather, it is that poor
> states today assert both negative and positive norms at one and the same
> time. ... And contemporary international society is trying to operate with
> both.
>
> (Jackson 1993: 135)

15 Christopher Clapham, by contrast, argues that the international norms connected with sovereignty no longer afford any special protection to postcolonial
state elites and that 'the era of sovereignty as a universal organizing principle
for the management of the global system has ended' (1999: 537). The position
taken here is that the institution of sovereignty has been developed and modified to accommodate weak, postcolonial statehood.
16 That lack of stability is clearly demonstrated in the analysis by Clapham (1999).
17 There are now a number of analyses to support this view. See, for example,
Alter (1996, 1998) and Slaughter *et al.* (1998).

3 Law in the global polity

A. Claire Cutler

Introduction

The increasing significance of law in international relations, at both
regional and global levels, has led to an intensification of concern with the
globalization or internationalization of the 'rule of law' (Dezalay and
Garth 1996: 3; Scheuerman 1999a). Whether in the area of international
economics and the development of law through global institutions, like
the World Trade Organization (WTO) and the General Agreement on
Tariffs and Trade (GATT) and regional legal systems, like the European
Union and the North America Free Trade Agreement (NAFTA), or the
areas of human rights and the environment, there is considerable interest
among international relations and legal scholars in examining the nexus
between international law and international politics (Abbott 2000; Alter
2000; Goldstein *et al.* 2000; Goldstein and Martin 2000; Lutz and Sikkink
2000). Students of international society have traditionally believed that
the domain of international relations is characterized by principles and
rules that provide a normative framework for action (see Lauterpacht
1946; Bull 1977; Cutler 1991; Hurrell 1993). International law is thus
regarded as an essential component of global governance arrangements
and an 'institution' of global society that both shapes and is shaped by
global economic, social and political relations. However, the contemporary concern with the globalization of law reflects a sense that there has
been an intensification in the legal regulation of international relationships that is having an impact on the ways in which states and societies
govern themselves (Twining 1996; Fried 1997). For some, the globalization of the rule of law is a welcome development that is civilizing the globe
through uniform laws and practices that replace parochial systems of local
and national law (David 1972; Schmitthoff 1982). Others doubt the 'civilizing' role of globalized law and suggest that the transmission of predominantly First World laws throughout the globe engages questionable
practices of legal hegemony and colonial domination (Cutler 1995, 1997,
1999c, 2001b; Silbey 1997). For some the globalization of law signals a loss
of national and domestic control over significant policy areas, eroding the

foundations for democracy and participatory forms of governance, while empowering supra-national sites of governance that lack democratic traditions and credentials (Trimble 1985; Habermas 1998: 151 and 155). This suggests that increased legalization is thus not necessarily linked with greater democratization. Yet others regard the globalization of law as filling governance gaps created by economic globalization and thus providing much needed public goods in the forms of economic security and certainty (Ruggie 1993; Moravcsik 1998). Finally, some focus on changes in the nature of global capitalism that are altering the context for international commerce and obviating the need for traditional law. The enhanced significance of soft law, informal, discretionary, and *ad hoc* and private legal regulation is quite inconsistent with and, perhaps, even eroding the foundation of the rule of law as a system of global governance (Scheuerman 1999a; Cutler 2001b).

This diversity of opinion suggests that there is very little clarity regarding the nature and significance of law. Indeed, this chapter argues that there is neither analytical nor theoretical agreement about the role of law in the global polity. Students of both international law and international relations contest the precise nature of the role of law in global governance. While international lawyers have long debated the nature and significance of international law, agonizing over the analytical issues of the formal 'sources' and proper 'subjects' of legal obligation and debating whether international law may be regarded as law 'properly so-called' (Austin 1954; Hart 1961; Kelsen 1961), contemporary theorists reflect similar debates over the status of informal or 'soft' law sources of law and the authority of non-state actors as subjects of law (see Cutler 1999b and c). In addition, different theoretical approaches or schools of thought contribute often incompatible views to the debate over whether law matters in the regulation of global relations (see, generally, Beck *et al.* 1996).

International relations scholars also debate the significance of mechanisms of global governance, although in the past the concern has been predominantly with the efficacy of international regimes. While both mainstream and critical approaches to the study of international relations are concerned with whether international regimes really influence state behaviour or are epiphenomenal and part of the superstructure of the global political economy (see Krasner 1983b; Keohane 1997; Cutler 2002a), they disagree about who makes law and shapes the global polity. Mainstream approaches to international law and organization and international political economy posit that states are the main 'subjects' and agents or voices of the global polity and that state consent is the prerequisite for a 'source' of legal regulation (Keohane 1984; Franck 1990). Others challenge this state-centric approach with the increasing authority of transnational corporations, private associations, non-governmental organizations, global social movements, and transnational class and gender relations and the forms of regulation they generate (see Cutler *et al.* 1999; Cutler 2002a).

In addition, in both fields there is much disagreement over the nature of the outcome or effect of law on the global polity. For some, international law creates an interest-based order, facilitating the achievement of national interests and objectives through multilateral cooperation. Such thinkers eschew the proposition that there is a necessary relationship between law and morality or between politics and morality, positing international law to be neutral in normative impact. This position is associated generally with legal positivism and political realism, approaches to law and politics considered below (see generally, Beck *et al.* 1996). In contrast, a diverse number of theorists regard international law as inherently normative in both design and impact. Natural law theorists, feminists, historical materialists and critical thinkers in both law and politics reject the analytical and theoretical separation of law and morality, positing law to be a social construct and thus capable of progressive social change (Kennedy 1988; Kratochwil 1989; Charlesworth *et al.* 1991; Cutler 1991, 1995). As a normative order, international law may advance a multiplicity of ends, whether they be democratic or undemocratic and equitable or inequitable. It may, indeed, be instrumental in advancing the interests of private capital, transnational corporations and classes, patriarchy or hegemonic states, thus promoting and deepening asymmetrical rather than homogeneous economic, social and political global relations. However, the law may also be used to achieve emancipatory projects and reconciling tensions in relations between national and global political economies, between classes, between genders, and between peoples. In this regard, it is useful to conceive of international law as *praxis*: as political practice informed by emancipatory objectives.

This chapter reviews these debates in order to clarify the nature and role of international law in the global polity and to advance an understanding of the potential for law to work towards progressive ends. The discussion first presents the different theoretical views on the nature and role that law plays and considers contestation over who creates and shapes the global order. Then it considers the impact and effect of law and reviews why we should care about law in the global polity.

Theorizing the nature and role of international law

Although legal theorists are less inclined than international relations scholars to doubt the efficacy of international law, there is remarkable symmetry in conventional approaches to both fields. In international relations these debates are often framed in terms of the significance of international regimes, institutions, norms and degrees of legalization (Krasner 1983b; Keohane 1989a and 1997; Mearsheimer 1994–1995; Abbott *et al.* 2000), while international lawyers tend to talk about the formal sources and subjects of the law and the problem of legal obligation (Brownlie 1990; Shaw 1994). Many international relations scholars regard international legal regimes to be epiphenomenal and external to the material power relations of states. Susan Strange (1983) probably best articulated this position in her trenchant and now classic critique of regime analysis. To Strange the study of regimes was an American fad, conceptually woolly and imprecise, reflected a value bias in favour of finding order in the world, and produced a static and state-centric view of international relations. The focus on state-led regimes thus obscured rather than clarified processes of governance in the global polity by ignoring the underlying structures of power and influence. Others also question whether international regimes influence political outcomes autonomously and directly or are mediated by state interests and goals (Krasner 1983b). They question whether regime norms have any compliance-pull or normative influence of their own, or are used instrumentally by states to achieve their particularistic interests (Keohane 1997).

Similar concerns over the efficacy of legal rules are expressed by legal theorists who adopt conventional approaches to international law (Franck 1990). This symmetry is due in no small part to three fundamental tendencies shared by conventional approaches in both fields that produce a state-centric view of the global polity, inhibit the recognition of non-state subjects and sources, and reject the moral foundations of the law. The first tendency is the general application of the domestic analogy and related presumptions of international anarchy to international relations (Suganami 1989). This involves the application to international relations of a hierarchical model of rule derived from domestic legal orders that precludes conceptualizing pluralism in legal regulation. The second tendency is legal formalism and the association of authority with the formal authority of the state as both the subject and the legitimate source of law (Cutler 2001a). The third is belief in the relative autonomy of the law. The term the 'relative autonomy' of the law is used here in the specific context used by liberal theories about the rule of law which posit law to be relatively independent of social, political, moral and religious influences.[1] Berman (1983: 8) notes that belief in the relative autonomy of the law is the first principal characteristic of the Western legal tradition. It provides the foundation for positing that law operates in an objective and neutral manner as the rule of law and not the rule of man.

The similarity in approach begins to decrease, however, as analysis moves to less conventional and more critical approaches. Unconventional approaches identify increased pluralism in legal governance arrangements, net in a broader range of legal subjects and sources, and posit the inherent normativity and subjectivity of the law.

Conventional theoretical approaches

There is a remarkable unity between conventional international legal theory and international relations theory in terms of the tendencies to apply the domestic analogy, to exhibit formalism over the subjects and sources of the law, and to conceive of the law as relatively autonomous, neutral and objective.

The conventional approach to international law today is legal positivism (see generally, Beck *et al.* 1996: Chapter 3 and Malanczuk 1997: Chapter 1). Legal positivism emerged as a reaction to natural law theories that were current during the formative time of modern international law. Legal positivists tended to approach the question of whether international law mattered by inquiring into its status as 'law properly so-called'. Proper law was, of course, domestic law. Applying the domestic analogy, John Austin articulated a hierarchical or 'command theory of law' that associated proper law with the command of a sovereign backed by the force of sanctions. Law was theorized to be a body of neutral rules that are applied in an objective manner through adjudication. Thus Austin concluded that international law could be no more than 'positive morality' because it lacked the necessary features of an adjudicatory system. Other positivists answered the question of whether law matters with a qualified 'yes'. Hans Kelsen theorized that international law was a primitive legal order in which enforcement was achieved through decentralized sanctions (self-help and reprisals), while H.L.A. Hart theorized international law to be a primitive system of primary rules (stipulating obligations), but lacking the secondary rules (governing recognition, change and adjudication) common in advanced legal systems (Beck *et al.* 1996: 56–59).

Most mainstream contemporary legal scholars, although positivist in approach, tend to impute more efficacy to international law than did the early positivists. The Austinian preoccupation with commands of a sovereign enforced by sanctions has given way to more nuanced understandings of the source of legal obligation and compliance. Compliance is theorized to be related to concerns for reputation, reciprocity, perceptions of legitimacy, trust and the like, which do not rest on coercion or sanctions (see Franck 1990; Chayes and Chayes 1995; Cutler 1999b: 292 *et seq.*). In addition, developments in the institutional foundations of international law in the post-World War II period make its analytical status as a primitive order lacking secondary rules highly questionable. However, the legal positivist attributions of legal subjectivity to states and the sources of law to products of state consent persist, as too does the presumption that the worlds of law and of morality are separately existing domains. These tendencies are evident in the doubts that many have about the prospects of achieving anything more than procedural, as opposed to substantive, justice in the world comprised of a multiplicity of independent states. Law thus matters, but only insofar as it regulates procedural and not substantive legal/political matters involving competing normative systems (see Bull 1977; Young 1979; Nardin 1983; Franck 1990; Cutler 1999b: 289–292). This is a rather minimalist view of the extent to which law matters.

In international relations the conventional approaches, political realism and neo-liberal institutionalism, reproduce many of the reservations expressed by legal positivists about whether law matters. Classical realists, applying the domestic analogy, echoed the Austinian preoccupation with the anarchy problematic and the theoretical impossibility of regarding international law as a 'real' binding legal order. The suspicion that it is a dangerous form of 'positive morality' is clearly evident in the work of E.H. Carr (1946) and Hans Morgenthau (1948). Neo-realists share similar doubts about the efficacy of international law and with neo-liberal institutionalists, are preoccupied with the extent to which cooperation in international regimes is thwarted by cheating, problems of enforcement, and inter-state competition (Krasner 1983; Keohane 1984). Neo-realists reproduce many of the classical realist objections, illustrating a continuing debate over the nature and role of law, regimes and institutions, which concepts tend to be used interchangeably. Stephen Krasner (1983b) identifies three broad approaches to the significance of international regimes. Structural realism, at one extreme, posits the irrelevance of regimes to state behaviour. State action is regarded as interest-based, and not norm-driven. At the other extreme are Grotians who posit the ubiquity of regimes wherever there is regularized state behaviour. In the middle lie the modified structuralists who are prepared to accept that regime norms and institutions can influence state actions by intervening between state interests and outcomes. The structural realist position is articulated most powerfully by Joseph Grieco (1988) and John Mearsheimer (1994–1995) in the attempt to discredit the position of modified structuralists or neo-liberal institutionalists. They argue that legal regimes have a negligible impact on state action for two reasons: states' fear of cheating and competitive concerns about their position *vis-à-vis* other states (relative gains) limit their willingness to cooperate in international institutions. Neo-liberal institutionalists, in contrast, believe that cheating and concern over relative gains, while problematic, do not rule out the effectiveness of regimes and institutions. Indeed, neo-liberal institutionalists counter that institutions may be even more significant when distributional issues arise for they can assist in balancing unequal gains from cooperation and in mitigating fears of cheating (Keohane and Martin 1995: 45). Notwithstanding such differences, there is thus a fair degree of unity in the application of the domestic analogy and the anarchy problematic and institutional efforts to mitigate the effects of anarchy as the defining conditions of whether law and institutions matter (see generally, Mearsheimer 1994–1995; Keohane and Martin 1995; Ruggie 1995; Wendt 1995; Zacher with Sutton 1996).

In terms of the subjects and sources of international law, legal positivists adopt a state-centric approach that regards states as the only subjects under the law with full and original legal personality and that associates the legitimate sources of law with state consent. A brief review of the law governing subjects and sources is necessary here in order to provide the legal framework for analysis.

The doctrine of international legal personality determines what entities possess rights and duties enforceable through law (Shaw 1994: 135). Traditionally, only states may enter into treaties, be parties to contentious proceedings before the International Court of Justice, be full members of the United Nations, claim the right to territorial integrity, appoint ambassadors, and declare war. Other entities, like international organizations, have only the degree of personality that is vested in them by states. This usually includes as much personality as the institution requires to perform the tasks assigned to it. However, such personality remains a derivative of state personality. While states and to a limited extent international organizations have legal personality as 'subjects' of the global polity, other entities like individuals and corporations are only 'objects' of the order (Higgins 1985: 478). According to legal doctrine, states are the proper subjects of international law, while individuals are the proper subjects of their domestic, municipal legal system (Janis 1984: 61). Individuals can at best be the recipients of benefits as objects of the international legal order (Higgins 1985: 477). The situation for business enterprises, like transnational corporations, is analogous to that of individuals, although there are some exceptions to the limited legal personality of both individuals and transnational corporations (Cutler 1999b, 2000).

As the proper subjects only states can create international law and so doctrine on the sources of law mirrors the state-centricity of that regarding subjects. While the matter of the sources of law is not usually problematic in domestic political orders where there are legislatures and parliaments who are the legitimate law-making institutions, this is not the case in the global polity. The institutions of the global polity, while possessing many government-like capacities, do not function as a supranational government. The United Nations General Assembly, while broadly inclusive of states, has only limited law-making capacities. The General Assembly, with rare exception, can only make recommendations and cannot issue resolutions that are binding on states. Only the United Nations Security Council, which is hardly a representative body given the veto power of the five permanent members, can issue binding resolutions. The European Parliament probably comes the closest to a truly supranational legislature that can legally bind member states; however, its authority is limited regionally.

Article 38 of the Statute of the International Court of Justice is generally regarded as a definitive statement of the formal sources of international law. It identifies the two primary sources of law as international conventions (treaties) entered into by states and international custom, as evidence of a general practice of states accepted as law by states. The two subsidiary sources include general principles of law recognized by civilized nations and judicial decisions and teachings of the most highly qualified publicists. Somewhat predictably, given the state-centric nature of the law governing legal subjects, sources doctrine also constitutes a state-centric order. Positivist international lawyers tend to prefer treaties over custom as authoritative sources because the former are based on positive acts of state consent, while the latter is harder to fit into a consent-based legal order (Kennedy 1987: 24–25). In order to do so, positivists have reinterpreted custom in a manner consistent with consent-based sources: custom binds only those states that have consented to it. Clearly, proving consent to be bound by historic customs proves problematic when new states are concerned and when there is no historical record. As a result, positivists have implied state consent through the repeated practice of the custom by states and the belief that the conduct is legally obligatory (ibid.: 25–26). Legal positivists thus rank the sources in a hierarchy of declining consent and, hence, declining strength. The strongest sources are treaties; next comes custom; next comes general principles of law; weakest are judicial decisions and the writings of publicists. Moreover, unlike in many domestic legal systems where the principle of *stare decisis* (the binding force of judicial decisions upon subsequent proceedings) applies, under international law such decisions are only subsidiary and not primary sources. This leaves states very much at the centre as the sources of law, for not even the judicial decisions of the International Court of Justice can upstage state consent as a legal source. Notably, the resolutions of international organizations do not figure in this hierarchy of sources. Nor do the normative claims of individuals, human rights, or environmental movements constitute sources of law. More often than not, these appeals rest upon extra-consensual sources like appeals to 'justice', 'equity' and 'fairness' that do not figure in traditional sources doctrine. Nor do transnational corporations or private business associations figure as legitimate sources, notwithstanding the significant accretion of legal personality by corporations under global and regional regulatory regimes that confer the legal rights normally associated with states alone (see Cutler 2001a). Sources doctrine thus both reflects and supports the doctrine on subjects.

Whereas international lawyers talk about subjects and sources, international relations scholars refer to agents or actors, conflating the analytical concepts of source and subject. States as the essential actors in international relations are also the legitimate voices of the global polity. Conventional analysis in international relations thus mirrors the state-centrism of subject and sources doctrine. Structural realists remain steadfastly committed to the view that states remain the essential actors, notwithstanding what appears to be a proliferation of other entities claiming significance (see Krasner 1993, 1995; Mearsheimer 1994–1995). Neo-liberal institutionalists also continue to regard the state as the main agent of international regimes, despite the fact that the generally accepted definition of international regimes did not limit them to participation by states but to norms, rules, etc. 'around which *actors*' expectations converge' (Krasner 1983b: 2) (emphasis added). The initial promise of regime analysis to net in a broader set of actors was not met as regime analysis became progressively more state-centric. This led Miles Kahler to observe that regimes analysis was 'captured' by a neo-realist synthesis of realism and neo-liberalism. Neo-liberals had initially challenged the excessive state-centrism of realism in studies of interdependence and transnational relations that were the precursors to regime analysis. However, over time a synthesis emerged and '[n]eo-liberalism was redefined away from complex interdependence toward a state-centric version more compatible with realism' (Grieco 1988; Kahler 1997: 35).

Structural realists clearly regard states as the legitimate voices, recognizing the authority of the pronouncements of international organizations only insofar as states have empowered them to speak. Recognizing the voice of individuals is regarded as potentially subversive of the authority of states and is thus discouraged (see Cutler 1999b: 290–291), while the activities of transnational corporations are ultimately regarded as conditioned by states (Krasner 1995: 279). The voices of non-state actors cannot possibly be regarded as authoritative as that would be inconsistent with the formal logic of state sovereignty. For neo-realists, the discourse on sources thus tends to run into and become indistinguishable from the discourse on subjects.

The neo-liberal institutionalist treatment of international regimes does raise some of the issues addressed by sources doctrine. The contemporary focus on 'explicit' regimes and international treaties reflects a similar preoccupation with formalism. Curiously, an approach that initially embraced the authority of 'implicit and explicit principles, norms, rules and decision-making procedures' (Krasner 1983b: 2) has become increasingly formalistic in narrowing regimes to explicit acts of state consent. Robert Keohane (1989b: 4) defines international regimes as 'institutions with explicit rules, agreed upon by governments, that pertain to particular sets of issues in international relations'. Andrew Hurrell (1993: 54) notes that the 'apparently growing stress on explicit, persistent, and connected sets of rules brings regime theory and international law much closer together'. It is most paradoxical that international regimes analysis has moved in the direction of the 'formalism' and 'legalism' of law, accusations once lobbied with such disdain at international lawyers by classical realists. For both disciplines formalism concerning subjects and sources precludes theorizing about the authority of non-state actors and sources of law (but see Abbott *et al.* 2000 and Abbott and Snidal 2000).

In terms of the relative autonomy, neutrality and objectivity of the law, conventional theory in both international law and international relations reflects an *a priori* distinction between the world of state interests and *realpolitik* and the world of morals and normativity. As we saw for some of the early positivists, the chasm between law and morality, when combined with the application of the domestic analogy resulted in profound doubt about the status of international law as law 'properly so-called' and led to its treatment as 'positive morality'. In an interesting inversion of this conceptualization, more contemporary legal positivists accept that law is law 'properly so-called', but regard it as separate and autonomous from morality, polity and religion. In international relations theory, classical realists shared the early positivist doubts about the legal status of international law. Such doubt is also evident in the work of many structural realists in the context of the efficacy of regime norms and international institutions in regulating state behaviour (Mearsheimer 1994–1995). In general, structural realists and neo-liberal institutionalists alike have a hard time accepting the binding force of non-material influences like laws, norms and ideas, a position separating them from more unconventional approaches (see Krasner 1983b; Goldstein and Keohane 1993).

Unconventional and critical theoretical approaches

The unconventional approaches in international law are numerous and include natural law theory, the New Haven approach, critical legal studies, feminist and other approaches drawing on critical theory. In general, these approaches contemplate considerable pluralism in both the subjects and sources of legal regulation.

Natural law theory predated legal positivism and in many ways precipitated the latter's rise to prominence. For natural lawyers like the Stoics, Cicero and Aquinas, there was no question that law mattered. Indeed, belief in the existence of universal transcendent legal principles that could be apprehended through right reason formed the foundations for the earliest forms of international law (*jus gentium*), predating the formation of the state system (Cutler 1991 and Beck *et al.* 1996: Chapter 2). Grotius is probably the best known natural lawyer, whose work paved the way for legal positivism and an increasingly state-centric view of both the subjects and sources of the law (Lauterpacht 1946; Cutler 1991). Grotius theorized law to be based upon both universal principles *and* state consent, anticipating the advent of legal positivism as the theory most consistent with the emerging doctrine of sovereignty. Early natural law theorists clearly accepted the individual as a subject of international law, although by the time of Grotius the state was clearly beginning to assume greater centrality (Lauterpacht 1946; Cutler 1991). In terms of the sources of law early naturalists drew upon divine law, transcendental natural law principles, and state-made law, reflecting considerable pluralism in legal regulation. They also regarded law as infused by morality and as an integral element in a larger social totality. Significantly, though, they imputed considerable neutrality and objectivity to its operation by virtue of its link to transcendent and rational principles.

Although natural law thinking has receded in importance, it continues to influence modern thought. Natural law beliefs in a plurality of legal subjects and sources and the infusion of law with moral values inform international human rights and environmental laws, theories on just war and humanitarian intervention, the prosecution of war crimes trials and other approaches, like the New Haven, critical legal studies, and feminist approaches (see Beck *et al.* 1996: 36). However, most of these approaches developed in response to perceived inadequacies in both natural law and positive law theories. At root was a suspicion that law did not operate neutrally or as an objective system of rules. Critics emphasized the socially constructed, subjective, and even indeterminate nature of law.

The New Haven approach originated in the work of two Yale professors, Myres McDougal and Harold Lasswell, who sought to develop a 'policy-oriented jurisprudence'. The approach is interdisciplinary, drawing on law, political science, sociology and psychology (see generally, Beck *et al.* 1996: Chapter 5). It challenges the legal positivist view that law is a body of rules, positing that it is an 'authoritative decision-making process' involving a multiplicity of participants and choices between competing norms and values (McDougal and Lasswell 1959; Lasswell and Reisman 1968). New Haven scholars thus reject the conventional identification of the state as the only proper subject, arguing that there are many 'participants' involved in the process of authoritative decision-making (McDougal and Lasswell 1959; Higgins 1985; Artz and Lukashuk 1998). These participants include states, individuals, groups and basically any collection of entities seeking to make claims and realize values in the international arena. New Haven scholars thus reflect the natural law position that membership in international society is not limited to states, but extends to individuals as well (Cutler 1991).

They also reject formalism concerning the sources of the law, asserting the legal status of General Assembly resolutions and arguing that subjects doctrine does not adequately account for the status of individuals under international human rights law (Higgins 1985). Presumptions of the separation of law from society and morality are also rejected and the law is defined in terms of its normative content. This reflects the natural law position on sources, subjects, and the moral content of law. However, New Haven scholars reject naturalist claims about the objectivity and neutrality of the law. Rather, law is posited to be a construct of states and other participants and is said to promote the values and norms they adopt. Law is thus not an objective and neutral order and its efficacy turns on the extent to which the participants, subjectively, regard it as authoritative and, objectively, behave in accordance with its precepts.

Critical legal studies in international law, also referred to as the 'New Stream', adopt the insight that law is constructed by participants in the law-making process. Drawing on eclectic and interdisciplinary insights from 'normative philosophy, critical theory, structuralism, anthropology, prepositional logic, literature, sociology, politics, and psychiatry' (Purvis 1991: 88–89) the New Stream is regarded as a 'postmodern approach' to international law (Carty 1991: 66), with significant roots in the European critical theory tradition (Purvis 1991: cf. 89). Critical legal scholars reject the naturalist appeals to transcendent, universal and neutral legal principles and the positivist premise that law operates as a body of rules. Rather, law is regarded as a 'discourse' and as an 'ideology' that transmits imagery about the world through legal rhetoric. As such, we can study it through linguistic analysis, focusing 'upon the hidden ideologies, attitudes and structures which lie behind discourse, rather than upon the subject matter of the legal talk' (Kennedy 1980: 355). Moreover, central to the constructed and ideological nature of law is the dialectical tension between law's role in constituting and empowering the state (through legal doctrines associated with state sovereignty including those governing the use of force, acquisition of territory, sources and subjects of law, etc.) and its role as a regulator and critic of state action. David Kennedy (1988), who first developed this approach, posits that international legal discourse is characterized by the rhetorical movement between these two competing roles (see also Cutler 2001a). There is thus no objective content to law; its content is indeterminate and a function of the ideological uses to which it is put. As Beck *et al.* (1996: 229) note, 'because doctrinal arguments merely mask ideological forces, international law is incapable of playing the neutral role traditional approaches prescribe for it. It cannot resolve dilemmas. Instead, it mirrors and reinforces them through its rhetorical structure.'

Central to the New Stream is a critique of the liberal foundations of international law, which posit the nature and role of law to be the impartial settlement of disputes through the application of objective legal principles. The liberal 'rule of law' for New Stream scholars is an impossibility given the indeterminacy and ideological nature of legal argument or 'rhetoric'. Critical legal scholars also object to the 'exclusionary' nature of state-centric subject and sources doctrines, which operate as 'mechanisms of exclusion' excluding 'actual social difference' in the face of the 'logic of state orthodoxy' (Kennedy 1988: 25). Critical legal theorists reject the state-centricity of international legal doctrine governing subjects, arguing that this simply does not describe adequately the role of the individual as a subject of international law, particularly in the area of international human rights law (Janis 1984).

The idea that international law does not operate neutrally, but serves to promote particularistic interests and values is carried forward into other critical approaches. Feminist theorists of international law believe that law matters, however, not as an autonomous, neutral or objective legal order (Charlesworth *et al.* 1991).[2] Rather, international law is theorized as promoting patriarchal institutions, structures and methods of legal reasoning. Like the critical legal studies approach, feminist approaches are highly interdisciplinary and tend to focus on both the doctrinal and practical dimensions of patriarchy. The former involves critical analysis of the gendered basis of concepts that regulate the substantive content of international law to exclude matters of particular concern to women (see Charlesworth *et al.* 1991: 276–279; Wright 1991; Kim 1993). The focus on doctrine involves, for example, a critical review of limitations on the scope of legal concepts like torture, slavery, war crimes, crimes against humanity, and the like, that exclude actions having a disproportionate effect on women, like rape, forced pregnancy and prostitution (Byrne 1991: 214; Gardham 1991; Kim 1993). The focus on the practical aspects of patriarchy involves analysis of the ways in which law-making institutions exclude women. Feminist scholars in both international law and international relations have challenged the state-centricity of conventional approaches and the way in which national governments and international organizations have typically excluded specifically women's issues from emerging human rights norms. Exclusionary hiring and consultation practices of national governments and international organizations and the limitation of conference diplomacy to participation by states and international organizations have generated considerable concern that there should be provision for the inclusion of individual and group participation in international legal fora (Charlesworth *et al.* 1991; Whitworth 1994). These feminist scholars argue that the increasing participation of women and women's groups in the decision-making structures of national governments and in international governmental and non-governmental organizations is assisting in the practical inclusion of women in the development of the normative foundations of the global polity. However, until there is a rethinking of the doctrinal foundations of international legal personality, the formal inclusion of women as subjects will not occur. Moreover, the efficacy of the whole human rights regime rests upon developing a sounder foundation for individuals to assert their rights against states under international law by opening up all relevant human rights fora to participation by individual litigants.

For feminists, law matters both as a source of exploitation and as a source of potential emancipation. Feminist scholarship rejects legal positivism as a theory of law that is unsuitable for promoting social change. Positive international law is defined and enforced by states whose interests militate against empowering those who might use the law to challenge the conduct of their own state. Natural law theory is faulted as well for its narrow and limited definition of rights drawing upon exclusively Western and male standards (Kim 1993: 65–66). Feminists thus reject that states are the proper subjects or sources of the law and embrace its socially constructed and potentially emancipatory nature.

The idea that law is a social construct and has an integral role to play in emancipatory politics is also reflected in a new generation of critical scholarship in international law and international relations (McCormick 1999; Cutler 2001a; Scheuerman 2001). Building on the insights of critical legal studies and feminist analysis, law is posited as playing a generative role in constituting the underlying structure and normative framework for the global polity. According to this view, law exists not as a fixed body of neutral and objectively determinable rules, but as a construct of and thus deeply embedded in international society. William Scheuerman (1999a, 1999b, 2000) emphasizes the interplay of economic, political and social worlds in the constitution of international law. He argues that forces of globalization and changes in the nature of global capitalism are influencing the nature and role of international law. Economic globalization and the process of time–space compression associated with post-Fordist developments in capitalist production[3] are creating an increasingly discretionary, *ad hoc*, privatized and non-transparent legal order. 'International capital's preference for porous, open-ended law' is evident in the areas of international business arbitration, business taxation, finance and banking regulations, and the WTO (Scheuerman 1999a: 4). This development is quite inconsistent with liberal conceptions of the predictable, non-arbitrary, and public 'rule of law'.

Others also note that the process of time–space compression is transforming the nature and role of law, rendering traditional positivist forms of legal regulation quite anachronistic and even irrelevant (de Sousa Santos 1993: 115). This suggests that there is increasing pluralism in the nature and source of legal regulation in the proliferation of informal and 'soft' legal sources and the resistance of the major commercial participants, like transnational corporations, to traditional legal forms in the regulation of international economic relations (Kline 1988). Indeed, the virtues of soft law in the forms of model laws, optional codes of conduct and statements of principle are that they are easier to implement, to modify, and to agree upon by commercial actors and are more cost-effective than are hard laws (Abbott and Snidal 2000). This reflects the preferences of commercial participants for flexible, discretionary, private and *ad hoc* standards that allow maximum freedom in commercial relations. However, such standards do not necessarily provide for equity or fairness and so Scheuerman (2001) advocates the 'constructive task' of developing a 'normatively legitimate' or more equitable form of transnational legal regulation.

The increased significance of private authority in the legal regulation of international commerce is emphasized by others as well (Cutler *et al.* 1999). Picking up on the themes that law is a social construct playing both exploitative and potentially emancipatory roles, my work adopts an explicitly 'critical' perspective (see Cox 1981, 1987; Linklater 1986, 1990; Gill 1993).[4] Drawing on the insights of critical international relations scholarship and critical legal theory, conventional theories are argued to obscure the significance of international law is a constitutive element of global capitalist relations of production (Cutler 1995, 1997, 1999a). Conventional subject and sources doctrines fail to capture the centrality of private business corporations and informal and soft legal sources in the construction of the transnational legal order. International law establishes systems of property and corporate rights that advance the interests and neo-liberal ideology of a global 'mercatocracy', or a transnational merchant class. The mercatocracy is comprised of a mix of public/state and private/non-state authorities and elites who are engaged in the unification of transnational commercial law (Cutler 1999a; 1999c). These efforts promote property rights that advance the interests associated with the transnational expansion of capital over those associated with national accumulation (Cutler 2002a). The preference for maximum flexibility and soft legal standards that provide for maximum capital mobility is favoured by the mercatocracy and not by developing states or weaker market participants who want hard laws that bind and work to level the playing field. African states, for example, would have preferred commercial arbitration law to have been unified through a binding treaty rather than through an optional model law (Sempasa 1992).

Unified laws also expand the rights of transnational corporations under international law in unprecedented ways without a commensurate expansion of corporate accountability. The provision for direct legal claims by transnational corporations against states under the dispute settlement mechanisms of the International Center for the Settlement of Investment Disputes (ICSID), the Canada–US Free Trade Agreement (FTA), the North American Free Trade Agreement (NAFTA), and the failed Multilateral Agreement on Investment (MAI) evidence a significant accretion in the legal subjectivity and personality of corporations (Cutler 2001b). In addition, the expansion of corporate legal authority in the increasingly privatized field of dispute resolution and international commercial arbitration reflects a profound expansion in the legal and political authority of corporations (Cutler 1995; Dezalay and Garth 1996). This is resulting in the privatization of justice in areas traditionally regarded as part of the public domain such as taxation, antitrust, intellectual property and securities regulations (McConnaughay 1999). However, legal doctrine remains blind to these developments as transnational corporations are invisible as 'subjects' under the law (Johns 1994).

While critical legal scholarship in international law is helpful in displacing legal positivist and natural law fictions about the neutrality and objectivity of law, it does not sufficiently enable the recognition of the centrality of class interests in the formulation of global economic law. The adoption of a class-based, dialectical mode of reasoning and historical analysis is crucial to critical theory conceived of through historical materialist analysis as an emancipatory project (Neufeld 1995; Smith 1996). Arguably, critical legal theorists in international law are uncomfortable with the traditional Marxist distinction between the economic base and the ideological superstructure of capitalism (Purvis 1991: cf. 89). Their efforts to establish the effective role of law as ideology in the creation of relations of dominance and exploitation in the world could not be achieved if law remained merely part of the superstructure. However, this is a contested view of Marx's position on the nature and role of law under the capitalist mode of production (see Vincent 1993; Cutler 2002a). Marx clearly contemplated the law as constitutive of the political, social and material relations of production and that it is therefore appropriate to inquire into the relationship between legal concepts and the property relations to which they give rise.[5] One might thus conceive of a 'looser materialism' that conceptualizes Marxism as a form of 'praxis' uniting theory and practice in a symbiotic and reciprocal relationship, denying unidirectional claims of the base over the superstructure or the material over the ideational (Klare 1979; Vincent 1993; Cutler 2002b). This approach rejects the domestic analogy as an adequate account of global law and law-making, both in terms of the subjects and sources of the law. While states may be the formal subjects of the law (*de jure*), private corporate actors are increasingly operating as subjects (*de facto*) in creating new forms of legal regulation, like soft laws, model laws, optional codes and statements of principal that advance the interests of the mercatocracy. This may appear to reflect increasing legal pluralism in legal regulation both as to legal subjects and sources (Kline 1988). However, a more critical view reveals the underlying unity provided by the globalization of neo-liberal disciplinary legal norms and the dialectical tension between class interests associated with national capital accumulation and those associated with the transnational expansion of capital (Cutler 2000a; Cutler, under review).

The globalization of the rule of law is an integral aspect of neo-liberal discipline, which is expanding the private sphere of capital accumulation, while constraining potentially democratizing influences. Indeed, the notion of 'a rule of law' advances the rhetoric of globalization, which posits that the expansion of private corporate authority is a natural, organic, efficient, and ultimately more just means of adjusting to the challenges posed by globalization. However, conventional theory remains blind to the increasing significance of private subjects and sources due to its commitment to legal formalism and a state-centric model of rule. Movement away from the hierarchical model of rule and analysing the tensions and counter-trends in contemporary legal regulation provides a clearer analytical understanding of the multiplicity of legal subjects and sources constituting law in the global polity. It also provides a more critical theoretical understanding of the nature and operation of the law. This is significant for identifying potential sources of transformation in the global polity, because it reveals spaces in which the globalization of neo-liberal discipline may be contested. The emergence of new legal subjects and sources offer potentially fertile sites of resistance and transformation. There is no compelling analytical or theoretical reason why a business corporation should possess any more legal personality than a human rights organization. Nor is there any reason for the *prima facie* elevation of the value of cost-effectiveness over justice as the criteria for legal sources. In this regard, critical scholarship has much to offer in developing an understanding of the nature and role of law in the global polity.

We see as we move away from conventional approaches to international law that the law gains more efficacy. The law clearly matters to more critically minded theorists, but not as a neutral and objective arbiter of disputes, fixed through transcendent natural law processes or through positive law acts of state consent. Rather, the law matters as an integral part of social, political and economic life. As such, it is a source of global exploitation and, significantly, a potential source of transformation and change. This, however, is the unconventional and not the conventional view and so we must turn to consider why conventional thinkers might want to reconsider the dominant modes of thought.

Evaluating the effects of law in the global polity

Thus far we have argued that there are a number of conventional and unconventional approaches to assessing the nature and significance of law in the global polity. These approaches reflect different and often competing analytical and theoretical traditions in law and in politics. Conventional approaches, like legal positivism and neo-realism, generate different answers to the question of whether law matters than do the unconventional approaches of New Haven, critical legal, feminist and critical international relations scholars. These approaches also identify different subjects and sources or legitimate voices of the global polity. Conventional approaches identify states as the legitimate subjects and state consent as the authoritative source or voice in the polity. However, as we move away from the dominant approaches, we see increasing diversity in the authoritative subjects and sources of the global polity. Unconventional approaches identify a number of non-state entities as effective subjects, including individuals, global social movements, women and women's groups, transnational corporations and private associations, and a corporate mercatocracy or transnational capitalist class. Indeed, the expansion of regional and global human rights regimes and of corporate legal personality is challenging the doctrinal foundations of legal personality and broadening the scope of individual and corporate claims under international law. Increasingly, individuals and non-governmental organizations are participating in the negotiation of international human rights and environmental laws. Individuals have direct recourse in some regional and global arenas to assert legal claims against states for the infringement of human rights. The prosecution of individuals for war crimes, crimes against humanity, genocide and other offences creates a direct line of responsibility of the individual under international law. These developments resonate in the growing scholarship in international relations on emerging global civil society and the proliferation of non-governmental organizations and social movements involved in developing global environmental and human rights regimes (Lipschutz 1992; Shaw 1994; Clarke *et al.* 1998). This scholarship illustrates the increasing participation of non-state actors in the United Nations conference system and in other fora where international law is being negotiated and developed. When combined with the expansion in corporate legal personality and the pro-liferation of private non-governmental governance arrangements brought about by the privatization, deregulation and globalization of many sectors, industries and businesses (Cutler *et al.* 1999), subjects and sources doc-trine appear entirely inadequate analytically and theoretically. This has led one legal scholar to conclude that the 'concept of legal personality, an old favourite in Austinian analytical jurisprudence, may be ripe for a revival in a global context' (Twining 1996: 60). However, we must ask why we should care about the analytical and theoretical inadequacy of the con-ventional understandings of law. This takes us into the normative dimen-sion and moral content of law in the global polity.

For legal positivists, classical realists and neo-realists there is little concern over the moral content of the law. The assumed separation of morality and law, like that between morality and politics, renders the moral content of the law a non-issue. The law is created by and a reflec-tion of the interests of states. Indeed, state consent disciplines the content and impact of law, ensuring that there is no room for appeals to extra-con-sensual, higher principles. Legal formalism and political realism endow this picture with legitimacy as an objective state of affairs generated by the demands of positivist international law and state sovereignty. International law, under the liberalist rule of law, thus functions in a morally neutral manner to adjudicate disputes between conflicting state interests.

In contrast, the critics of the dominant approaches, like natural law theorists, New Haven scholars, feminists and critical legal and inter-national relations scholars, challenge that the global polity comprises a purely interest-based order in which law functions neutrally to adjudicate disputes between states. They emphasize the subjectivity and indetermi-nacy of law, resting much of their argument on the necessary moral content of the law. Indeed, their emancipatory projects rest in many cases upon their appeals to extra-consensual sources of law which are promoted by non-state subjects and actors. This is necessary in order to escape the disciplining role of the state and statist logic. For these critics, we need to care about the theoretical and analytical adequacies of the conventional approaches because they promote the values and interests of a very narrow set of subjects, actors or identities and marginalize others. The dominant approaches thus determine winners and losers; who can play the game and who counts in the global polity. Theory and law thus operate as mechanisms of inclusion and exclusion, but presumptions of objectivity and neutrality obscure these roles and the normative judge-ments they entail. Analytical and theoretical deficiencies in the conven-tional approaches blind us to the moral content and impact of the law and to its distributional consequences. They limit our ability to understand contemporary transformations in the global polity that are enhancing the empirical and normative influence of non-state subjects and sources of political authority. The role of law in deepening asymmetrical relations between genders and classes does not figure in the dominant analytical and theoretical frameworks. Nor does the law's role in attenuating the links between law and society and between the rule of law and democracy constitute part of the dominant view. The exclusion of women, global social movements, transnational corporations, private business associations, the global mercatocracy, and the transnational capitalist class as effective subjects of the global polity precludes any inquiry into the way in which law operates to perpetuate inequalities and exploitative relations. The exclusion of private structures and processes of governance and soft law as effective sources of law similarly forecloses inquiry into the way in which law facilitates the expansion of private power in the global polity. These subjects and sources simply do not figure in the analytical and theoretical nets cast by the dominant approaches, which are in any case rendered resistant to moral examination by assumptions of the value-neutrality of the law.

The dominant approaches are thus incapable of inquiry into the moral content and impact of the law and are therefore blind to the critical insight that law, like '[t]heory is always *for* someone and *for* some purpose' (Cox 1981: 87). This means that an adequate understanding of law in the global polity must include a critical understanding of the analytical, theoretical, and normative dimensions of the legal order, including reference to both the deficiencies of conventional theories and the promise of the unconventional.

Notes

1 Marxists used this term rather differently in their analysis of the nature of the relationship between law and capitalist society (see Balbus 1977).
2 There are clearly many feminist approaches to law, including liberal feminism, radical feminism, social/psychological feminism, Marxist feminism, socialist feminism, existentialist feminism and postmodern feminism (see Kim 1993).
3 David Harvey (1990: 147) associates post-Fordism with enhanced capital mobility and flexibility which he refers to as 'flexible accumulation' ('flexibility with regard to labour processes, labour markets, products and patterns of ownership, the emergence of new sectors of production, new financial services and markets, and intensified rates of commercial, technological, and organizational innovation') and the resulting time–space compression as the time horizons of decision-makers shrink.
4 Critical theory is here defined in keeping with the Frankfurt School which

> tended to focus on an intertwined relationship between the concepts of 'ideology' and 'legitimacy'. Critical theorists argued that the subordinate classes, against their own interest, accept the ideology of the ruling class, because they somehow came to see that ideology as legitimate and as their

own. True to its Marxist roots, the Frankfurt School tended to treat law as an agent in social life, often a reflection or institutional incarnation of the prevailing ideology. Law was a mechanism of legitimation. 'It was seen as the locus of conspiracy or the reproducer of false consciousness.'

> (Purvis 1991: cf. 89, quoting David Kennedy 1985–1986: 244–245)

The Frankfurt School was also concerned with the gap or disjuncture between theory and action and attempted to overcome the gap so that theory could become an active agent of liberating change in the world.

5 Marx emphasized that legal relations flow from the 'material conditions of life' and not from the 'human mind'. Many have interpreted him as believing the law to be part of the superstructure of capitalism. However, in analysing the origins of civil law in the practices of medieval merchants and later the bourgeoisie, it is clear that he regarded law as linked to the mode of production in that it served the interests of the powerful by creating institutions of private property which in turn led to the development of new relations of production and new property rights (see Cutler 2000a).

4 Societal denationalization and positive governance

Michael Zürn

Introduction

The study of the effects of globalization, or societal denationalization, on the national capacity to govern on the one hand and the study of international institutions on the other, are peculiarly separated. It would seem, however, more logical to combine these efforts for a more thorough understanding of governance, and thus to build another bridge across the 'great divide' (Caporaso 1997) between national order and international anarchy. Do international regimes arise especially in those issue areas in which national intervention has become counter-productive? To what extent is international governance a response to the decline in the effectiveness of national policies? Do international regimes systematically favour certain policy types and governance goals over others?

Rationalist theories of both international institutions and the democratic welfare state offer a number of objections to the notion that governance beyond the nation-state can overcome the current deficits of national governance. These objections state that the effectiveness of international institutions, when measured against more general governance goals, is highly conditional on structural prerequisites that are very unlikely to be met outside of the national context. First, both neo-realist theorists of international politics and a good many theorists of continental jurisprudence hold the view that the right of governance is structurally or constitutionally reserved for a central power, and they draw a categorical line between the national and the international sphere. Governance, in this view, is bound to the existence of a superior power, which most of the time is lacking at the level beyond the nation-state. According to another set of objections, it is pointed out that international institutions can only enforce certain types of regulation. Although, it is argued, international institutions do play a role, it is restricted to the creation of markets and facilitation of free cross-border exchanges. Measures that intervene into such exchanges are only possible within a hierarchical national structure. The structural problem here with governance beyond the nation-state is thus that for the purposes of social welfare, economic efficiency is prioritized and market control and distributive justice are systematically neglected.

According to all these objections one should expect that the demand for international institutions will not be met beyond the nation-state and thus that the realization of governance will remain deficient. According to the first objection, international institutions arise as a consequence of the power distribution in the international system, but they do not respond to the challenges of societal denationalization. According to the other objections, we should observe the absence of market-correcting institutions beyond the nation-state, or at least, a growing gap between market-making, or 'negative', and market-correcting, or 'positive' international institutions.

This chapter aims at demonstrating that these expectations are only partially met. To this end, the objections against the notion of governance beyond the nation-state are put into the context of rationalist theories of international institutions and discussed in more detail. It will then be demonstrated that market-correcting international regulations have indeed grown roughly in parallel (albeit with small delays) with societal denationalization. By using some quantitative measures and a qualitative survey on the state of governance beyond the nation-state, it is furthermore argued that the (nonetheless existent) gap between market-making and market-correcting international regulations is not widening, but in fact closing in some areas.

Societal denationalization and global governance: concepts and theoretical expectations

Governance is the purposeful management of problematic social relations and conflict situations by means of reliable, durable regulations and institutions rather than the direct application of power and force. Governance in the developed OECD countries centres on aims such as maintaining the physical integrity of the people and their political organizations from internal as well as external risks and threats (security) and maintaining a balance between economic efficiency and distributive justice (social welfare). The democratic welfare state that developed in the so-called OECD world in the 1970s has been uniquely successful in contributing to these governance goals. It is the heyday of this ideal-type OECD-state that serves here as a standard for the achievement of these governance goals (Zürn 1998: Chapter 2).

The success of the democratic welfare state in achieving these governance goals depended, among other things, upon the *spatial congruence* of political regulations with socially integrated areas. When social spaces transcend national borders and the jurisdiction of national governments remains confined within their old borders, it is often very hard to formulate policies that reach their objectives. However, this is exactly what happens when so-called globalization or societal denationalization takes place. Societal denationalization[1] namely can be defined as a process in which social spaces, which are constituted by dense transactions, extend beyond national borders, without them necessarily being global in scope. Consequently, a shift in the boundaries of socially integrated areas – boundaries being defined here as the place where there is some critical reduction in the frequency of social transactions (Deutsch 1969: 99) – constitutes a challenge to the effectiveness of national regulations and creates demands for regulation beyond the nation-state.

Societal denationalization challenges both market-making and market-correcting regulations on the national level. On the one hand, as national borders no longer encompass sufficient territory to function as self-contained markets for large multinational companies, many national regulations that are not harmonized at the international level separate markets and create barriers for the efficient development, pursuit and sale of goods and services. Larger markets and unhindered cooperation with other enterprises are therefore seen as essential to remain competitive: in a denationalized world the 'static efficiency costs of closure' (Frieden and Rogowski 1996: 35) increase. In general, economic integration will create further demands to maximize the gains from economic exchange by overcoming the disadvantages of political segmentation and harmonizing national policies or by common rules that prohibit national intervention (*negative international regulations*).

On the other hand, political regulations may have little impact if they only cover a part of the relevant social space. A national regulation by Australia alone, for instance, can do little to prevent increasing cancer rates due to the depletion of atmospheric ozone (externalities). Moreover, the establishment of a regulation that does not apply to all social actors within an integrated social space can be economically counter-productive. In particular, policies that create costs for the production of goods may turn out to be self-defeating in terms of competitiveness for the area to which the policy applies. Against this background, the widespread fear of a downward spiral in national social and environmental standards is not surprising (race to the bottom). Rising externalities and fears of a race to the bottom create demands for common policies to intervene in free societal transactions (*positive international regulations*).

Whereas *negative international regulations* contain an agreement that states refrain from certain activities, *positive international regulations* oblige states to actively undertake certain activities and intervene in line with a coordinated strategy.[2] With negative regulations, states often only agree to refrain from certain actions. For instance, they may not hinder free exchange by rules of their own, or – in the reciprocal acknowledgement of regulations – must carry out a certain amount of 'interface management'. The situation with positive regulations is completely different. Here, the participating governments undertake to implement certain policies or to reach certain objectives. Typically, an agreement aims to *harmonize* national policies at a level slightly above the lowest common denominator. At least some of the participating governments feel obliged to take some form of action (rather than to desist from taking action) in order to comply with the agreement. Furthermore, this action is almost always necessary to bring societal actors to change their behaviour. Therefore, positive regulations require a 'double implementation', that is the implementation of international policies at the national level and the implementation of national policies so that the target groups in fact change their behaviour.

Is it possible to meet this demand for negative and positive regulations beyond the nation-state in order to overcome the governance challenges due to societal denationalization? By distinguishing *governance* and *government*, the purposeful regulation of social processes (governance) becomes conceivable outside of a hierarchical setting characterized by the notion of a government.[3] This notion liberates governance from its national constraints, making governance beyond the nation-state, be it negative or positive, all the more conceivable. 'Governance beyond the nation-state' (Zürn 1998) or 'global public policy' (Reinicke 1998) can, at least theoretically, restore the effectiveness of regulations by establishing new political institutions that match the relevant social spaces.

Governance beyond the nation-state cannot take the form of governance by government, but, more realistically, governance with governments, as in international institutions, or governance without government, as in transnational regimes. So far, however, *governance without government* does not seem to play a significant role in international relations. Therefore the focus is on *governance with governments* regulating state and non-state activities the effects of which extend beyond national borders. Central to international governance are *international regimes*, defined as social institutions consisting of agreed-upon and publicly undeclared principles, norms, rules, procedures and programmes that govern the interactions of actors in specific issue areas.[4] As such, regimes contain one or more specific regulations and engender recognized social practices in international society. Regimes contain both substantive and procedural rules and are thus distinct from mere *networks* which frequently only contain informal, procedural rules. Such networks meet on a regular basis and may develop coordinated responses to specific situations, but they do not govern behaviour in a given issue area for a prolonged period of time.[5] Other components of international governance are *international organizations*, which are material entities and can act as vehicles for both international regimes and inter- or transgovernmental networks.[6] *Supra-national* institutions are a special form of governance with government. Supra-national institutions develop rules that are considered superior to national law and involve servants that are independent of national governments. The demand for supra-national governance increases with the growing density and scope of international governance. Any of these components of governance beyond the nation-state can be regional or global in scope. The sum of all such institutional arrangements, including the existing transnational regimes, make up regional or global governance systems. Moreover, the interplay of different forms of governance beyond the nation-state with the cooperation of nation-states can produce political systems of a new quality, as attested by the European Multi-Level Governance System (Marks *et al.* 1996; Jachtenfuchs and Kohler-Koch 1996).

Do these different international institutions meet the demands induced by societal denationalization? Can governance beyond the nation-state compensate for the deficits of national governance? Are all global public policies feasible? Different rationalist theories of international institutions tend to answer these questions quite differently.

Functionalism

Following functionalist *theory*, it is only consistent to answer all the above questions in the affirmative. This is because, from a functionalist perspective, political institutions are an adequate – if slightly belated – response to the problems arising out of societal denationalization for the realization of governance goals. In this view, functioning institutions evolve through competitive selection or the inevitable adaptation to changing circumstances and demands. Thus, in the seventeenth and eighteenth centuries the nation-state prevailed over other forms of political organization because it best matched the functional requirements of the time (see North 1990; Spruyt 1994). To the extent that national political systems can no longer fulfil today's requirements, it is expected from a functionalist point of view that new, more adequate political institutions will develop. The logical conclusion of this is that in a denationalized world with transnational social spaces, the demand for (and subsequently the provision of) international institutions, be they negative or positive, will grow.[7] While Keohane's (1984) quasi-functionalist theory of international regimes avoids the causal shortcuts of other functionalist approaches, it leads to the same prediction:

> as long as technological change prompts increased economic interdependence and as long as threats to the global environment grow in severity, we will observe a continuing increase in the number and complexity of international institutions and in the scope of their regulation.
> (Keohane 1993: 284–285)

Inter-governmental power theories

Power theories diametrically oppose functionalist reasoning. Waltzian Realism (1979) essentially denies that international institutions play any role in world politics. Modifying this proposition, the theory of hegemonic stability suggests that international institutions may help to maintain a liberal and peaceful international order (Kindleberger 1973; Krasner 1976; Keohane 1980). However, the creation and maintenance of international institutions depend upon a hegemon. Only a clearly superior power is in a position to provide the means for maintaining international order. With the relative decline of the hegemon's power, its willingness and capacity to maintain these institutions decrease. However, historical and theoretical analyses have led to a consensus that hegemony is neither necessary nor sufficient for the creation or the persistence of international institutions.[8] Nonetheless, it is still a widely believed argument that the absence of a strong power hierarchy poses an obstacle for the creation of international institutions. In operational terms, one may expect that international institutions, be they negative or positive, will develop parallel to the relative power and reflect the interests of the United States.

Transnational power in world economy

According to this view, 'political measures aimed to change or correct market outcomes can only be implemented within the boundaries of the nation state.... Economic globalization undermines the conditions for such intervention and only allows de-politicized, privatized and market-induced forms of economic order' (Streeck 1995: 60, my translation; Lange 1992; de Swaan 1992). This expectation rests on an assumption about class relations according to which the nation-state provided a unique institutional setting for balanced economic interests. Without this setting, the democratic civilization of capitalism is likely to become obsolete (Cerny 1995; Offe 1998; Streeck 1998). Among other things, the democratic civilization of capitalism depends on strong labour unions, national solidarity and majoritarian decision-making, all of which are non-existent at a level beyond national societies. At the transnational level, interest representation is therefore completely biased in favour of economic interests and the social purpose of international institutions can be expected to reflect the interests of a transnational business class (Cox 1987; Gill 1993; van der Pijl 1998). The rise of international institutions that respond to efficiency pressures and improve exit options for businesses is thus likely, while the rise of international institutions to correct market outcomes contrary to the interests of capital owners is extremely unlikely. In operational terms, while the rise of negative international regulations should develop parallel to societal denationalization, positive international regulations cannot be expected at all.

Rationalist institutionalism

Rationalist institutionalism builds on the quasi-functional theory of international regimes, but is more sensitive to the implications of varied preferences involved in international negotiations. One implication is the recognition that a Prisoner's Dilemma (PD) is only one type of problem affecting collective action. Another implication is an increased sensitivity to distributional issues even if the underlying structure of the interest constellation resembles a PD type of game.[9] Employing such a framework, Fritz Scharpf (1999), for instance, maintains that governance beyond the nation-state (international and European) cannot offset the declining effectiveness of national policies. In this view, market-building regulations arise, at least with respect to larger economies, against the background of a constellation of interests that resembles a coordination game. In order to avoid the possibility of 'cheating', which may come about as a result of domestic pressure by particularistic interests, executives lock in negative international regulations through the creation of supra-national bodies.[11] Since negative integration is both to a large extent self-enforcing *and* supra-nationally safeguarded, it is comparatively easy to achieve and extremely resilient to change.

Positive international regulations, in contrast, are much harder to achieve and less resilient. The problem they have to deal with is much more 'malign' (Underdal 1997, 2000). The need for positive international regulations frequently arises within a constellation of interests that resembles a collaboration game. This does not rule out institutionalized cooperation *per se*. Indeed, EU regulations have been passed on issues such as health, product quality and consumer protection, which at first glance all appear to be positive regulations. At this point, however, Scharpf introduces a further distinction:

> The bordering line between consensual and confrontational [interest] constellations can roughly be drawn parallel to the distinction between the harmonization of product and mobility-related regulations on the one hand and the harmonization of production and locational regulations on the other.... The decisive reason for conflict over production and locational regulations is – inevitably – the extreme differences in the economic development of the member states.
>
> (1996a: 117; see also Scharpf 1996b: 19–25)

Accordingly, positive international regulations are possible only in the relatively scarce cases when the underlying interest constellation can be made self-enforcing. This is the case when discriminating product regulations are respected by negative international institutions and can thus be the basis for the exclusion of products of inferior quality – the so-called California effect (Vogel 1995). It may also happen when the costs of implementing the policies are so low that they do not seriously affect the competition for foreign investment. In the majority of positive regulations, the PD type of constellation of interests is, however, additionally burdened by serious distributional conflicts. These distributional conflicts may be due either to different national economic capacities (which standard is affordable and appropriate) or to different regulatory and cultural traditions (which instruments do we use and why do we need to change them, Héritier *et al.* 1996). In sum, while negative regulations and simple positive regulations often arise out of inter-governmental interest constellations that resemble coordination games, and sometimes collaboration games without distributional implications, genuine interventionist measures need to overcome an interest constellation that resembles a dilemma game, mostly with serious distributional implications. In its operational form, the hypothesis is as follows: effective international regulations related to production and location are not realizable between states with significantly different productivity levels and/or with different regulatory traditions. Positive regulations will therefore be scarce and a growing gap between negative and positive international regulations can be expected.

The development of governance beyond the nation-state

The lack of congruence between national political regulations and denationalized areas of social transactions calls into question the capacity of the nation-state to provide that which made it the dominant political institution in the first place. In this predicament, governments can regain control by establishing new international regimes, networks and organizations to coordinate and harmonize their policies, i.e. to establish governance beyond the nation-state. The question then is whether, and to what extent, governance beyond the nation-state has grown parallel[11] to societal denationalization. To answer this question, an understanding of the speed of societal denationalization is first necessary. Then, in a first cut, the aggregate growth rates of international organizations are analysed. In a second cut, I discuss to what extent governance goals have been attained by international institutions.

Societal denationalization

The degree of societal denationalization can be operationalized as the extent of cross-border transactions relative to transactions taking place within national borders. Social transactions take place whenever goods, services and capital (constituting the issue area of economy), threats (force), pollutants (environment), signs (communication) or persons (mobility) are exchanged or commonly produced. An empirical investigation carried out against the background of this conceptualization shows that denationalization is not a uniform, but rather a jagged process that differs notably among issue areas, countries and over time.[12] Nevertheless, for the purposes of this chapter the developments may be summarized as follows: societal denationalization has been taking place in mild forms since the 1950s, especially in the field of force with the employment of nuclear weapons. From the 1970s on, the growth of cross-border exchanges accelerated with respect to goods and capital, information, travel, migration and regional environmental risks. Surprisingly, the growth of some of these exchange processes levelled off for a few years in the early 1980s. Veritable denationalization thrusts, however, occurred in a number of very specific issue areas such as global environmental dangers, finance and digital communication areas just as the slowed-down growth in some cross-border exchanges was reversed, that is from the end of the 1980s on. This aggregate picture of societal denationalization serves as a measure of the demand for international regulations.

International organizations and treaties in the aggregate

Does the development of international institutions match that of societal denationalization? A first measure for the extent of international governance is the number of international governmental organizations (IGOs). Up until the early 1980s this figure grew continuously to a total of 378, thus reflecting the permanent growth in the importance of cross-border transactions. In the late 1980s, as the growth of some cross-border transactions slowed down, the overall number of international organizations declined rapidly to less than three hundred. Only recently has the number of international organizations been increasing again. Currently the number of IGOs is still below the figure for the 1980s, unless IGO emanations are counted.[13]

The decline in the absolute number of international organizations during the 1980s can at best be partially explained by the breakdown of the Socialist bloc and its organizations. A look at the development of memberships in international organizations of the G7 countries alone shows for all countries a more or less parallel development to the overall number of international organizations, with only two differences. The rise in figures was less sharp and the temporary decline set in five to ten years earlier (Figures 4.1 and 4.2). It is noteworthy that the development of international organization (IO) memberships of the G7 countries is uniform, irrespective of whether they are European countries or not.[14] Moreover, the number of regional IGOs declined in the 1980s even faster than global and inter-regional IGOs (see Shanks *et al.* 1996: 596).

The number of international organizations is only a very rough measure of the development of international governance. It is easily conceivable that a relatively constant number of IGOs should have produced a higher regulatory output and thus strengthened international governance. Indeed, the overall number of multilateral treaties as deposited at the United Nations has grown in a linear fashion from less than 150 in 1960 to well over 400 in 1998. The same applies to the annual ratification of multi-

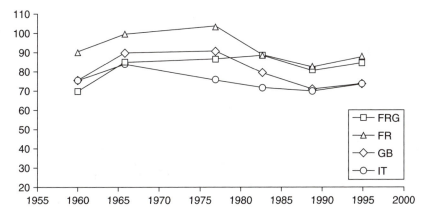

Figure 4.1 Membership of international organizations by Germany, France, Great Britain and Italy

Source: Beisheim *et al.* (1999: 353–355).

Note: We use the following abbreviations: FRG = Federal Republic of Germany, FR = France, GB = Great Britain, IT = Italy.

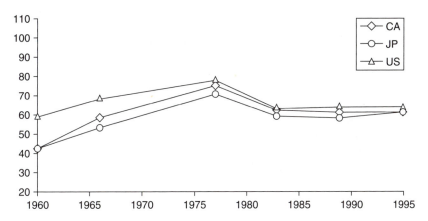

Figure 4.2 Membership of international organizations by Canada, Japan and the USA

Source: Beisheim *et al.* (1999: 353–355).

Note: We use the following abbreviations: CA = Canada, JP = Japan, US = United States of America.

lateral treaties (Hirschi *et al.* 1999: 40). Along the same lines, the number of EU directives, regulations and decisions grew significantly up until the 1980s, when IGO membership of the G7 countries had already begun to decline. The total number of directives, regulations and decisions increased from 36 in 1961, to 347 in 1970 and 627 in 1980. The number of

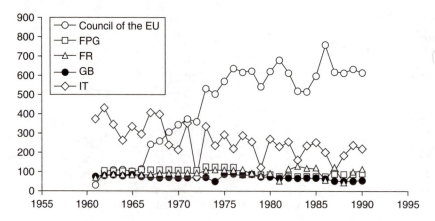

Figure 4.3 Acts of the Council of the EU and legislative output in Germany,
        France, Great Britain and Italy

Source: Beisheim *et al.* (1999: 328–330).

Note: We use the following abbreviations: FRG = Federal Republic of Germany, FR = France,
GB = Great Britain, IT = Italy.

EU rules has remained quite constant since then, with a temporary peak of
almost 800 in 1986. It is especially noteworthy that the relative weight of
EU legislation clearly increased when compared to national legislation in
Germany, France and Great Britain, where the yearly legislative output has
remained more or less constant since the 1960s (Figure 4.3).

The development of international institutions in the aggregate runs to
a large extent parallel to societal denationalization. A more or less linear
growth up until the early 1980s, was – with respect to some indicators –
briefly interrupted before it continued. Current growth rates in international institutions may, however, be slightly slower than in some fields
of societal denationalization. This aggregate picture of the growth of
international institutions matches surprisingly well the functionalist prediction of a growth more or less parallel to societal denationalization.

International institutions in security and social welfare

Is this aggregate development reflected when we look at the extent in
qualitative terms to which international regulations are a response to the
deficits of uncoordinated national endeavours to accomplish their goals?
Or is the gap between negative and positive international regulations
growing? Do we see a rise in positive international regulations at all? In
approaching these questions, I focus on two of the most important goals
of governance, that is, the attainment of internal and external security
and of social welfare by providing conditions favourable to growth and
restricting social inequality by market-correcting measures.

Social welfare

All the challenges that societal denationalization poses for national governance seem to be relevant for attaining 'social welfare'. On the one hand, the pressure for the establishment of rules to offset the disadvantages of national segmentation by prohibiting national intervention has led to demands for negative international regulations. On the other hand, the fear of a regulatory race to the bottom and the ineffectiveness of national policies when faced with insurmountable externalities has created demands for positive international regulations.

Negative international regulations

The establishment of legal certainty in the economic sphere has been a major means to increase the efficiency of economic activities and exchanges and thus foster economic growth and prosperity. The liberal nation-state effectively achieved legal certainty in the economic sphere by establishing property rights, by guaranteeing the free movement of labour, goods and capital, by standardizing weights, measures and education, and by drawing up necessary product regulations in a non-discriminatory way. In doing so, national economies with more or less uniform price levels emerged as transportation and communication costs decreased. In the course of economic denationalization, these national regulations come under efficiency pressure, in turn creating a demand for the establishment of common rules that prohibit national policies or intervention to overcome the disadvantages of national segmentation. Many international economic institutions arose in direct response to such efficiency pressures. The development of the GATT regime is a case in point. The early GATT removed government intervention at the borders, that is, tariffs on manufactured goods. Over time this increased the importance of non-tariff barriers, thus inducing demands for a new type of market-making regulations that focused on behind-the-border issues. The Tokyo Round of negotiations (1973–79) began to deal with non-tariff barriers such as anti-dumping, government subsidies, government procurement, and custom and licensing procedures. The results of the Uruguay Round (1986–94) were a major step forward in this respect. Above all, the section of the new WTO on the manufactured goods trade brought in new monitoring and dispute settlement procedures to deal more effectively with behind-the-border issues, with the Dispute Settlement Body and the Appellate Body developing towards a supra-national institution. Moreover, regulations on technical standards aim at introducing the principle of mutual recognition of national standards and, where necessary, some international harmonization. Furthermore, an institutional framework has been established for the services industry that resembles those of other sections of the new WTO, and the Trade-Related Aspects of International Property Rights (TRIPS) Agreement regulates an essential field in any market-making process.

Finally, the Trade-Related Investment Measures Agreement mainly contains regulations that facilitate foreign direct investments (FDIs), but do little to control the conduct of multinational corporations (MNCs). In sum, the successful conclusion of the Uruguay Round increased the number of participants, radically enlarged the range of regulations, introduced a new organization profile and above all introduced supra-national elements (see Kahler 1995: 46; Jackson 1999).

Similar institutional changes have taken place at the regional level. The most prominent example is the Single European Act, which established the four liberties of the EU with the purpose of completely eliminating national obstacles to the Common Market.[15] In other regions of the OECD world, it is a similar picture: 'NAFTA's goals, like those in CUSTA, were largely a clearing away of obstacles to exchange, not the construction of a framework for positive policy coordination' (Kahler 1995: 103). The same is true of Asian attempts at regional integration such as APEC, ASEAN and ANZCERTA. Common to all the regional agreements are their relatively strict monitoring mechanisms with regard to *issues behind the border*.

The branches of industry which provided the necessary infrastructure for transnational exchange also came under increasing efficiency pressure. Up until the 1970s, air cargo services, the postal services and telecommunications in most OECD countries were under state control. In the course of the last decade the elimination of obstacles to transboundary transactions and increased economic efficiency came to be the central issue in these services. In particular, the monopolies over telecommunications and air traffic were rescinded in favour of competitive management and regulation by independent transnational agencies, mainly by the establishment of international standards (Genschel 1995; Zacher with Sutton 1996).

Overall, the provision of regulations that ensure legal certainty and make economic efficiency possible has been successfully internationalized.[16] Negative international institutions initially lent force to the process of societal and especially economic denationalization, but were then additionally strengthened themselves when societal denationalization accelerated in the last decades. Rigorous information and monitoring mechanisms that increasingly contain supra-national bodies render these institutions very effective. With respect to the economic efficiency challenge, supply meets demand to a remarkably high degree. At the same time, the interplay between negative international regulations and societal denationalization seems to be a dynamic process in which both elements strengthen each other, possibly at the cost of positive international regulations.

Positive international regulations

Apart from improving economic efficiency through negative regulations that help to make and maintain markets, social welfare also requires *posit-*

ive regulation in order to alleviate the undesirable effects of unregulated markets. On the one hand, the democratic welfare state implemented macro-economic policies with a view to reducing the economy's crisis-proneness and maintaining a high level of employment. On the other hand, the welfare state corrected the market distribution by re-distributing resources in a way that protected the weakest members of that society. With the rise of new transnational economic spaces and stiffer competition for investments, the respective national policies face new challenges.

With regard to macro-economic steering, supply still falls short of demand when measured against the activities of the democratic welfare states in the 1970s. Although national steering policies hardly have any impact today (Scharpf 1987), the meetings of the G3 and the G7 countries have produced few remarkable results with respect to the coordination of economic cyclical policies. The last serious endeavour to regulate macro-economic steering at the international level was back in 1978, when the Summit Conference was held in Bonn. The situation does not look much better within the European context, although the European Currency Union could prove to be a step towards a common European cyclical policy.

The emergence of global financial markets in particular has given rise to a large demand for regulation in the financial and monetary sectors (O'Brien 1992). The new markets must be regulated to at least ensure macro-economic stability, whereby two issues are of special importance (Sachs 1998). One problem is the need for sufficient capital standards to prevent serial bankruptcies. This task has been tackled to some extent by the Committee on Banking Supervision and Regulatory Practices, which is organized by the Bank for International Settlements (BIS). The 1988 Basle accord contains an agreement that harmonizes the capital standard requirements at an acceptable level using private agencies to overcome the related information problems (Genschel and Plümper 1996). In 1995 the Committee announced new rules to be implemented by the end of 1997. In order to control a rapidly evolving and increasingly complex industry, the private sector was heavily involved in the policy formulation, but also in the private–public partnerships for implementation. In addition, some regulations issued by the International Organization for Securities Commission have stabilized international banking and stock exchange transactions to a certain degree (see Lütz 1997). In spite of these achievements, the dynamics of the financial service industry and its spatial expansion means that regulators permanently lag behind demand (see Reinicke 1998: Chapter 4).

Another problem is posed by the dynamics of panic reactions, which have been exacerbated by the increase of purely speculative activities on the financial and equity markets. Transboundary financial and monetary relations appear to be severely under-regulated (Helleiner 1994). To a certain extent, monetary relations are supervised at the Summit meetings of the G7, although up until now these meetings have not so much produced substantial rules as an inter-governmental network that reacts in an *ad hoc* manner to crises (Hirst and Thompson 1996: 131). Despite these efforts, many other areas in need of regulation have remained untouched – compared with the heyday of the welfare state. For example, the goal to curb speculative activities without inhibiting other capital flows – for instance, through the introduction of a so-called Tobin Tax (cf. Eichengreen *et al.* 1995) – has not triggered any appropriate institutional responses on the international level. The formulation of international policies to offset the deficits in this area is a very sluggish process.

Social policy is also an area with substantial regulatory deficits despite an increasing number of attempts at the international level. On a global scale, new initiatives such as the Social Summit in Copenhagen have not led to regimes of any substance. The United Nations Social Pact is subject to the proviso that each state implements the social rights gradually and only 'to the maximum of its available resources'. The WTO has up until now evaded socio-political questions as far as possible. Hence, so far only the International Labour Organization (ILO) has sought to ensure the inclusion of socio-political dimensions in the formulation of international policies. From 1919 until May 1998, the number of member countries of the ILO increased from 45 to 174. By 1997, the International Labour Conference had adopted 181 agreements on numerous issues such as working hours, minimum wages, mandatory insurance, contractual freedom, and the protection of children, young people and women, of which an average of around 60 per cent was ratified by OECD countries (see Senghaas-Knobloch 1998). Although the number of conventions ratified per OECD country and year is today significantly higher than it was in the 1960s (2.35 per country), figures were highest in the 1970s (6.35) and have since then gradually dropped again (3.6 for the first half of the 1990s) (Senti 1999: 23). Moreover, the effectiveness of ILO regulations is controversial. It therefore comes as no surprise that the transnational lawyers interviewed in a study by Harry Arthurs did not see a *lex laboris* in the making.

> Only a very few lawyers, for example, acknowledged having ever raised, or been directly confronted with, an ILO convention in the course of a legal argument. None acknowledged having encountered the non-binding 'codes of conduct' for MNCs operating abroad, which have been adopted by both the OECD and the EU.
>
> (Arthurs 2001)

In sum, it seems fair to say that the international coordination of positive national policies for preventing a socio-political deregulatory spiral in reaction to economic denationalization is at best only in its initial stages.

Regionally, this process has made more headway. The North American Agreement on Labor Cooperation (NAALC), a supplementary agreement to the Free Trade Agreement between the USA, Canada and Mexico, has in a number of cases already proven to be an effective mechanism for enforcing minimum social standards (Hornberger and Dombois 1999). In the European Union, the indications of a positive trend are most significant. Most importantly, the overall number of social regulations has grown significantly over the last few years, especially since the Maastricht Social Agreement and its extensions in the Treaty of Amsterdam. Significant measures at the European level have been taken as regards issues of gender equality (Ostner and Lewis 1995; Liebert 1998; Falkner 1999) and health and safety in the workplace, both already on the basis of Art. 119, Treaty of Rome (now Art. 141). For instance, the 'General Specifications for Protection at Work 89/391/EWG (ABl. L 183/1)' established a comprehensive set of regulations with Union-wide minimum standards, that are the exact opposite of social dumping (Eichener 1996: 265). Both of these fields were enlarged with the Amsterdam Treaty (they now cover the general fields of 'working conditions' and 'labour force') and have been placed under qualified majority voting (bringing in a supra-national element). Moreover, a whole set of new topics is now *explicitly* part of European social policy (see Leibfried and Pierson 2000). It also should be recalled that mechanisms for regional redistribution (see Anderson 1995; Rieger 1995) are part of the European system. Whether the – pre-Amsterdam – judgement is correct that despite the Social Charter of 1991 'a real social community is still a long way off' (Sieveking 1997: 207), or whether this is already an expression of a 'transformation of sovereign welfare states into parts of a multi-tier system' (Leibfried and Pierson 1995: 45), still largely remains a question of interpretation. It can, however, be concluded that the EU is certainly much further ahead in introducing social regulations than any international institution. Moreover, the Amsterdam Treaty marks a watershed in the development of European social policy: 'EC legislative activity is now at least as extensive as, for example, federal social policy activity was in the United States on the eve of the New Deal' (Leibfried and Pierson 2000: 15).

When it comes to positive regulations in the field of social welfare, it can be stated with certainty that, as a whole, supply still falls short of demand. This also applies to the EU. Fritz Scharpf's (1994: 219) observation that 'the policy-making capacities of the Union have not been strengthened nearly as much as capabilities at the level of member states have declined' still seems true. At the same time, it is clear that positive regulations do exist. Moreover, they not only exist as product regulations, but also as production regulations, which apply to the location in which a product or service is produced, and regularly have considerable distributional implications. The Basle capital standard requirements and the EU regulation on protection at work are two such examples. Most of these positive international regulations are very recent and some analysts have detected a change in the attitude of economic decision-makers. The new post-Washington Consensus redefines the relationship between markets and politics in a way that leaves much more room for political interventions in form of global governance (see Higgott *et al.* 1999).

This development is also reflected in quantitative terms. Although the implementation of the Uruguay Round and the Single European Act – two important market-making projects – have more or less come to a conclusion, there has still been no decline in the annual number of new international economic regulations. The renewed increase in regulations beyond the nation-state in the economic field during the first half of the 1990s (as indicated in Figure 4.4) can therefore be interpreted as an indication of an emergent re-regulation of the markets on levels beyond the nation-state. What is more, the number of positive international regulations has increased from one between 1970 and 1985 to seven since 1986,[17] while the number of negative regulations remained constant.

Security

Policies for protecting the physical integrity of both the national territory and the population against internal and external threats and risks are generally seen as central to national politics. In the course of societal denationalization, however, new challenges appear that can hardly be tackled by unilateral national policies.

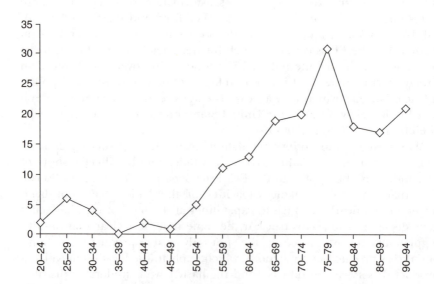

Figure 4.4 Number of significant new international economic treaties

Source: Beisheim *et al.* (1999: 352–353) with reference to the treaty collection of the International Trade Law Site (ITL) of Ralph Amissah, University of Tromsø, Norway; http://itl.irv.uit.no/trade_law.html/. 'Significant' means major, law-relevant agreements.

Negative international regulations

The stockpiling and proliferation of long-range nuclear and other weapons of mass destruction after World War II heightened the challenge for existing security policies. It was no longer possible to maintain national security just by building up a strong defence. The risk of inter-state wars had to be reduced by means of negative international institutions, which prescribe states to refrain from certain actions. These security institutions could be built on principles such as non-aggression, arms control, consultation and information mechanisms that have been developed before, but until the post-World War II period mostly lacked consolidation into rules and norms.

The international security institutions that were established in response to the proliferation of new weapons – such as the CSCE Final Act of Helsinki (1975), the Agreement on the Non-Proliferation of Nuclear Weapons (1968) in connection with the IAEA (founded 1957), the Partial Test Ban Treaty of 1963 and the first East–West Arms Control Agreements (the ABM Agreement and the SALT Agreements) – all aimed to reduce the risk of war, either by the prohibition of secrecy and the instalment of improved information and consultation mechanisms, or by the prohibition of certain weapons systems. Further arms control agreements have been signed since the 1970s. The INF Agreement of 1987 on conventional arms in Europe, the START Agreements between the Superpowers, the Chemical Weapons Convention of 1993, the renewal of the Non-Proliferation Agreement (1995) and the comprehensive prohibition of Nuclear Tests (1996) largely remained within this existing institutional framework. The same would apply to a possible extension of NATO.

After World War II, international security institutions also took over new tasks. For the first time, they were commissioned to protect individuals from state violations of their basic human rights – measures which, however, still fall into the category of negative regulation. The Universal Declaration of Human Rights, passed by the General Assembly of the United Nations in December 1948, was a milestone in history in this respect. The European Convention on Human Rights, passed by the Council of Europe in November 1950, went a step further in terms of binding obligations and monitoring mechanisms. In 1966, the Universal Declaration was reinforced by the International Covenant on Civil and Political Rights and the International Covenant on Economic, Social and Cultural Rights, both of which were unanimously ratified by the UN General Assembly and made internationally binding in 1976 as a result of national ratification processes. Back in Europe, some of the more generally formulated human rights standards were taken up in the Final Act of the CSCE in Helsinki in 1975 in the context of East–West relations.

The accelerated societal denationalization process over the last two decades has led to a refinement of the existing institutional mechanisms and instruments and a large number of new conventions and declarations in the field of human rights (see Figure 4.5). Moreover, procedures for individual complaints about violations of the Civil Rights Covenant, the Convention on the Elimination of Race Discrimination and the Convention against Torture have also been drawn up. ECOSOC Resolutions 1235 and 1503 also improved the monitoring mechanisms. Finally, there has been a rapid increase in the number of signatory states to human rights agreements since the late 1980s. Although these institutions cannot be seen as examples for especially effective regulations, it can be stated that the output of negative international regulations with respect to the goal of security also appears to run more or less parallel with societal denationalization.

Positive international regulations

From the second half of the 1980s onwards, societal denationalization accelerated to a significant level in certain issue areas. In particular, global environmental risks, organized crime and terrorism are among such areas that are of particular relevance to security policy. As opposed to older security problems, which were mainly due to *threats by states*, these constitute *risks that are generated by society* – i.e. challenges to security posed by the mainly unintended side-effects of societal activities (in contrast to state-generated threats). The new security problems need thus to be regulated by positive international institutions (cf. Zangl and Zürn 1999). How far

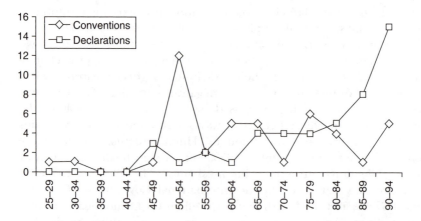

Figure 4.5 Number of newly implemented UN Conventions and Declarations on Human Rights

Source: Beisheim *et al.* (1999: 343).

Notes: Here, all legally binding 'Human Rights Instruments' conditional on formal ratification are coded as 'conventions'. They especially include 'conventions' and 'protocols'. All non-legally binding 'instruments' are coded as 'declarations'. These include 'declarations', 'standard rules', 'recommendations' or 'principles'.

have international institutions been able to meet the challenges provoked by this shift in problems?

Indeed, international security institutions have increasingly turned their attention to the risk problems of guaranteeing internal security and securing the state monopoly of force in the last two decades. The UN task of upholding the state monopoly of force has become more compelling than that of supporting states in their foreign defence. The UN were more often involved in civil wars than in inter-state hostilities, as shown clearly, for example, by a closer look at the increase in peacekeeping operations in recent years (well over half the operations took place after 1990). The Security Council has even – in line with Chapter VII of the UN Charter ('Action with Regard to Threats to the Peace, Breaches of the Peace and Acts of Aggression') – occasionally intervened in domestic conflicts, if they were seen as a threat to *international* security. The number of Security Council Resolutions has increased proportionate to the increase in *peace-keeping* operations, again with a clear emphasis on domestic conflicts.[18]

A similar trend can be observed in Europe. The CSCE, originally established to reduce the risk of inter-state war, is today known as the OSCE and is chiefly concerned with threats generated by civil wars. The OSCE section concerned with inter-state wars has more or less the same function as that of the CSCE, and chiefly deals with procedural matters for facilitating a more up-to-date, better-quality information flow (see Schlotter *et al.* 1994). Moreover, anti-terrorism has become a central issue for many international organizations. Whereas in the 1950s and 1960s there was hardly any notable inter-state cooperation in the struggle against terrorism, there were new developments during the 1970s. Eight out of nine multilateral agreements on anti-terrorist measures were signed after 1970, the majority only in recent years.

Organizations coordinating endeavours to combat organized crime, especially drug trafficking, have been greatly reinforced by international measures. In the 1950s and 1960s, Interpol was more or less a private 'policemen's club', mainly concerned with the exchange of professional experiences. From the 1970s onwards, however, Interpol was systematically expanded into an international governmental organization, whose task it increasingly became to lend states assistance in intercepting criminals. Interpol now runs a computer-aided network for police use that was set up in 1985. Developments were very similar within the EU. After World War II, the Council of Europe was assigned the task of coordinating crime control, which led to a multilateral extension of the bilateral agreements concluded before the war. The establishment of TREVI in the 1970s as well as the Schengen Accord, the Maastricht Treaty and especially the Treaty of Amsterdam in the 1990s are unmistakable signs of a trend towards an intensification of coordinated European endeavours to fight crime, particularly organized crime (Busch 1995).

International environmental institutions dealing with transboundary environmental risks have also gained increasing importance since the 1970s. International organizations such as the United Nations Environment Programme (UNEP) and the EU, but also the OECD, the Council of Europe, the G7, the WMO and the WTO (the former GATT) all deal with regulations for the protection of our natural environment. Most international environmental agreements and instruments were signed in the 1970s and 1980s – as a direct response to accelerated denationalization in this field (see Figure 4.6). Among the most prominent examples are the Vienna Convention to protect the ozone layer (and the subsequent protocols) and the Convention on Long-Range Transboundary Air Pollution (and the subsequent protocols).

This trend is also visible within the EU. In cooperation with those European states with traditionally strict environmental legislation, the European Commission has reached an astonishing level of regulation in favour of environmental and health protection (Vogel 1995, 1997). While the EEU passed on average one environmental bill per year in the 1960s, this number rose to over five in the 1970s and over twenty per year in the 1980s.

Altogether, there has been a clear shift in emphasis in international security institutions. While for a long time they were predominantly concerned with state-induced insecurity factors, the focus has shifted over the past twenty years to human rights issues and particularly to overcoming threats and risks generated by society. These changes can be seen as a reaction to societal denationalization patterns. In addition to human rights, transboundary pollution, transnational terrorism and organized crime have gained in significance in the course of societal denationalization. Today, OECD states are supported by an astonishing variety of inter-

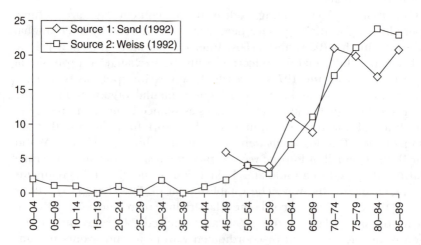

Figure 4.6 Number of new international environmental agreements

Source: Sand (1992), Weiss (1992) and Hewett (1995).

national institutions, not only in fulfilling their defence function, but also in maintaining internal security. It certainly would be premature to argue that all of these regulations were effective. However, it can be stated that the rise of new international security institutions runs more or less parallel to societal denationalization in the fields of force and environment.

The majority of new international security institutions are *positive international regulations*. Traditional international security institutions prohibited the deployment of certain types of weapons, military aggression, the procurement of certain arms types, the infringement of individual rights, etc. In contrast, the institutions concerned with new transnational risks do not impose constraints, but demand positive action. Thus, the growth of new international security institutions shows that positive regulation beyond the nation-state is indeed possible, not just in individual cases, but as a systematic pattern of reactions to particular challenges. With regard to security as a goal of governance there is – in contrast to social welfare – no evidence of a divergence between negative and positive international regulations.

Conclusion

Empirical findings have shown that governance beyond the nation-state is already well established. It has been possible to respond successfully to efficiency pressures arising out of societal denationalization by establishing a growing number of remarkably effective negative international institutions. Some of them even contain elements of supra-nationality in order to lock in institutional commitments. While in that respect demand for international governance has been met, the picture regarding positive regulations is much more complex. Although it can definitely be stated that structural restraints do not completely rule out the possibility of positive international institutions, they are comparatively rare with respect to the governance goal of social welfare. In addition, a significant proportion of them are 'product regulations' and are thus easier to achieve than regulations relating to production or location. More sophisticated production process policies (with significant distributive implications) seem to be a very recent development, more or less restricted to the EU. On the other hand, however, it has been possible to meet the demand for positive international institutions much more easily within the realm of security.

These observations correspond remarkably well with rationalist theories on international institutions. Although *inter-governmental power theories* are weakest in explaining the growth patterns of institutional institutions, they help account for an interval in growth for some fields in the late 1970s and early 1980s, when US power was briefly considered to be in decline. Much more importantly, the *functional hypothesis* that the significance of international institutions has increased in parallel with societal denationalization is not as far from the truth as many would expect. It certainly seems to hold when we focus on the rise of formal organizations and treaties in the aggregate. Moreover, it also holds with respect to negative international regulations alone. Up until the late 1970s, when the moderate growth of transboundary exchange processes only created a demand for negative regulations, international institutions developed more or less in parallel with the growth of societal denationalization. Only when societal denationalization accelerated and thereby aggravated the problems of externalities and the race-to-the-bottom dynamics, did societal and political denationalization begin to diverge with respect to the governance goal of social welfare.

This divergence coincides exactly with the expectation of the theory that focuses on *power in the world economy*. Indeed, part of this divergence can be accounted for by the bias in interest representation in favour of capital owners at the international level. The strong hypothesis, however, that market-correcting regulations do not work at all beyond the nation-state, does not hold. With the help of Rationalist Institutionalism the complex picture of positive international institutions can be explained better. Negative international institutions are based on 'benign' interest constellations and the institutionalization of cooperation thus hardly poses a problem. Moreover, positive regulations without strong distributional implications often approximate simple collaboration games, which still makes the establishment of institutions quite likely if the parties concerned are reasonably certain that all will comply with the regulations and none will be disadvantaged. It is only in the case of positive international regulations with strong re-distributive implications that the underlying constellation of interests is usually particularly obstructive (see Table 4.1).

Two developments, however, are puzzling to all the theories discussed here. First, even Rationalist Institutionalism predicts a growing gap between negative and positive international institutions. A closer look at the most recent developments in the 1990s, however, seems to question this hypothesis. Second, the rise of positive regulations in the field of international security is even more remarkable. Since the mid-1970s, the number of positive international institutions has grown faster in this field than negative international institutions. It seems that rationalist theories

Table 4.1 The rise of international institutions as a function of societal denationalization

Type of regulation, theoretical expectations and empirical finding	Negative regulations beyond the nation-state	Positive regulations beyond the nation-state
Realism	−	−
Functionalism	++	++
Transnational power	++	−
Rationalist institutionalism	+	−
Empirical finding	++	+/−

of international institutions must be complemented by constructivist theories to account for this development. Constructivists point to two aspects that may be able to explain the recent rise in positive international institutions. On the one hand, they point to ideas as an independent force that may help to overcome rationalist obstacles of cooperation. The notion of global governance and the fears about uncontrolled globalization may have exactly this effect. On the other hand, they point to the impact of institutions on the interests and identities of actors and thus leave room for institutional dynamics. These dynamics may lead – intentionally or unintentionally – to a transformation of international relations and thus to an extension of governance. It would be worthwhile exploring these constructivist concepts without neglecting the quite impressive insights of rationalist theories of international institutions.

Acknowledgements

This chapter draws on different arguments that I have developed at different occasions, at which I have received numerous helpful comments. Especially helpful for the purposes of this chapter were comments by Mathias Albert, Karen Alter, Markus Jachtenfuchs, Ron Mitchell, Craig Murphy, Morten Ougaard, Fritz Scharpf, Georg Sørensen and Gregor Walter. In addition, I owe thanks to Peter Arnhold and Vicki May for their effective assistance. Major parts of this chapter were written at the Centre for Advanced Studies, Oslo. Thanks to Arild Underdal for giving me this opportunity.

Notes

1 For a number of reasons the term societal denationalization seems more apt than the term globalization. First, 84 per cent of world trade is transacted between countries inhabited by approximately 28 per cent of the world population. This OECD focus is even more apparent if one looks at direct investments (Hirst and Thompson 1996: 67) or communication flows (Beisheim *et al.* 1999: 65). Second, the 'placeboundedness' of social transactions is not transformed by what many call globalization. Sassen (1998) correctly asks why, after all, if knowledge workers can telecommute so easily, so many of the world's desktops are to be found in a few square kilometres in New York, Tokyo, London and a few other places? Societal denationalization term refers to the classic works of Karl W. Deutsch (1969) and Eric Hobsbawm (1992) on nationalism. According to them, a nation is a political community sustained by intensified interactions, which stands in a mutually constitutive relationship to the nation-state and is thus an expression of the national constellation. Consequently, denationalization is an indication of the weakening link between territorial states and their corresponding national societies.

2 This distinction goes back to Tinbergen (1965) who generally distinguished between positive and negative economic integration and Pinder (1968) who applied it to European integration. By contrast, I utilize this conceptual distinction in specific connection with regulations, maintaining that integration

processes or even international regimes may contain positive and negative regulations in parallel. See Corbey (1995: 263) for a recent employment of this distinction that is very similar to my use. Distinctions like the ones between market-making and market-correction (used in the field of political economy), between enabling and restricting institutions used in the general theory of institutions, and between negative and positive rights of freedom (used in legal theory) are closely related and only marginally diverge.

3 See Rosenau (1992), Kohler-Koch (1993) and Mayer *et al.* (1993) and Young (1994) for contributions to the theme 'governance without government'.

4 See Krasner (1983b: 3). See Hasenclever *et al.* (1997) and Levy *et al.* (1995: 267–330) for further elaborations on the definition of international regimes.

5 This distinction between international regimes and international networks is similar to the one drawn by Mayntz (1996: 148–168), between networks for the management of *ad hoc* problems and institutions for the regulation of recurring problems.

6 The formal term is International Governmental Organizations (IGOs), as opposed to Transnational Non-Governmental Organizations (TNGOs). The latter consist of any kind of professional association, like the International Political Science Association, for instance, as well as profit-seeking TNOs, that is multinational enterprises. For the purposes of our study on international governance, we need to focus here exclusively on IGOs, while the growth of NGOs is mainly an indication of denationalization.

7 See Ougaard (1999c) for an excellent study of the OECD in light of functional expectations.

8 See Keohane (1984), Snidal (1985), Eichengreen (1989), Rittberger and Zürn (1990) and Young and Osherenko (1993).

9 See e.g. Hasenclever *et al.* (1997) for a very detailed discussion of different strands of rationalist theories of international institutions. They also distinguish between the quasi-functional theory of international regimes (especially Keohane 1984) and approaches that build on that perspective but focus on different interest constellations (see Martin 1993; Stein 1983; Zürn 1992, 1997).

10 See Goldstein (1996) with respect to NAFTA and Moravcsik (1998) with respect to the EU. A similar argument can be made with respect to the new Dispute Settlement Body of the WTO.

11 This – admittedly – rough operationalization is based on contestable assumptions. First, the starting year of the data series is assumed to characterize a certain balance of demand and supply of international regulations. In this sense, this operationalization follows the stylized and contested notion, especially by neo-liberals, in the literature that the third decade of embedded liberalism featured such an institutional balance – the heyday of the democratic welfare state. Second, the quantitative growth of transnational transactions increases demand for international regulation in a somewhat linear manner. Although it certainly does not apply to each case on the micro-level, this assumption refers to the macro-level and is to some extent corroborated by experience with the nationalization of societies and national regulations.

12 The following is summarized by Beisheim *et al.* (1999), who have developed seventy-two indicators to determine the extent of denationalization in different issue areas and different OECD countries. For a similar undertaking with similar results see Held *et al.* (1999a).

13 Emanations include those organizations that have another IGO's name in their title, have been created by a provision in another IGO's charter, are a joint or internal IGO committee or an international centre or institute. See Shanks *et al.* (1996: 597).

14 The only exception is West Germany. Its membership grew slightly after 1975, mainly because of agreements with the GDR, which in turn made it possible to join the United Nations and some special organizations.

15 See Moravcsik (1998: Chapter 5) for a most useful account. Joerges (1996) used the phrase 'market without state' to characterize the dominance of negative over positive European regulations in the early phase of SEA implementation.

16 An exception to this is the regulation of property rights in Internet transactions, although it must be said that national regulations have hardly progressed any further than international regulations. Others see the regulation of cross-border contractual relations as deficient. In this field, however, transnational regimes such as the *lex mercatoria* seem to be quite effective (see Applebaum *et al.* 2001).

17 We coded only those regulations as positive which implied direct costs for producers. Data comes from the Chronological List of International Trade Instruments of the University of Tromsø's Faculty of Law (http:lexmercatoria.org/).

18 See http://www.un.org/documents/scres.htm for Security Council Resolutions and http://www.un.org/Depts/dpko/ for Peace-Keeping Missions.

Part II

Non-state actors in the global polity

5 Discursive globalization

Transnational discourse communities and New Public Management

Hans Krause Hansen, Dorte Salskov-Iversen and Sven Bislev

[T]he cities of the 'International Network for better Local Government' see themselves as national and international mediators and multipliers in the reform process in local governments.
(www.stiftung.bertelsmann.de/english/projekte/bereiche/refkommv
2000)

Introduction

A discourse of management – usually referred to as New Public Management (NPM) – has arrived on the public sector scene, with noticeable consequences for its organization and institutionalization. This chapter sets out to investigate an important vehicle for the generation and dissemination of this discourse: the transnational discourse communities (TDCs) concerned with public sector reform.

As globalization is believed to change the roles and situations of the nation-states, and thereby to establish new premises for the operation of public sector organizations, these TDCs recommend the introduction of management practices, with a specific view to making the public sector more efficient and responsive. NPM presupposes subordination of traditional, legally oriented principles of the public sector to new, more pragmatic values (Hood 1998; Salskov-Iversen *et al.* 2000). And it is evidently part of a global trend that brings market mechanisms into spheres of society not hitherto permeated by the market rationality, such as the personal sphere, the family and the public and voluntary sectors. In the public sector, this process does not imply the unravelling of regulation as such, but the implementation of new forms of regulation reflecting new societal realities – reflexivity and risk (Beck 1992), the global multiplication of organizational forms (Pieterse 1995), flexible accumulation and global specialization (Harvey 1990).

NPM is one such form of regulation. It resembles 'public administration' in that it aims at the organized, governed disposition of resources. But where 'administration' is tied to public bureaucracy, public sector values and rule-based organizational technologies, 'management' is based on private sector ideas. It is more role-based (instead of rule-based) and foregrounds organizational techniques such as competition, cost efficiency, and orientation towards performance and results. When it comes to actual implementation, NPM appears in many different versions and is of course ideologically contested. Unsurprisingly, viewing public sector organizations through the lens of private sector management rationalities invariably clashes with the more traditional perspectives on how public sector organizations operate, engendering conflict and complex processes of negotiation at the national and local levels (Salskov-Iversen *et al.* 2000).

In terms of the definition of a global polity set out in the Introduction to this volume, the TDCs that we explore form part of an emerging 'thin community': specialized and professional communities, not quite globally encompassing, but nonetheless boundary-transcending. Their thoughts and actions connect and involve a significant number of people at the global, national and local levels. Interestingly, the TDCs can be seen as important contributors to the emerging global polity along several lines. For one thing they penetrate and in some respects even weaken traditional nation-state institutions, providing the settings within and through which knowledge-based interaction with public sector organizations is being articulated. Moreover, they disseminate the partially harmonizing discourse of NPM, proposing a type of regulation that challenges traditional public sector values. Before exploring in more detail the TDCs concerned with public sector reform it is important to conceptualize their transnational and discursive character, and to discuss why it makes sense to view them as communities.

Forms of global connectivity: transnational discourse communities as a conceptual tool

The field of public administration is rapidly becoming involved in transnational relations, as are, at an even brisker pace, the expert organizations related to this field. Public administration professionals – public administrators, academics and consultants – have engaged in the formation of international organizations, associations and networks dealing with questions related to public administration. These professionals or experts possess a relatively autonomous status in relation to territorial space as the knowledge they define and generate can be asserted across territorial divisions. To grasp the meaning and importance of all these forms of interaction and connectivity (Tomlinson 1999), it is tempting to look at them not as organizations, which would imply studying their formal structures, material activities and resources, but as networks of people.

However, while the network metaphor neatly captures the independence of expert activities in relation to territorial space – transnational networks extend beyond two or more national territories – it works less convincingly as an analytical device to examine the collective, transnational organizational forms that incorporate specific shared interests and meanings. The 'network' concept addresses connections, but does not speak about their substance and dynamics. To comprehend the dynamics of this minefield of competing, complementing and overlapping transnational organizational forms – each of them having its own set of goals and strategies – we use the concepts of 'community' and 'discourse'. As conceptual tools, these terms strike us as capable of capturing the construction and dissemination of NPM.

As regards *Community*, we take its defining element to be the formation and articulation of a set of collectively shared identities across a group of individuals. In this case it also crosses the divisions among national identities, otherwise the most important ones in modern society. National identities have been formed and fortified by two centuries of institution building and legitimization efforts, and the national community is routinely regarded as pre-eminent. Critical theory has pointed out that the national identity is just an imagined one – meaning that it stretches beyond the immediate experience of personal relations. The nation embraces far more people than those with whom citizens are personally related but is nevertheless characterized by a 'deep, horizontal comradeship' (Anderson 1991: 6), holding a claim to ultimate allegiance.

Public sector professionals, traditionally expected to represent a specific national view on any issues treated in their international activities, no longer do only that. In fact, by foregrounding their professional identity, they transcend the power of the nation-state system to impose its categories of identity upon them. They also tend to assume a global or regional rather than national outlook on key issues related to public administration.

Within and across transnational communities, professionals engage in a variety of *communicative practices*. Each community has a broadly agreed set of common public goals, mechanisms and genres for communication among their members, as well as a specific lexis. Face-to-face communication at conferences and meetings is complemented by written and electronic forms of communication – papers, documents, websites, emails, etc. Increasingly, these imagined communities take the shape of 'virtual communities' (Featherstone *et al.* 1995: 7). In principle, everybody now has access to the textual material produced by these communities, as well as to some of the expertise provided by them. But from the viewpoint of the community, not everybody is considered an 'expert' – there are specific requirements to participate fully in the activities of the community.

These communities of identity, communication and expertise have been characterized as 'epistemic communities' – i.e. communities of professionals with a 'shared belief or faith in the verity and the applicability of particular forms of knowledge or specific truths' (Haas 1992: 3, n. 4). The networks described here fit very well that designation. Our public sector professionals certainly develop shared understandings about the nature of public administration and the conceptual tools to analyse it. However, they also share conceptions of the right practices of public administration and management – appropriate processes, adequate structures, suitable institutions, efficient techniques. To capture the rationalities underlying such shared conceptions we prefer the term transnational *discourse* community.

First, the concept of *discourse* implies viewing language as a form of social practice, socially shaped but also socially shaping, i.e. constitutive of social identities, social relations and systems of knowledge (Fairclough 1995: 131). David Harvey conceives of discourse as one of five fundamental 'moments' that make up social processes in their totality: power, beliefs, institutions, material practices and social relations. From this perspective, discourse refers to the 'moment of resort to the vast panoply of coded ways available to us for talking about, writing about, and representing the world', i.e. representing the other 'moments' (Harvey 1996: 78).

Harvey's 'discursive moment' refers to forms and processes of organizing meaning which are often, but not only realized through language. Although the discursive moment is part of all the other moments of social practices, internalizing and suffusing them, there is still more to social life than language. The capacity to both internalize other moments and to permeate and affect them is what makes the discursive moment and the games played within a discourse such a complex phenomenon.

Second, among Harvey's five moments, we focus on the relationship between discourse and the moments of 'knowledge' and 'power', following Foucault's perspective on discourses as constructing knowledge and power. From this perspective, a major characteristic of discourses is their ability to map out what can be said, thought and done about different aspects of life – discourses generate 'effects of truth'. And by normalizing or naturalizing specific ways of thinking and doing things, often with a claim to scientific or other expertise, discourses produce 'effects of power' (Foucault 1982)

Third, 'community activities' and not least those in professional communities are quintessentially discursive. Professionals create a transnational community through a boundary drawing discourse that defines who and what is to be considered inside and outside the community, establishing a distinction between professionals and non-professionals, and between good and bad professionals. The specific vocabulary and jargon, the speech and meeting rituals, etc. create possibilities for the professionals who master them. And the perceptions and evaluations of different subjects – e.g. about public administration and the variety of actors involved in it – are generated by referring to professional knowledge. By drawing on the experience of state professionals and consultants, and on the scientific knowledge of academics, TDCs are capable of and authorized to construct particular discourses which serve to establish the goals of public administration reforms and innovations, to justify the necessity of change, to describe the means to achieve better results, etc.

The management discourses disseminated by these TDCs carry a clear normative charge – the necessity of change in a context of globalization. It should be noted, however, that these discourses are rarely directly and specifically translated into reforms at the local level. There, management discourses are subjected to a process of adaptation and selection in order to make sense. Their overall normative charge, however, can be used to legitimize reform. At the same time, managerial discourses are met with counter-discourses, scepticism and organizational friction – a reflection of the nature of discourse and power/knowledge.

At any rate, the extent to which public managerialism, as it is currently being imagined by TDCs, is actually translated into organizational practices in concrete public administrations is and remains an empirical question. To that end we have investigated the discourse of a number of municipalities in Germany,[1] Britain,[2] Denmark,[3] the USA[4] and Mexico[5] (Bislev 1999; Salskov-Iversen 1999; Bislev *et al.* 2000; Hansen 2000; Hansen *et al.* 2001; Salskov-Iversen *et al.* 2000). In various ways, the authorities in our case studies consider themselves at the cutting edge of local government and among their peers (e.g. officers from other municipalities and central government, professional organizations and journals) they enjoy a reputation as reformers. Thus, they are all actively pushing a reform image, as part of their efforts to modernize their internal organization, to revitalize the local citizen–state relationship, and more generally, to bear upon socio-economic developments in the local area and relations with central/state/federal government. Furthermore, in all cases, the concern with image has been crowned with different types of external verification: prizes for excellence, best practice, participation in prestigious networks and schemes. In other words, the municipalities in our inquiry into the nature and dynamics of the alleged '*global shift in the direction of management*' were selected because of their articulateness about administrative reform.

In the course of our visits to these localities, our interviews with management and scrutiny of their discourses, it became apparent that in most cases some sort of relationship to different (trans)national public administration discourse communities had played a role in instigating, legitimizing or maintaining the momentum of local reform projects – whether in the form of actual membership of a community, or by way of regular contact or interaction with such a community. Clearly, among officers and political leaders, ideas about more systematically to pursue managerialism could often be traced to the workings of discourses originally transmitted to them via their connections to professional networks. Gradually, imports from and exposure to these discourses had naturalized hitherto contested notions such as efficiency and customer orientation. It had become knowledge – rather than a highly contested and ideologically grounded approach – that the means to obtain the ends of efficiency and legitimacy were managerial techniques like performance budgeting, performance-related salary systems, outsourcing, benchmarking, etc.

While much of the networking and dissemination of discourse that we came across does happen through formal organizations, other manifestations of ideational travelling and professional interaction take place in and through *ad hoc* fora that are more fluid, less habitualized, less institutionalized, and, per definition, very idiosyncratic. The concept of discursive community fits both fora, which, despite their different realizations, constitute sites for some of the same processes.

Our focus on TDCs flows directly from these studies of local administrations, in which we encountered references to sources of inspiration for the NPM reforms conducted. In other words, being mentioned and being perceived as influential and/or inspirational by the individuals in local government we have spoken to, have qualified certain TDCs for further investigation in which we focus on the world-views that these communities can be seen to construct, project and disseminate, as evidenced by the discourse that emanates from them. Empirically, we rely mainly on written documents and webpages. To get their history right and to clarify their position on a number of issues of importance for our study, we have also conducted a questionnaire survey of eight of these TDCs.

Our investigations into the world of TDCs disseminating the discourse of the new public managerialism uncovered the following three types of communities, each having their own status, positions and features (see also Bislev *et al.* 2000):

1   Those that are related to the UN complex of organizations: the UNDP, the World Bank, the International Monetary Fund and the Latin American-based and oriented CLAD (see Hansen 2000). These are the big, resourceful international organizations with a political mandate to advise nations and national institutions, mainly in the developing world and in the transitional economies, on a broad range of policy areas – among them, problems of good governance and efficient public management. In their different capacities they are international organizations, formally constituted as such

2   The second group is smaller but composed mainly of representatives of the wealthiest countries. It consists of the OECD and affiliated organizations: the OECD itself, its Public Management Committee, the Eastern Europe-oriented SIGMA organization. These are organizations with lesser political mandates, officially charged with the provision and exchange of information. Wealthy OECD countries typically possess large public sectors; public sector reform has been very much on the agenda in OECD countries, and the OECD has taken the lead in developing NPM notions.

3   Finally, a very broad group of professional organizations for practition-

ers and academics exists. Some organize politicians and/or civil servants at different levels in the organization: the International Union of Local Authorities, the International City/County Management Association, and the Public Sector International. Some have a political–ideological mission: the neo-liberal think tanks in the UK and the USA, and softer ones like the American-based Reinventing Government Network and the Bertelsmann Network for Better Local Government of German origin. A number of these organizations participate in the race to be *the* academic or *the* professional network, *the* meeting place of ideas for improving public management. The International Institute of Administrative Sciences and its sister organizations along with the International Public Management Network, the European Institute for Public Administration and several lesser ones all aspire to be just that.

To illustrate our discussion, we have chosen three TDCs – one from each group, and each one with an important organization at its core – that have struck us as particularly salient for our discussion. Especially the two first examples, the TDCs associated with the World Bank and the OECD, may not come as a surprise to the reader, as their power is widely acknowledged. The last example, the Bertelsmann Network, is perhaps less obvious. What they share, however, is a capacity to intervene from outside the specific politically and historically generated logics that any given governance institution, whether sub-national, national or supra-national is embedded in, and provide these institutions with notions about governance unmediated by territorial politics. Even if these notions are subsequently negotiated locally, the very power to place them on the agenda in multiple contexts and at different levels constitutes a potentially globalizing force. By looking more closely at how these three TDCs organize their discursive intervention into specific local contexts and by unravelling the underlying premises of the discourse that they peddle we hope to be able to qualify our contention about their role in the global polity. Our three cases portray three TDCs at work in changing the public sector. To different degrees, they push for a concern with management instead of administration, and support the use of market mechanisms instead of political institutions. We analyse their positions on these continua while asking:

- in which ways, and how much does each TDC contribute to the supranational connectedness of polities – where is it positioned in terms of formal and informal status, resources, etc., in relation to other actors in the world of international organizations and states?
- How do these TDCs connect with state and sub-state institutions – local institutions where NPM is adapted, spoken and practised?
- To what degree do the TDCs contribute to the formation of a global community – are their discourses becoming globally valid, and through which processes does that happen?

The World Bank

Our Mexican case study of Tijuana, Baja California, turned up a number of references to the World Bank as a source of ideas and norms for public management. And in reverse, in World Bank materials one finds references to Tijuana as one example of NPM or rather, in WB discourse, Good Governance.

Founded in 1944 to ensure cooperation among nations on international monetary and financial issues, the international context in which the World Bank operates has changed radically over the years, and so has the role of the Bank. A major marketization of the world's financial markets was undertaken in the 1970s, private lending to the developing countries increased, and by the early 1980s, many developing countries found themselves in a serious debt crisis (Agnew and Corbridge 1995; Hoogvelt 1997). As direct government intervention on the part of the leading developed countries was out of question, the WB, together with the IMF, was commissioned to engage in the establishment of debt rescheduling arrangements. Having acted previously mostly as a provider of loans and grants, the WB now also appeared as a 'debt collector', with a specific view to exacting payments from the developing countries. The two roles were subsumed under the concept of 'structural adjustment' – a series of economic *and* political measures to be undertaken by the crisis-ridden countries in return for a new wave of loans.

Since the heyday of structural adjustment, the WB's public sector discourse on the public sector has had two strands. First, one, which incorporates the economy-centred rationality of the early structural adjustment programmes: the performance of government is measured against purely economic variables – a narrow and one-sided version of NPM (Haltiwanger and Singh 1997). A second strand in the WB public sector discourse is broader and has become the most influential since its emergence in the early 1990s. Its core conceptualization revolves around 'good governance', a notion similar to New Public Management but with more political content. Since then, loans, grants and technical advice have been received on conditions framed by the 'good governance' agenda, and checked by supervising and inspecting missions sent out by the Bank, in collaboration with local academics, consultants and state officials. In local and national politics this kind of intervention has been met with acceptance or resistance, or, more often than not, combinations of the two, depending on the specific local context (see Salskov-Iversen *et al.* 2000).

The official WB discourse on 'good governance' begins with the booklet *Governance and Development* from 1992. Four major components of 'poor governance' are identified: poor public management, lack of accountability, the absence of a legal framework for development, and problems of information availability and transparency. Improved governance on each of these areas is seen as a key developmental goal. In the booklet, the Bank argues that its governance perspective implies a move away from a narrow focus on the Bank's own intervention, to a broader perspective including the country context (WB 1992: 48). Overall, however, the WB tends to view governance in terms of development policy management, leaving the impression that achieving 'good governance' is actually more a technical than a political matter.

The vocabulary and framework used in *Governance and Development* set the stage for the goals outlined in the Bank's later publications. By the late 1990s, an adjustment of WB's original 'good governance' perspective can be found in several WB publications, most notably in the Bank's World Development Report from 1997, *The State in a Changing World*. It departs from the assumption that there is a global move towards greater reliance on market mechanisms: the state has not been able to deliver on its promises, reflecting the failures of state-dominated development strategies. And the Report presents a more nuanced picture of the role of the state than earlier WB publications. In the words of the staff director of the Report:

> Many observers feel that the logical conclusion to be drawn from these failures is that the ideal state is the minimalist state. But . . . this extreme view is at odds with the evidence offered by the world's success stories, recent and past . . . Development requires an effective state that can play a catalytic role, encouraging and complementing the activities of individuals and private businesses
>
> (Chibber 1997: 1)

The renewed focus on the state is predicated upon the assumption that the global economy and the spread of democracy have changed the environment in which states operate, narrowing the scope for 'arbitrary and capricious behaviour'. 'Responsiveness' on the part of the state has become crucial:

> Taxes, investment rules, and economic policies must be ever more responsive to the parameters of a globalized world economy. Technological change has opened new opportunities for unbundling services and allowing a larger role for markets. These changes have meant new and different roles for government – no longer as sole provider but as facilitator and regulator. States have come under pressure even where governments have previously seemed to perform well . . . Markets – domestic and global – and citizens vexed by state weaknesses have come to insist, often through grassroots and other non-governmental organizations, on transparency in the conduct of government
>
> (World Bank 1997: 2)

This conception of the world as becoming more liberal and open, economically and information-wise, leads the World Bank to propose a strategy to make the state a more 'credible' and 'effective partner' in the development process. The state's role must be matched to its capability. And state capability must be raised by reinvigorating public institutions:

> This means designing effective rules and restraints, to check arbitrary state actions and combat entrenched corruption. It means subjecting state institutions to greater competition, to increase their efficiency. It means increasing the performance of state institutions, improving pay and incentives. And it means making the state more responsive to people's needs, bringing government closer to the people through broader participation and decentralization.
>
> (ibid.: 7)

Here, state reform is seen as contributing directly, not only to financial improvements, but also to political goals, to democracy: checking arbitrariness and combating corruption. The Report also points to the power of political interests 'to maintain an inequitable and inefficient status quo, whereas those who lose out from this arrangement may be unable to exert effective pressure for change'. By drawing attention to conflicts and contradictory political and economic interests, the Bank is as close as it can be to recognizing the fundamentally political character of its project and suggestions.

One of the basic arguments made by the Report is that governments need to 'listen to businesses and citizens and work in partnership with them in deciding and implementing policy'. If governments are not capable of listening, they are not 'responsive to people's interests', in particular to the interests of the poor. The direct participation of potential users of government programmes is necessary for efficiency: 'Evidence is mounting that government programmes work better when they seek the participation of potential users, and when they tap the community's reservoir of social capital rather than work against it. The benefits show up in smoother implementation' (ibid.: 11). In such formulations, the World Bank verges on expressing a directly political agenda, recommending some forms of democracy rather than others.

This probably stretches the legitimacy of WB discourse as its political mandate is nailed to its economic one. The dilemmas created by this manoeuvre spring from the conflict between recommending a specific policy and invoking knowledge whose credibility rests on scientific methods (Ramamurti 1998: 11). Transnational discourse communities may sometimes, as members of/participants in international organizations, possess political legitimacy and power through material resources and formal authority, but more typically they trade in knowledge. The WB tries to do both, but has to walk a fine balance. Additionally, the Bank has come under some criticism from academics and NGOs for not practising what it preaches: transparency and accountability are not always prominent in the processes of the World Bank (Raffer and Singer 1996: 172).

At any rate, the transnational reach of the WB discourse is unquestionable. Not only is it difficult to find any academic work on the economic, political and social situation of developing countries that does not draw on or relate to the Bank's statistical representations, to its key words and world-views. More specifically, WB discourse is also echoed at national and local levels of government in developing countries. In Latin America, for example, national and local governments in many countries integrate the WB discourse in their programmes, refer to the reception of WB missions and to the collaboration with WB officials in a number of policy contexts (e.g. Campbell 1997; Hansen 2000; Salskov-Iversen *et al.* 2000)

The Organization for Economic Cooperation and Development

The local governments among our cases rarely mentioned direct inspiration from the OECD. Inspiration was said to come from national sources such as state organizations – relevant ministries, especially – and national municipal associations and consultants. Or from international networks of municipal managers and politicians. The position of the OECD as an important framework for transnational NPM discourse was, however, confirmed in contacts with those mediating links – the national and international networks and state administrators: their discourses refer frequently to OECD sources as authorization, inspiration, etc.

Like the World Bank, the OECD is a developing organization. In its own words:

> the OECD vocation has been to build strong economies in its member countries ... After more than three decades, the OECD is moving beyond a focus on its own countries and is setting its analytical sights on those countries ... that embrace the market economy ... But its scope is changing in other ways too ... analysis of how various policy areas interact with each other, across countries and even beyond the OECD area.
>
> (www.oecd.org)

The OECD has been cultivating a special relationship to two broadly recognized international trends, where it sees itself as having had a head start: globalization (the OECD started out trying to enhance economic interaction) and the knowledge economy (when re-organized in 1961, analysis and data collection were the main items on OECD's agenda).

Before globalization and the knowledge economy became established truths, the OECD succeeded in creating a strong position in economics,

and was part of the process that established a special position for economists. In the 1960s, macro-economic planning was seen as the main tool of
government, and the economists' rationalistic models recognized as a
privileged knowledge, a technology for social engineering. The OECD
built a status for itself as the purveyor of authoritative data on economic
developments and its series of regular reports on economic themes and
policy areas became standard fare for decision-makers. The OECD has
become a discursive authority on economic matters, and exercises this
authority not only in its main areas of economic policies, including trade
and technology policy, but also – with considerable self-confidence – in
broader policy areas.

In economic policy discussions, in discussions about a possible global
investment regime, in questions of development policy and in the labour
standard issue as connected to trade, the OECD can justifiably claim a
significant share of the parentage of new ideas (Ougaard 1999c). And in
the area of corporate governance, OECD's guidelines for multinationals
are an important part of the discourse.

In the area of Public Management, the OECD has been carrying the
torch since the early 1980s. It entered the field following a 1979 conference in Madrid (OECD 1980). The justification in terms of OECD's economic mandate was the expansion of welfare states during the 1970s, and
the ensuing emergence of very large public sectors. Both the dominant
schools of economic policy theory – Keynesian and neo-liberal – would
point to some concern over growing public sectors. New Public Management became the answer.

After a slow start in the 1980s, PUMA, the OECD's public management
committee, was officially established in 1990 and soon became an important site for the development of what has become known as NPM discourse. PUMA is a practitioner's forum inserted into an international
organization, with no politicians or academic members (most other practitioners' fora are more mixed in this respect, but also lack the powerful
organizational background of something like the OECD). It launches
itself as a knowledge network – 'Collecting, analyzing and disseminating
information . . . Publishing analyses, case studies and best practice guidelines. Facilitating exchange of information' (www.oecd.org/puma). Most
member states have sent professionals with high status in national public
administration, and the ideas and networks they have cultivated have permeated national institutions, establishing NPM as the norm for public
sector reform (Lerdell and Sahlin-Andersson 1997; Bislev *et al.* 2000).

In the beginning, the OECD had to take great care to appear ideologically and culturally neutral, '*there cannot only be a single solution of these problems* . . . different cultures, constitutions and administrative traditions'
(Eldin 1980: 46; emphasis in original). Gradually, normativity crept into
the OECD's formulations and recommendations: NPM became knowledge, the managerial notions became internalized, house-trained into

public service. In the 1993 report (OECD 1993) and subsequent ones, a wide raft of different elements of the NPM jargon were developed, tried and recommended to members. Already in 1993, the original mantra of 'national specificity' had given way to a normative concept of One Best Way to Reform. Finally, in a 1995 report, PUMA confidently declared that '*A new paradigm for public management has emerged, aimed at fostering a performance-oriented culture in a less centralized public sector*' (the Public Management Service of the OECD (PUMA) 1995; emphasis in original)

Thus, in the mid-1990s, PUMA had arrived at a confident declaration stating that management was the substance of administration, and that improving management was essential to better administration. Among its conclusions:

> the challenge for governance at the end of the 20th century is one of institutional renewal ... requires a reappraisal of the rationale for government intervention and a re-examination of the cost-effectiveness of public sector institutions ... governments must strive to do things better, with fewer resources, and, above all, differently.
>
> (PUMA 1995: 7)

In the 1980s, the OECD had still been cautious in the public management field, perhaps for political reasons: public management reform was being politicized as a choice between the contradictory notions of politics and the market. Neo-conservative governments used public sector reform as a spearhead for their political ideas – Reagan, Thatcher and Mulroney. But there was no consensus on this point, no unanimity around the neo-liberal version of NPM which the chief conservatives propounded (Savoie 1994). Behind the official reports, no consensus had existed, either, on the exact role of NPM: was managerialism the only truth, or did specific public sector values exist that pointed in another direction? In other networks, we have observed that public sector values tend to survive and reassert themselves when public sector professionals meet (Bislev *et al.* 2000). They may have survived inside the PUMA, too. And following the lead of the World Bank, PUMA in 1999 sent a signal about public sector values: for public management to serve both citizens, customers and, crucially, the common good, it needed a public sector ethos (www.oecd.org/puma).

The Bertelsmann network

Our local government case study has used the Bertelsmann network and award system as a clue to finding interesting local sites – making it less surprising that the same localities mentioned the network as a source of inspiration for their reforms. Bertelsmann Stiftung publications list some of the achievements in German local government reform as connected with their efforts – which is very likely to be true.

The Bertelsmann Network for Better Local Government is an international network of self-proclaimed world-class local authorities, which on a continuous basis produces evidence of excellence and best practice in local government, to be emulated not only by the international members, but more generally by the world of local government in the member cities' countries. The discourse of Bertelsmann Stiftung is not much different from the WB's and the OECD's, but its mode of operation is more typical of practitioner-based discourse communities, using the discourse of 'excellence' and 'best practice' and the awarding of prizes and distinctions as ways to carry out its missions.

Compared with the World Bank and the OECD, the Bertelsmann network operates at a much smaller scale and at a very different level. It also works solely with local governments, whereas the others reach local governments primarily through national administrations (the OECD) or economic development projects (World Bank). However, its mode of intervention, notably its strategic use of the globalization discourse, makes it a particularly modern kind of TDC. While its ultimate objective is to make German local government more efficient, more businesslike, its authority on the domestic scene, realized via a more recently created national network of carefully selected German authorities, rests very much on the knowledge and truths about local government generated by the international network. As such, this network constitutes an interesting and very concrete transmission belt between the global and the local. This is how the Bertelsmann Foundation describes the mission of the international network:

> Since [the network's] beginnings 'New Public Management' has become a global movement. Hence, the cities of the 'International Network for Better Local Government' see themselves as national and international mediators and multipliers in the reform process in local governments. The strictly practice-oriented work of the network makes it particularly useful for the participants.
> (www.stiftung.bertelsmann.de/english/projekte/bereiche/refkommv 2000)

'Cities of Tomorrow', the Bertelsmann Network for Better Local Government, is founded and funded by the Bertelsmann Foundation, a creation of Germany's mighty Bertelsmann media group. The network is a legacy of the Carl Bertelsmann Prize, which is awarded annually for 'exemplary approaches to solving social problems in order to give new impulses to the public and political discussion' (Carl Bertelsmann Prize 1993: 9). In 1993, the theme of the prize, Democracy and Efficiency in Local Government, was designed to stimulate Germany's plans to reorganize local government in the wake of unification. The event was organized as an international competition and it was the ten municipalities from Northern

Europe (Herten in Germany, Hämeenlinna in Finland, Braintree in Great Britain, Farum in Denmark, Delft and Tilburg in the Netherlands and Neufchâtel in Switzerland), Quebec in Canada, Phoenix in the USA, and Christchurch in New Zealand nominated for the prize that in 1995 formed the network. The very practice-oriented activities undertaken in the Network all serve to identify, develop and communicate excellence and best practice in local government administration, management and service provision across national/regional borders and different welfare state models. In the words of the Network itself: 'A growing number of cities in Germany and abroad are experimenting with new concepts of management and organization in an attempt to reform their administrations and convert them into modern public service companies' (Pröhl 1997). This is the world-view that frames the Network's activities. For the ten network cities, the overall objective of exchanging experiences, transferring knowledge, and ensuring mutual learning is realized in three-year work cycles. At the beginning of each work cycle, the member cities get together with the Bertelsmann Foundation and decide what issues to pursue, working groups with members from each city agree on project designs and schedules and then set out to discuss and analyse their own achievements as well as relevant input and examples from 'leading local government associations, business consultants as well as from other well-managed cities of their nations' (www.stiftung. bertelsmann.de/english/projekte/bereiche/refkommv 2000). The Foundation is responsible for publishing their results, initiating discussions, holding symposiums and advising and supporting members in the working groups.

A competition announced by the German Bertelsmann Network in 1998 for the most Community-Oriented Local Government in Germany exemplifies how the new regime instrumentalizes lower-level governance institutions and their employees to pursue the quest for reform (Deetz 1998: 164). The winning municipalities are now taking part in a two-year pilot project in the area. Incidentally, this and other recent initiatives suggest that the network's initial *de facto* preoccupation with the management end of the administration–management continuum and its foregrounding of market rather than democracy concerns have given way to a hybrid discourse where issues of policy and governance techniques are mixed across the entire spectrum and thus, perhaps, herald the eclipse of the dichotomies between administration–management and democracy–efficiency. The Network's explicit international profile enables it to embed the alleged need for reform of Germany's municipal systems in a particular understanding of globalization, an understanding which makes a particular kind of reform in Germany appear natural and inevitable. As such, the Network can be viewed as a vehicle that enables both communication about and acceptability of managerialism in a context – especially at the federal level – which has been known as very sceptical of *das Neue Steuerungsmodell* and very hesitant to embrace, let alone permit, ideas viewed as essentially antithetical to German administrative culture.

Outside Germany, the network is less well known and only in the member cities' home countries. This is understandable as you become a member or contribute to its projects by invitation only. However, non-German member cities all sport membership of the Network in every conceivable way: on their homepage, in the City Hall, in official reports and publications, etc. To be ranked among the best managed cities in the world is a valuable asset for cities concerned with the role of image, reputation and identity in generating competitive advantages and adding to their symbolic capital and leverage *vis-à-vis* their employees, their citizens and the world outside (whether potential citizens, investors, tourists or other levels of government). For these cities, membership of the Bertelsmann network serves as external verification of their own claim to excellence – a resource and a lever to gain more influence and more legitimacy.

Conclusion

Globalization is in part realized through the growing number of international regimes and regulations, intensified flows of goods, money and knowledge. All these processes are uneven, spatially as well as temporally. The dissemination of New Public Management is an excellent illustration of most of these points, and is made all the more interesting by evincing the postmodern features of reflexivity and discursivity.

The transnational discourse communities we have analysed are part of the growing global connectivity because they are part of the international organizations and networks that transport these connections – supranational organizations, transnational corporations, professional associations, networks of experts and practitioners.

The prime actors in international networks remain states and state professionals, but increasingly, corporations, non-governmental organizations and other non-state actors take part. Our three types of TDCs also connect with sub-state organizations – especially city governments. Local authorities everywhere play an increasing role in the delivery of public services, and they are developing international connections as part of the modernization and effectivization process currently under way. Numerous international conferences and other communicative practices connect local government officials. The Bertelsmann project uses local government networking on an international level as a means of influencing the agenda of administrative reform in Germany.

The supra- and sub-national patterns of connection are part of the framework for the communicative practices developing a global discourse of public administrative reform. Our three cases are all producers and disseminators of 'knowledge', but they also represent different types of TDCs possessing other types of resources. The World Bank attaches conditions to its loans and demands 'good governance' from the recipients of loans and moratoria. Officials in recipient countries pay attention to the norms propounded by the WB because of the financial weight behind the words. The OECD is also a site of considerable economic and political resources, but is more indirectly involved with money and political power. In the area of public management, the OECD operates with 'softer' means than the WB conditionality process. The Public Management Committee organizes communication between public officials – exchanges of experience and analytical insight. The Bertelsmann Foundation works with an international network of its own creation, purposefully established to infuse its agenda in Germany with authority and legitimacy. Importantly, the Bertelsmann network exemplifies a bottom-up process, not uncharacteristic of reflexive society: participating local governments proclaim themselves to be best in the world and utilizing the global discourse of NPM, they define the parameters whereby excellence is to be measured.

In this way, our TDCs and their discourse contribute to making the global community slightly thicker. Civil servants, hitherto working nationally, come to be aware of each other's existence, and to think and act in broadly similar ways. They also contribute to harmonizing the practices of governments everywhere. Not through the hard ways of sanctions-based rules and financial appropriations, but through the processes of reflexivity, the discursive modalities of communicating professionally. The contributions of the TDCs are to open up communication across the national borders and to inject doses of a liberal, market-inspired discourse into the world of politico-administrative discourses.

The Transnational Discourse Communities, although connecting in different ways and using different methods, do to a certain extent walk in step: the notion of New Public Management had its most uncompromised versions in the 1980s, concomitant with the existence of conservative governments in the wealthiest countries. The early 1990s saw its culmination. In the late 1990s, there is a collective retreat from the most outspoken market-driving positions, and 'good governance', meaning a support for liberal political values, comes back. The value of democracy appears again on a par with economic values.

In this process, the nature of both global and national polities is affected. The role and functions of the state, the nature of statehood, changes as values, identities, concepts and practices are negotiated in TDCs where governments no longer hold exclusive rights to be heard and heeded.

Notes

1 Heidelberg, Saarbrücken and Herten.
2 York, Newham, Lewisham, Oldham and Torvaen.
3 Skanderborg.
4 Phoenix and San Diego.
5 Tijuana.

6 Knowledge networks and policy expertise in the global polity

Diane Stone

Introduction

Increasing political inter-connectedness is running in tandem with another related process of change in the global order, that is, the growing role of knowledge and expertise in social and political life. A focus on this later trend brings issues of knowledge and power to the forefront of analysis of the global polity. Indeed, the two trends are deeply intertwined since knowledge creation and dissemination have been an international affair for centuries.

Accordingly, this chapter outlines sources of knowledge that have some impact upon global modes of governance.[1] The discussion also investigates aspects of the relationship between power and the internationalisation of political life, particularly the manner in which research and consulting advice can help shape global and regional policy agendas. Moreover, the proliferation of international knowledge networks is integral to the globalisation process. Within these networks, knowledge actors – research institutes, experts, consultants, scientists, professional associations, etc. – exchange resources (knowledge and expertise) with other actors (decision-makers, opinion-formers, producers) to pursue shared interests. However, asymmetries in power relationships within the global polity are reproduced within these knowledge networks as well as occasionally modified by them.

Drawing on the themes outlined in the Introduction to this volume, these networks contribute to increased interconnectedness and represent instances of 'thick community'. The 'depth of consciousness of the world as a single place' is often well formed among network agents. Indeed, participation in these networks can be a learning mechanism to heighten such awareness. However, little attention has been given to issues of accountability and participation in this mode of governance where 'global knowledge elites' become key actors in a thickening web of global institutions, regulatory activities and policy practices. The growth in the supply and spread of knowledge and expertise has an impact not only on the character of knowledge but also on channels into and participation in the global polity. Knowledge-based authority is one foundation behind the 'enforceable societal relations' and sets of hegemonic ideas within the global polity. As such, this chapter largely concurs with the views expressed in the previous chapter about the presence of a hegemonic 'new public management' discourse.

The chapter is structured into four parts. The first section is an overview of some salient sources of knowledge. In the second section, a brief critical account of some conceptual approaches towards networks, knowledge and policy precedes the development of the idea of 'knowledge network'. The third section is a broad-brush description of three very different global network styles in which the creators and possessors of knowledge play a central role and acquire authority in the global polity. In the final section, reflections on these three examples provide some lessons concerning knowledge, power and political internationalisation.

Global sources of knowledge and expertise

Knowledge moves relatively freely in the global domain aided by the massive proliferation of the number of experts, consultants, advisers and professionals and the expansion of their respective industries. Similarly, the Internet has meant easy transmission of 'codified' knowledge. However, traditional, 'grass-roots' and practitioner knowledge is frequently less amenable to such transfer, rooted as it may be in communal understandings or local practices. This results not simply because of problems in the supply of such knowledge but as consequence of the interests of the sources of demand and their funding priorities. Demand provides opportunity for knowledge providers and policy research entrepreneurs but the nature of demand also shapes organisational responses and knowledge creation.

Ideational or knowledge actors with a policy orientation and increasingly involved in the global spread of knowledge include philanthropic foundations, scientific associations, training institutes, autonomous university centres, think tanks, professional associations and consultancy firms as well as non-governmental organisations (NGOs) and pressure groups with a strong research capacity. They are complemented by individual academic entrepreneurs, intellectuals and experts. Only four examples of knowledge producers will be addressed here. These are: universities and colleges, think tanks, foundations, and the consultancy industry. While the functions are overdrawn, they represent respectively producers of knowledge; knowledge communicators and policy entrepreneurs; funders of knowledge creation; and commercial applicators of knowledge.

Universities and colleges

The spread of ideas, knowledge and information among intellectuals and scholars is not a new phenomenon. Transnational knowledge networks were established generations ago for the exchange of knowledge. The role of the so-called 'Chicago boys' transmitting monetarist ideas is well documented (Valdes 1995). Similarly, the international movement of Keynesian ideas is widely recognised (Hall 1990). What is different is the intensity of exchanges. The opportunity to attend international conferences or workshops is taken for granted by a significant proportion of the academy. Moreover, the Internet has facilitated scholarly exchange and the spread of knowledge and information allowing the global 'invisible college' to communicate with speed. Increasingly, many academics are becoming de-linked from the national context identifying with transnational disciplinary communities.

There have always been academics who take their scholarly interests beyond the realm of disinterested research and scholarly debate. That is, some academics have sought a dialogue with those in power. While recognised at the national level, this phenomenon is now very apparent in regional and global fora. Academics seek appointment to international advisory bodies and expert committees, secondment to international organisations such as the World Health Organisation (WHO) or International Monetary Fund (IMF) and they provide scholarly support and some legitimacy to international NGOs. In addition, many universities are mindful of the policy implications of academic work and have established institutes or research centres that address policy issues.

Think tanks

Conservative estimates put the number of think tanks worldwide between three and four thousand (McGann and Weaver 2000). Think tanks vary dramatically in size, structure, longevity, policy ambit and political significance. Some think tanks are 'academic' in style, focused on research, geared to university interests and in building the knowledge base of society. Other organisations are overtly partisan or ideologically motivated. Many institutes are routinely engaged in advocacy and the marketing of ideas whether in simplified policy relevant form or in sound bites for the media. Specialisation is a more contemporary development with environmental think tanks (e.g. the Thailand Environment Institute), economic policy think tanks (e.g. the Lithuanian Free Market Institute) or regionally focused think tanks such as the Centre for European Policy Studies (CEPS) in Brussels. Most think tanks produce policy-related research or advice which tends to differentiate them from universities that more often produce academic or theoretical research less amenable to general consumption. This interplay of knowledge and policy is complemented by strategic practices to develop advisory ties to government, industry or the public as brokers of policy ideas.

International interaction among think tanks prior to World War II was rare but not unknown. For example, historians have recently given attention to the links between the national branches of the Institute of Pacific Relations (Akami 1998). In general, however, during the first three-quarters of the last century most think tanks catered to government departments, trade unions and other pressure groups, the local media and other state-bound constituencies. Not until the late 1980s did institutes begin to operate transnationally; that is, extending their activities to function within the domestic political system of more than one state (Stone 2000).

An example of technical exchange between institutes is the European Information Network on International Relations and Area Studies (EINIRAS) (Thunert 2000).[2] Global ThinkNet is a dialogue forum for the heads of the world's leading think tanks (JCIE 1997).[3] Regionalisation has also prompted the creation of think tanks with a regional focus rather than a national identity. The European Union acts as a policy magnet that has prompted the 'Europeanisation of think tanks' (Sherrington 2000b). Today, transnational networks of think tanks are dense and very active. These institutes also seek to introduce themselves or be co-opted into official policy dialogues, treaty negotiations, and are often pro-active as transnational policy entrepreneurs.

Foundations

Foundations range from relatively small organisations to large international bodies like the Ford Foundation. Similarly, they have diverse mission orientations: some fund community programmes or development projects where other bodies might be geared to supporting education or medicine. These bodies are often regarded as significant sources of private and public support to knowledge creation. For example, the role of the Ford Foundation in promoting 'management studies' in Europe in the post-World War II period is well documented (Gemelli 1998).

Another difference is the degree of independence they operate with in relation to the state, corporations or political parties. Political foundations are quasi-governmental actors that tend to provide support to political parties (as in the case of the German Stiftungen) or governments.[4] For instance, the Canadian International Center for Human Rights and Democratic Development and in the UK, the British Westminster Foundation for Democracy have been pro-active in exporting democracy and Western values. Although reliant upon government for most of their funding, they are semi-autonomous and function with greater freedom of action and legitimacy than state agencies in the spread of ideas and funding of community and other groups. They encounter fewer legal and diplomatic problems of interference than official aid agencies in the pursuit of certain national interests (Scott and Walters 2000).

Independent foundations, by contrast, have a greater degree of autonomy by virtue of their financial independence. As is well known, the Soros foundation network is concerned to promote 'open societies' by introducing programmes developed in the West into countries of the former Soviet Union, Haiti and South Africa. More generally, a number of foundations have been involved in 'exporting democracy' to the post-communist states of Eastern and Central Europe (Quigley 1997). Philanthropy, especially American philanthropy, has moved offshore to fund libraries, scholarship programmes, new universities and various forms of educational exchange.

Consultancy advice

The consultancy industry is extensive. Consultants are an accepted part of the business world but they have also become entrenched in the public sectors of OECD countries and a major interlocutor in development processes. A consultant is 'a person who gives expert advice'. Consultants can be found in financial companies and banks, law firms, and within universities, most notably the business schools. Management consultancy firms are best known as suppliers of advice for business rather than for governments or international organisations. However, the spread of this form of sub-contracted activity has become extensive. With the advent of managerialism and its stress on exploiting the tools of financial management for efficient government, political executives and the senior officials of management consultancies have increasingly come in close contact with one another (Bakvis 1997). Consultancy companies have acquired a high profile in the transport of policy ideas, management principles and social reforms from one context to another.

The implementation of the Marshall Plan in the immediate post-World War II era relied upon consultancy companies to help provide 'technical assistance' in the form of American management knowledge and know-how (Saint-Martin 1998: 13). More recently, consulting firms have been presented with enormous opportunities by rapid changes in information technology, downsizing and outsourcing, as well as the political transformations and move towards market economies in the former Soviet states. The large consulting firms such as Coopers & Lybrand, KPMG Peat Marwick or Andersen Consulting are establishing 'government consulting divisions' that produce policy relevant research, liaise with public servants and advocate the adoption of 'a more managerial approach in government'. They play a role in packaging, selling and implementing reforms. Through extensive networking with others to diffuse ideas and cultivate links to international organisation – such as the public management committee (PUMA) of the OECD – they have been instrumental in international policy transfer on reinventing government (Osborne and Gaebler 1992). The NPM ideas were 'rapidly spread around the globe because of the existence of a global "fashion-setting" network of management consulting firms and because of growth in the use of external consulting services by governments' (Saint-Martin 1998: 26). As noted by Hansen *et al.* in this volume, they help mould the language in which public sector reform is understood.

Outside the OECD, global consultancies have contributed to the globalisation of the core values of Western culture generally, and the transmission of the idea of liberalisation specifically. In Indonesia, this 'transmission' of ideas was supported by significant USAID funding by Price Waterhouse and Andersen Consulting. They signalled to a wider international audience of investors and financial institutions that Indonesia was 'a serious and prudent economic manager' and 'that the right kind of people are involved in the process' who 'understand the global standards and are in compliance' (Nesseth 1999: 22). Similarly, in Eastern and Central Europe, consultancy firms have been prominent in providing advice throughout the transition processes. With US government funding, the Harvard Institute for International Development has been a central adviser in privatisation, legal reform and financial liberalisation in the post-communist states (Wedel 1998). Sub-contracting by multilateral and bilateral agencies, often with conditions on use of technical advice/support, has spurred the growth of this industry with attendant criticisms emerging about 'contractor-driven programs' and inadequate understanding of local conditions on the part of these contractors.

'An intellectual is a man without a trade'

The previous discussion has sought to belie this old Confucian saying in the focus on foundations, think tanks and consultancies in the diffusion and advocacy of ideas. Yet, to focus solely on a category of organisation is to lose sight of their interactions. Much of their impact comes from the formal relationships and informal ties that are developed with other actors. The trade in ideas has resulted in a myriad of societal relationships across borders and has also been a source of policy innovation. Possession of knowledge resources often represents a passport into the global order; a means of occupational advancement with the growing pre-eminence of the professional and technical classes; and the creation of new 'intellectual technologies'. Organising knowledge to inform and develop policy through networks is one such intellectual technology and a manifestation of the 'globalisation of political life'.

Global policy networks

The term 'network' describes several interdependent actors involved in delivering services. These networks are made up of individuals and organisations that need to exchange resources (capital, authority, personnel, information, expertise) to achieve their objectives, to maximise their influence over outcomes, and to avoid dependence on other network players. Networks represent structures to be managed by governments and by international organisations. They enable actors to operate beyond their domestic context and help generate 'a sense of global community'.

Network 'interdependencies cause interactions between actors which create and sustain relation patterns' (Klijn 1997: 31). While actors need each other because of interdependencies, they also have their own interests and preferences towards which they attempt to steer policy. As a consequence, networks are characterised by complex bargaining processes. This level of unpredictability is heightened in that networks are not static and actors' preferences may alter and be redefined in the course of interaction. In other words, social learning may take place. Furthermore, there is no actor with enough power to determine the strategic actions of other actors. Governments and international organisations are not necessarily the central managing actor but are merely one actor in the policy process. Regularised communication, the formation of rules and resource division coordinate the network. Indeed, over time the network may become institutionalised with the creation of formal arrangements such as advisory committees, consultation procedures and recognition by state and international organisations of their legitimate role in policy.

Networks can also be viewed as a mode of governance whereby the patterns of linkages and interaction as a whole should be taken as the unit of analysis, rather than simply analysing actors within networks. This approach focuses on the processes through which joint policy is organised. In short, there is a functional interdependence between public and private actors whereby networks allow resources to be mobilised towards common policy objectives in domains outside the hierarchical control of governments (Börzel 1998). Such forms of governance have been identified with global policy partnerships such as the Consultative Group on International Agricultural Research, the Roll Back Malaria Initiative and the Global Water Partnership (Reinicke 1999–2000). This tendency towards alliances, coalitions or partnerships is particularly noticeable in the global polity where governance structures are more diffuse and lack the central coordination hierarchies characteristic of national polities. Furthermore, the transnational character of many policy problems establishes rationales for research collaboration, sharing of responsibilities, regularised communication and consultation structures, and cooperation on other activities.

There are several competing and overlapping network concepts. They include: quasi-official *policy communities*, broadly participatory *transnational advocacy networks*, scientific *epistemic communities* or *discourse coalitions* defined by language, symbols and ideas. These policy network concepts are useful for conceptualising the manner in which non-state interactions with decision-makers help promote the international spread of policy knowledge. Network concepts also help to account for the incorporation of private sources of knowledge and authority in governance.

'Policy communities' are stable networks of policy actors from both inside and outside government which are highly integrated with the policy-making process. These communities are said to emerge and consolidate around specific policy fields or sub-systems such as education, tax or security policy and revolve around relevant institutions such as specific ministries or government agencies. Experts from universities, think tanks or law are likely to be accorded 'insider' status if they share the central values and attitudes of the policy community. A policy community is the most institutionalised variant of the policy network concepts. By definition, it is part of structures of governance (Klijn 1997).

A 'discourse coalition' is 'a group of actors who share a social construct' (Hajer 1993: 45) around which groups/networks frame political problems. First, discourse is an essential part of the process known as the 'mobilisation of bias'. In this view, discourse is a set of 'ideas, concepts and categories through which meaning is given to phenomena'. Discourses are important as they shape understanding and can pre-determine the definition of a problem. The focus is on who defines a policy problem, how it is framed and the discourse through which the problem is understood. Policy arguments are selective and shaped by power relations that involve interpretative struggles. Second, within a coalition, the discourse is amplified and carried beyond intellectual domains. The technocratic policy expertise of academics, think tanks and other experts is aligned with the interests of political and economic elites in a wider struggle to control the terms of debate. It is a concept very similar to Hansen *et al.*'s concept of 'transnational discourse communities'.

Discourse coalitions seek to impose their 'discourse' in policy domains. If their discourse shapes the way in which society conceptualises the world or a particular problem, then the coalition has achieved 'discourse structuration' and agendas are likely to be restricted to a limited spectrum of possibilities. If a discourse becomes entrenched in the minds of many as the dominant mode of perception, it can become distilled in institutions and organisational practices as the conventional mode of reasoning. This latter process is 'discourse institutionalisation'. (A stable policy community is characterised by an institutionalised discourse.) Various knowledge actors can be characterised as discourse managers involved in manufacturing the rhetoric essential to specialised policy subsystems.

An epistemic community is made up of experts who seek to translate their beliefs through a common policy project into public policies and programmes. They are networks of specialists with a common world-view of cause and effect relationships which relate to their domain of expertise and common political values about the type of policies to which they should be applied. Members of the community pursue what they consider to be true into policy domains. Since they come from diverse intellectual backgrounds and institutions, the ties that bind these individuals are neither bureaucratic nor based on vested interest. Instead, they have shared causal beliefs.[5]

Epistemic communities assert their independence from government or vested interest on the basis of their expert knowledge. The shared professional and educational pedigree is a socio-political barrier to the entry of others into the group. They need to share common causal methods or professional judgement, common notions of validity and a common vocabulary; that is, consensual knowledge. Consensual knowledge may be, for example, a commitment to ecological principles or the tenets of Keynesian economics (Haas and Haas 1995). The status and prestige associated with their expertise and their high professional training and authoritative knowledge regarding a particular problem are politically empowering and provide limited access to the political system. This is especially the case in conditions of 'uncertainty' where decision-makers cannot make decisions on the basis of existing knowledge or past experience.

The epistemic community framework has most often been used to explain the impact of scientists, particularly environmental scientists. However, the concept has been extended and applied to social scientists. That is, a trade in services epistemic community that targeted the GATT Uruguay Round (Drake and Nicolaidis 1992); the Club di Roma (Haas and Haas 1995: 261); macro-economists advocating structural adjustment programmes from the IMF and World Bank during the last two decades (Deacon 1999); and the monetary policy experts of the Delors Committee in the EU (Verdun 1999).

The epistemic community concept identifies an elite and relatively *homogeneous* network of actors. However, ideas, policies and practices are also transmitted through 'transnational advocacy networks'. Transnational advocacy networks include relevant actors working internationally on an issue, who are bound together by shared values, a common discourse and dense exchanges of information and services (Keck and Sikkink 1998). They are called advocacy networks because 'advocates plead the causes of others or defend a cause or proposition' (ibid.: 8). While they are organised to promote causes, ideas and norms, they are not bound by consensual knowledge founded upon common notions of validity based on inter-subjective, internally defined criteria for validating knowledge as in epistemic communities. Participants in an advocacy network can lack the status of recognised professional judgement. However, these networks have been prominent in 'value-laden debates over human rights, the environment, women, infant health and indigenous peoples, where large numbers of differently situated individuals have become acquainted over a considerable period and have developed similar world-views' (Keck and Sikkink 1998: 8–9). This kind of network is more effective in valuing 'grassroots', traditional and non-scientific knowledge.

Major actors in transnational advocacy networks include: (i) international and domestic non-governmental research and advocacy organisations; (ii) local social movements; (iii) foundations; (iv) the media; (v) churches, trade unions, consumer organisations and intellectuals; (vi) parts of regional and international inter-governmental organisations; and (vii) parts of the executive and/or parliamentary branches of government. A transnational advocacy network is a much broader collectivity than an epistemic community but not as broad as a social movement. Theorists of epistemic communities exclude activist groups stressing the scientific credentials of members of a community and their involvement in highly technical issues (Peterson 1992). The resources of a transnational advocacy network are not just technical expertise; 'for them it is the interpretation and strategic use of information that is most important' (Keck and Sikkink 1998: 31). These arrangements have more in common with discourse coalitions/communities, although the stress in this framework tends to be on alternative policy visions, reform and policy innovation.

Instead of addressing one network concept, it is important to keep in sight the very different power bases and policy capacities of different networks. This stance reflects the 'uneven and asymmetrical' character of the global polity. Furthermore, networks are organic evolving entities rather than static instruments. Epistemic communities can dissolve into policy communities just as policy communities can fracture. Experts from universities, think tanks or foundations participate in different kinds of network with their expertise and knowledge put to different effect. Depending on composition, the policy issue and the degree of incorporation into official circles through funding or patronage, networks provide an avenue for knowledge to inform policy.

Knowledge networks

The advantage of network concepts is that they factor in 'knowledge' in policy-making whether at the local level or the global. The growth of networks has helped make knowledge a basis for attaining power, class, social standing and official appointment to government or international organisations. The knowledge of an individual or group is important in itself. Accordingly, this section attempts more of a synthesis, addressing the interface between knowledge and different policy networks. Three examples are briefly outlined. First, the Trilateral Commission and the World Economic Forum (WEF) as elite consensus-forming organisations.

Second, the Global Development Network (GDN) of think tanks. Third, HIV/AIDS networks through which less traditional forms of knowledge are mobilised alongside scientific expertise.

The Trilateral Commission is one fading interface between corporate and government elites with knowledge elites while the World Economic Forum is a contemporary manifestation. The Commission is one of the most well-established post-World War II transnational non-governmental organisations.[6]

> When the first triennium of the Trilateral Commission was launched in 1973, the most immediate purpose was to draw together – at a time of considerable friction among governments – the highest level unofficial group possible to look together at common problems facing our three areas
>
> (Trilateral Commission 2002)

Towards this end, the Commission has sponsored a considerable amount of policy research as its publication list testifies. The Commission is a consensus-forming organisation for business and political leaders that draws on intellectual resources. If there is an 'international business class', then the Trilateral Commission represents a forum where some from this 'class' congregate. The Commission has also been portrayed as a tool of capitalist hegemony. That is, a medium for forging a common political identity among powerful individuals through research and dialogue activities. Also subject to conspiracy theories, the agenda-setting influence of this body has been over-stated.

The World Economic Forum (WEF) is arguably the world's premier economic exchange forum and assembles annually at the mountain resort of Davos in Switzerland. As a global partnership of 'business, political, intellectual and other leaders in society', it aims to 'engage in the process of developing and sharing ideas, opinions and knowledge on the key issues of the global agenda'. In the electronic bulletin of one group of critics, Focus on Global South:

> Davos is the place that every aspiring or arrived CEO wants to be. It's a must for anyone in the *Fortune 500*. It is also one of the best publicised (but rarely criticised) sites of 'informal' power where governments and the business world meet.
>
> (Focus on Trade, no. 45, February 2000)[7]

The Forum is yet another interface of various knowledges. Andersen Consulting has been a major sponsor of the WEF in Davos. The directors or senior scholars of a number of leading think tanks and foundations alongside a few academics are usually to be found in attendance. They are classed as Forum Fellows: 'world recognised experts from political, economic, scientific, social and technological fields' and deployed in 'consciousness-raising' for the leaders of the world's major transnational corporations and governments (quoted in Gill 1999).

This is not to suggest that WEF or the Trilateral Commission represent epistemic or policy communities. Participation is too diverse and consensus is absent. However, the meetings, seminars, study groups and various dialogues suggest the presence of a broad discourse coalition. The aim is to educate and advocate a certain way of looking at the world. This world-view is founded upon neo-liberal economics and a belief in the efficiency of market forces. In many instances, the discourse has policy structuration – it shapes policy agendas. Institutionalisation, however, is more variable and uneven partly due to the discursive challenges of groups like Focus on Global South and the International Forum on Globalisation, among many others.[8]

The Global Development Network (GDN) is one manifestation of the World Bank re-inventing itself as the 'Knowledge Bank'. Through developments such as the GDN initiative, its Distance Learning Programme, the Learning and Leadership Center and the Training Institutes managed by the World Bank Institute (WBI), the aim is to create partnerships not just with governments but increasingly with NGOs, training institutes and think tanks. In particular, the GDN attempts to allow greater scope for 'home-grown' policy, information-sharing and enhanced research capacity in and between developing countries (www.gdnet.org). It is intended to incorporate the 'research community' into development policy and is composed primarily of university research centres and think tanks. One intention is that the GDN becomes a coordinating mechanism – or network of networks – for various organisations, groups and individuals researching development. Accordingly, it is better described as a forum through which a variety of advocacy networks, epistemic communities and discourse coalitions intersect and interact.

The form of knowledge that is mobilised by the World Bank is primarily focused on economic liberalisation and market globalisation, albeit now with a stronger emphasis on transparency, good governance and social capital formation. As a consequence, the World Bank is prone to develop partnerships with other organisations that exhibit common values and norms. Alternative forms of knowledge – such as social democratic perspectives or radical ideas on ecological sustainability – are not excluded but can have a more difficult passage. The structural power of the World Bank in shaping not only the supply but also demand for development knowledge is significant. Political themes and policy approaches are reinforced by the multiplication of organisations at a domestic level and through building regional networks. To date, the GDN regional research networks are dominated by economists and economic policy institutes to the relative detriment of demographers, anthropologists, sociologists and other development specialists. It serves to amplify one discourse of economic development knowledge in preference to other voices and visions.

HIV/AIDS networks appeared in the late 1980s after the 'discovery' of AIDS. Initially, Western medical diagnosis and scientific evaluation dominated understandings of the disease, although grassroots groups engaged in care and service delivery provided assessments of cultural and social dimensions. From the epistemic community perspective, the HIV/AIDS pandemic was characterised by 'uncertainty' and lack of consensus on causes and consequences. The bio-medical discourse of scientists and medical professionals defined the policy problem in terms of clinical and epidemiological characteristics, seeing solutions in policies that targeted the agents of infection. That is, a hospital-centred, technological approach delivering individualised curative treatments where the problem is conceived as a 'lack of knowledge and its application'. The uncertainty generated huge demand for research and analysis. Another increasingly powerful AIDS discourse is one founded on neo-liberal economics where the policy problem is conceived in terms of impact on health care expenditures, loss to national economies and impact on local labour markets. That is, a focus on technical and allocative inefficiencies where health prospects can be improved by measures to reduce waste and corruption, cost-effectiveness studies of health interventions and increasing the operation of market forces in health service and delivery. In the case of developing countries, World Bank lending policies for AIDS programmes have encouraged a shift from public health response to a public–private mix of public, for-profit and not-for profit health care institutions (Lee and Zwi 1996: 367). Both discourses have epistemic-like features. By contrast, more diverse networks of social workers, NGOs, social scientists and AIDS activists were advocating better comprehension of sexual behaviour and drug cultures along with social and cultural attitudes towards the disease (the problems of denial, secrecy and stigma) and their impact on prevention strategies. These actors were more likely to promote equity, gender issues and human rights in the allocation of health resources and to address the normative issues that are less apparent in the technical and apolitical languages of bio-medical specialists and economists (ibid.: 364–369).

Many non-state organisations rapidly developed international links through sharing of information. Bodies like the International Council of AIDS Service Organisations (ICASO – 1990), the International AIDS Society (IAS – 1988) representing the scientific community and more specialised groupings like the International Association of Physicians in AIDS Care (IAPAC – 1995) emerged. Others included the 'global AIDS policy coalition', an independent research and advocacy organisation (see Mann *et al.* 1992) and the International AIDS Economics Network (IAEN – 1993). By the 1990s, international organisations were taking the policy initiative and seeking to coordinate the multiplicity of AIDS programmes.

The WHO Global Programme on AIDS (GPA) spearheaded developments. Later, the Joint United Nations Programme on HIV/AIDS (UNAIDS), the EU HIV/AIDS Programme for Developing Countries and the new ILO Global Programme on HIV/AIDS have become institutional poles around which HIV/AIDS experts and professionals are revolving and networks seeking routes of bureaucratic recognition.[9]

International policy coordination is consolidating and an AIDS transnational policy community is developing. The cross-hatching of networks, personal connections, joint representation on international committees or expert panels creates a multi-modal governance mosaic. International organisations have taken a central coordination role but the HIV/AIDS global policy partnership is characterised by interdependence and participatory management. The policy community incorporates multiple actors from all levels of the political process – ministries, local government, scientific and medical experts along with their associations, pharmaceutical companies, NGOs championing human rights, development specialists, health professionals and social workers as well as people living with HIV/AIDS.

> The management of HIV/AIDS also shows the way in which low-intensity, international quasi-legal instruments such as non-binding resolutions, declarations, guidelines and reports (sometimes referred to as 'soft law') can be deployed creatively by international governmental organisations (IGOs) ... [I]n highly emotional often confrontational settings like those created by the HIV/AIDS pandemic, quasi-legal approaches offer all parties the opportunity to move forward cautiously – allowing their disagreements and opposing viewpoints to exist.
>
> (Mameli 2000: 203–204)

It is also in this environment that different modes of knowledge can co-exist and fragment into policy niches in the management of the disease. A visit to HIV/AIDS websites indicates the degree of institutionalisation of professional niches in this field.[10] The policy agenda has moved from science to greater incorporation of the sociological and cultural insights into the disease. This suggests a relatively pluralistic policy environment but the policy community is characterised by unequal power relations.

HIV/AIDS networks are a much more dense set of arrangements than that represented by the GDN or WEF. Nevertheless, there are similarities. Within these kinds of transnational policy networks, knowledge organisations perform useful roles as information clearing-houses, initiating research and developing network infrastructure – starting newsletters, building databases, organising conferences and preparing submissions. This activity is often bank-rolled by foundations independently or in conjunction with multi-lateral initiatives of governments and international organisations. They also help create a common language and educate network participants into the values or consensus of the network. Indeed, knowledge resources are considered essential in making networks work. 'Acquiring information from diverse sources is not just politically correct hand-wringing – it is a key advantage in global public policy-making' (Reinicke 1999–2000).

The 'authority' of knowledge and expertise in the global polity

'Knowledge' does not signify a single body of knowledge that is commonly recognised. On the contrary, it implies a struggle between different 'knowledges' or what are often described as 'discourses', 'world-views' and 'regimes of truth'. For many, the issue is not simply the creation and dissemination of knowledge, but the kind of knowledge that is produced and the kind of knowledge that dominates. This requires recognition that knowledge and expertise are contained by and connected to material interests. Those who demand and fund the creation and supply of policy analysis, advice and research can have powerful sway over what is researched and the issues considered important.

There is also demand for information to be managed. International organisations and governments require knowledge organisations and reputable professionals to sift and vouch the welter of ideas, information and analysis pressed upon them by NGOs, governments, corporations and others.

> Editors, filters, interpreters and cue-givers become more in demand, and this is a source of power. There will be an imperfect market for evaluators. Brand names and the ability to bestow an international seal of approval will become more important.
>
> (Keohane and Nye 1998: 89)

Consultants, think tanks and academics represent legitimate and neutral vehicles to filter, to make sense of the conflicting evidence, sets of argument and information overload. The social status and reputation of academics, thinkers, experts and professionals are an important dimension of the trust that both the general public and official actors place with them as 'filters and interpreters' of information.

However, it is not only as mere filters that they gain power. Knowledge creation, dissemination and application bestow power. Foundations, professional associations, scientific assemblies, actuarial bodies advocate their own intrinsic intellectual value, policy relevance and knowledge capacities. However, it is not necessarily that the most sound knowledge or best ideas will inform policy developments. A danger in this kind of analysis is to privilege the influence of experts and over-state the power of ideas. Ideas matter but so do interests. Furthermore, as noted in a study of Eastern and Central European think tanks, 'It is the management of expert discourse and not in-depth research that has empowered think tanks' in post-communist transition (Krastev 2000). This statement need not be restricted to think tanks: academics, foundation executives, consultants, law firms and financial advisers adopt a discourse of intellectual authority and/or deploy their professional rhetoric in order to gain access, to influence and to benefit from global policy networks.

Certain practices and normative standards are essential in maintaining the public stature of knowledge producers or their 'brand name'. Some research is more rigorous, professional and scholarly, adhering to recognised standards of peer review. Standards need to be cultivated and protected as policy-makers and other users want policy research and analysis that meet professional standards. Attracting foundation support or funding from national (social) science regimes bestows credibility. Rhetorical resort to the professional and scientific norms of scholarly discovery, intellectual investigation and impartial advice is particularly important to think tanks and consultancies in order to set themselves apart from NGOs and highlight their superior knowledge base, professional standing or business experience. Practices such as peer review and professional accreditation are exclusionary processes in which only those with the relevant credentials can participate. Such authority and legitimacy is a necessary component in effectively diffusing ideas and propelling them into official domains.

The power and authority of those with knowledge when interacting in policy networks lies in knowing how to locate and juxtapose critical pieces of information and being able to organise certain modes of understanding that others will demand. In other words, they make ideas matter and use their intellectual authority to verify certain forms of knowledge as more accurate, persuasive or objective. For example, transnational knowledge elites are often attractive to local governing elites. They represent an authority beyond their borders to which to appeal in reform processes. The major bond-rating agencies like Moody's and Standard and Poor's set international standards in global financial markets (Sinclair 2000). In other circumstances, conditions attached to development assistance or foreign loans coerce governments into accepting foreign expert advice and international 'best practice'.

Here, the discourse coalition/communities literature is of use. A specific set of ideas of progress and reform – financial liberalisation and the NPM mentioned earlier – have prevailed over other paradigms. The discourse of certain think tanks and consultancies has come to be viewed as technical, expert and authoritative. This status is reinforced when foundations, governments and international organisations like the OECD direct funds and other resources to such experts. It bolsters their position and it serves to amplify favoured discourses throughout official circles and civil society. Accordingly, questions about what is deemed to be international 'best practice' come to focus on the mobilisation of bias, and why some ideas are selected and others systematically ignored. Global networks – and the individual experts and knowledge organisations in them – are instruments for the 'mobilisation of bias' in the global polity.

Networks are flexible, evolving, re-structuring arrangements that move within and around institutions. Connections, intersections and overlapping of networks present nebulous and opaque policy arrangements based on consensus, informal power and 'soft laws'. It is an assumption of responsibility and 'reinvention' of authority (Sinclair 2000). The global governance of HIV/AIDS, the definition of the world's development problems, and the dialogues of corporate and government leaders establish decision-making processes, lead to resource allocations and institute policy practices that are beyond existing structures of public scrutiny. Networks undermine 'political responsibility by shutting out the public' (Rhodes and Marsh 1992: 200).

Public representation in this mode of global governance has not been advanced as in many national polities. Accordingly, the global polity is responding better towards the well-organised, wealthy, skilled and knowledgeable who are organised through networks and other institutions rather than to disorganised, poorly financed, unskilled groups and those who target the institutional structures of nation-states. Moreover, members of the general public often have neither the expertise, nor the time, nor the inclination to be active participants in the policy at the national level, let alone participate in global policy debates. As a consequence of the lack of transparency and mechanisms for public representation, transnational policy communities are more able to act with relative autonomy. Additionally, they are more able to thwart the emergence of challenges to the dominant values or interests in the global polity, suppressing demands for change in the existing allocation of benefit and privilege.

Pluralists usually stress the openness and informal participation to decision-making offered by networks. This tends to be the flavour of transnational advocacy networks that are non-exclusionary in character and are often effective in exercising 'voice' in global policy debates. Networks can promote greater pluralism or representation of diverse views, but networks can also function as exclusionary devices that limit alliances and curtail exchanges to a select elite. As has been said of the epistemic community literature, but which applies to many other network approaches, the approach is 'a model of elites by elites for elites' (Jacobsen 1995: 303). It can also be said that a network approach accommodates Marxist perspectives that networks are dominated by interests representing capital (Smith 1993) and especially neo-Gramscian accounts that focus on knowledge creation and idea formation as central to the capitalist system of hegemony (Gill 1999; Sinclair 2000). However, the hegemony of established interests is incomplete, uneven and contested. While there are many question marks over the democratic accountability of networks, they also represent a medium through which alternative world-views and new policy thinking can be articulated, although discourse structuration and institutionalisation may remain elusive. This is the case with the GDN which is characterised by many schools of development research and knowledge. However, it is also a research association where certain mainstream liberal economic institutes have acquired a dominant position, have privileged access to resources and whose research agendas agree in considerable degree with the policy preferences and values of the main GDN sponsors. The asymmetries in the broader global polity are reflected inside networks in their internal power arrangements.

Conclusion

The different emphases in this overview of varying network concepts resurrects the problem as to what balance is to be given to interests compared to ideational forces. To some extent this problem can be minimised if the different network concepts are not treated as mutually exclusive. For instance, epistemic communities can act in conjunction with (or within) transnational advocacy networks (Keck and Sikkink 1998: 134, 161) and policy communities. Furthermore, epistemic communities of experts and professional advisers are not static. In some circumstances, they can dissolve into more structured and heterogeneous policy communities where greater recognition is given to the play of material interests. This is especially the case when it is recognised that 'knowledge hardly ever remains consensual once it passes out of the control of the initiating epistemic community' into the hands of a national or international bureaucracy (Haas and Haas 1995). With a high degree of participation and agenda control (discourse structuration) by international organisations and governments, as in the case of HIV/AIDS management, a network is more likely to resemble a transnational policy community where official actors mediate epistemic knowledge in recognition of other interests. In the relatively 'thin' community of the global polity, transnational policy communities are 'thick' concentrations of policy practices and understandings 'of the word as a single place'. In general, global networks are 'thick' linking structures composed of 'thickening' agents.

In sum, the political significance of global policy networks is that they are symptomatic of the evolving global polity. More specifically, the many expert discourses treated as sources of authority in global debates on health and welfare, market reforms, human rights or democratic development is a manifestation of the 'globalisation of political life'. Those who articulate these discourses often have local identities and national bases in university centres, consultancy firms and think tanks but they are also part of 'global knowledge elites'. Through transnational interaction, they help create a sense of global community, even if that is limited to a network. Through their incorporation into (or resistance towards) global policy networks, they help give shape to the global polity.

Notes

1 The focus is necessarily narrow. It is not possible to incorporate a discussion of the global trade in policy knowledge about biotechnology, genetic modification or other forms of commercialised scientific knowledge. Nor is the current corporate fetish with 'knowledge management' covered. Nor is this an essay about intellectual property. The impact of the Internet will only be addressed in passing as a means or instrument for spreading knowledge or facilitating the activities of knowledge elites.

2 EINIRAS pools information and documentation on international relations in research and political practice. The members of its steering committee are senior archival and documentation staff of major European international affairs think tanks such as SIPRI, Chatham House in London, the Center for Security and Conflict Studies in Zürich or the Foundation Nationale des Sciences Politiques in Paris.

3 Global ThinkNet is a major project of the Japan Center for International Exchange, funded by the Sasakawa Foundation, and meets annually with an international conference. The research carried out in the study groups and workshops organised as part of the project serve as a basis for discussion at the conferences. The conferences also provide a forum for leading individuals from policy research institutions around the world to discuss cutting edge global issues, share thoughts on the future research agenda, and develop collaborative activities. Further information about Global ThinkNet can be found at: http://www.jcie.or.jp/index2.html.

4 The US system of political foundations centres on the National Endowment for Democracy which is funded by Congress (about $30–35 million annually). NED works primarily through four 'core institutes': the International Republican Institute, the National Democratic Institute for International Affairs, the American Center for International Labor Solidarity and the Center for International Private Enterprise.

5 Interest groups are politically driven by interest rather than causal beliefs. Academic disciplines are too heterodox to be called epistemic communities. Professions lack the normative basis of an epistemic community and its policy enterprise. Epistemic communities also differ from groups of administrators and legislators by their unwillingness to advocate or participate in the implementation of policy that conflicts with their normative objectives (Haas 1992: 16–20).

6 The Trilateral Commission is composed of the EU, North America (USA and Canada) and Japan representing the three main democratic industrialised areas of the world. The Commission's members are approximately 335 distinguished citizens with a variety of leadership responsibilities; see http://www.trilateral.org. JCIE, convenor of Global ThinkNet, is the Tokyo hub for the Commission.

7 List owner: admin@focusweb.org.

8 WEF describes itself as an 'independent impartial not-for-profit foundation'. Its website is found at: www.weforum.org. The International Forum on Globalisation can be found at: www.ifg.org.

9 Jonathan Mann was founding director of the World Health Organization's Global Program on AIDS and a renowned authority on the disease. IAEN is sponsored by the World Bank. ICASO has UN recognition. By contrast, IAPAC has a significant level of 'unrestricted educational grants' from pharmaceuticals.

10 www.icaso.org; www.iaen.org; www.unaids.org; www.iapac.org.

7 Civil society and governance in the global polity

Jan Aart Scholte

Introduction

Recent years have regularly seen the spotlight fall on civil society involvement in global governance – the environmental movement, the landmine campaign, the 'anti-globalisation' protests, etc. Since the 1980s, and especially since the mid-1990s, more and more business associations, labour movements, non-governmental organisations (NGOs), religious groups and think tanks have turned their attention to the ways that we are managing (or mismanaging) transworld issues. By now, most politicians and officials acknowledge – however eagerly or reluctantly – that civil society mobilisation in respect of global policies is here to stay for the foreseeable future.

This activity arguably represents evidence of a global polity along the lines sketched by the editors of this book. Civil society initiatives on global governance involve 'political structures, agents and processes with transnational properties'. They also manifest 'thick interconnectedness' and 'thin community that transcends the territorial state' (this volume: 12).

This chapter elaborates this general point in five stages. First, it develops a notion of 'civil society' in relation to contemporary world politics. A second section then notes the large diversity that marks civil society activism on global governance issues. The third part of the chapter examines forces that have generated the recent growth of this mobilisation. The fourth section identifies the broad impacts that civil society has had on global governance in the late twentieth century. Finally, the chapter addresses questions of the legitimacy of civil society involvement in global governance.[1]

Defining 'civil society'

Like 'globalisation', 'civil society' is a buzzword of contemporary political commentary whose definition must be carefully specified if it is to have analytical purchase. This is not to promise an exact and definitive conception, but to seek a working definition of civil society that sheds light on current history.

Meanings of 'civil society' have varied enormously across time, place, theoretical perspective and political persuasion (Cohen and Arato 1992; Kumar 1993). In sixteenth-century English political thought, the term referred to the state, whereas present-day usage tends to contrast civil society and the state. Hegel's nineteenth-century notion of civil society included the market, whereas current concepts tend to treat civil society as a non-profit sector. Writing in the 1930s, Gramsci regarded civil society as an arena where class hegemony forges consent, whereas much contemporary discussion identifies civil society as a site of disruption and dissent.

This chapter engages with ideas of 'civil society' less as they have appeared in the history of political thought and more as they circulate in policy circles today. This is not to deny the historical importance of traditional western liberal and Marxist notions of civil society, but to suggest that the concept requires adaptation in relation to world politics of the twenty-first century. The aim is to examine talk of 'civil society' in present-day policy discussions and to sharpen it analytically to give a clearer understanding of current circumstances.

To this end, 'civil society' is taken here to refer to *a political space where voluntary associations deliberately seek to shape the rules that govern one or the other aspect of social life.* 'Rules' in this context encompass specific policies, more general norms, and deeper social structures. Thus civil society actions may target formal directives (such as legislation), informal constructs (such as many gender roles), and/or the social order as a whole. The 'aspect of social life' that concerns us in this chapter is the global realm.

To be sure, the lines dividing voluntary activities from official and market practices can blur. For example, some civil society associations may assist in the implementation of official policies, and some campaigners may engage in commercial activities to fund their advocacy efforts. Moreover, governments and companies may sponsor non-profit bodies to serve as front organisations. However, 'pure' civil society activities involve no quest for public office (thus excluding political parties) and no pursuit of pecuniary gain (thus excluding firms and the commercial mass media).

From the perspective adopted here, civil society can encompass many sorts of actors: academic institutions, business fora,[2] clan and kinship circles, consumer advocates, development cooperation initiatives, environmental movements, ethnic lobbies, faith-based associations, human rights promoters, labour unions, local community groups, peace movements, philanthropic foundations, professional bodies, relief organisations, think tanks, women's networks, youth associations, and more. In particular, this conception of civil society stretches much wider than formally organised, officially registered and professionally administered 'NGOs'. Civil society exists whenever and wherever voluntary associations – of whatever kind – try deliberately to mould certain governing rules of society.

An active political orientation is key to this conception of civil society. Some contemporary analysts speak of 'civil society' as covering any social activity that occurs outside of official bodies, political parties, firms and households. However, the more focused concept adopted here excludes those voluntary associations (for example, many recreational clubs and service NGOs) which do not involve conscious attempts to shape policies, norms and structures in society at large. Thus civil society activity is here regarded as only part of – rather than equivalent to – a so-called 'third sector' of non-official and non-commercial activities.

This conception of civil society encompasses considerable cultural diversity. In earlier Lockean, Kantian, Hegelian and Gramscian formulations, 'civil society' related to *western* politics in a *national* context. However, talk of 'civil society' today circulates all over the world and is sometimes applied to political practices (like kinship networks in Africa and so-called Civic Fora at the local level in Thailand) that derive largely from non-western traditions. Moreover, in contemporary politics civil society associations often operate in regional and global spheres as well as local and national arenas. Conceptions of 'civil society' need to be recast to reflect these changed circumstances.

Indeed, some critics have suggested that the very term 'civil society' is so laden with western cultural baggage that other terminology is needed to reflect – and nurture – pluralism in the relevant political practices (Hann and Dunn 1996). Whatever the merits of this suggestion, for the moment the language of 'civil society' has permeated the politics of global governance. This chapter opts to engage critically with existing language rather than to create new words.

The diversity of civil society

The point has already been made that civil society is not of one piece. Voluntary associations that engage questions of global governance are of many types, and the ways that civil society groups seek to shape rules show much cultural diversity. Wide variations are apparent in the internal organisation, geography, resources, strategies, decision-taking procedures and tactics of civil society bodies.

With regard to internal organisation, civil society activism on global governance involves formally constituted and officially registered groups as well as informal associations that do not appear in any directory. Civil society bodies can be large or small, permanent or ephemeral. Some civil society actors are unitary, centralised entities like the Ford Foundation and the Roman Catholic Church. Others like the International Chamber of Commerce and Amnesty International are federations where branches have considerable autonomy from the central secretariat. Other civil society groups like the Asian Labour Network on International Financial Institutions (which has linked trade unions in four countries to campaign on workers' rights and welfare issues) are coalitions without a co-ordinating office. Still other civil society associations like Slum Dwellers International (which has arranged periodic exchange visits between community leaders of poor neighbourhoods in major cities of Africa and Asia) are loose affiliations that maintain limited and irregular contacts (Patel *et al.* 2001). Meanwhile, recent 'anti-globalisation' protests have developed substantially out of online discussions and mobile telephone messages rather than formal decision-taking structures. Further complexity arises inasmuch as some civil society organisations shift their form over time between unitary, federal, network and coalition modes (Fowler 2000; Lindenberg and Bryant 2001).

Civil society activity on global governance also shows considerable variation in terms of its geographical character. An association may be local-centric, country-centric, region-centric or global-centric. Bodies are based in the North (mostly), the South (sometimes), or the East (occasionally). They can be rural or urban in focus. Civil society organisations may be territorially grounded in particular locations or – increasingly in recent years – web-mediated through cyberspace (Hill and Hughes 1998).

In terms of capacity levels, civil society includes some initiatives that are very generously resourced and others that struggle for survival, frequently without success. Some associations are richly endowed with members, funds, trained staff, office space, communications technology and data banks. Other groups lack these material means. Some civil society organisations have a clear vision and value orientation, a powerful analysis, an astutely conceived campaign, a set of symbols and language that can mobilise a broad constituency, and an effective leadership. Other groups lack such human and ideational capital. Some civil society bodies can exploit close links with elite circles, while others are completely disconnected from established power centres.

The theme of diversity continues when we look at the objectives and doctrines of civil society associations that deal with global issues. Civil society houses conformists, reformists and transformists. This general threefold distinction is important, although the lines can blur in practice. Conformists are those groups that seek to uphold and reinforce existing norms. Such groups may attempt to improve the operation of existing rules or to manipulate established regimes to their advantage, but they pursue no change in the rules themselves. Business lobbies, professional associations and philanthropic foundations have often (though far from always) fallen into the conformist realm. Reformists are those civil society entities that wish to correct what they see as flaws in existing regimes, while leaving underlying social structures intact. For example, social-democratic groups have rejected liberalist economic policies without challenging the deeper structure of capitalism. Many consumer associations, human rights groups, relief organisations and trade unions have promoted broadly reformist agendas. Meanwhile transformists are those civil society associations that aim for a comprehensive transformation of the social order (whether in a progressive or a reactionary fashion). These parts of civil society are frequently termed 'social movements'. They include anarchists, 'dark green' environmentalists, fascists, radical feminists, pacifists and religious revivalists, with their respective implacable oppositions to the state, industrialism, liberal values, patriarchy, militarism and secularism.

In pursuit of these different strategies, civil society organisations adopt diverse approaches to decision-taking. Some associations have staff-led policy-making, while others have a member-led culture. Some use hierarchical decision-taking frameworks, while others employ more horizontal dynamics. Personal relationships figure strongly in the operations of some civil society associations, while others adopt strictly bureaucratic processes.

Further diversity arises in the tactics of civil society activism on global affairs. Some campaigns rely on the 'head' (with elaborate analysis), others on the 'heart' (with emotional appeal), and others on the 'fist' (with the 'projectile reasoning' of direct action).[3] Some civil society associations target states, while others focus on multilateral institutions, markets or the public at large. Many groups directly lobby official agencies and commercial actors, while others also – or instead – put the emphasis on mobilising grassroots circles through symposia, rallies, petitions, letter-writing campaigns and boycotts. Quite a few civil society associations are adept users of the mass media (even hiring professional communications consultants for this purpose), while others rely more on direct interpersonal contacts with their target audiences. Some civil society initiatives favour public demonstrations, while others concentrate on behind-the-scenes lobbying. Some civil society groups pursue close collaboration with authorities, while others reject any engagement with official institutions and market agents as cooptation. Some associations are keen to make coalitions across different sectors of civil society (e.g. between NGOs, research bodies, business fora and trade unions), while others spurn such alliances.

In sum, civil society spans a large and multi-coloured canvas. It exists wherever people seek through voluntary associations to affect the ways that we manage our collective affairs. It involves a wide range of constituencies, institutional forms, geographies, capacities, doctrines, decision-taking procedures and tactics. Apart from this broad definition and the acknowledgement that civil society is highly diverse, it is difficult to generalise about the phenomenon.

The rise of civil society

Civil society operations have greatly expanded in contemporary history. Many countries now report tens of thousands of officially registered civil society organisations (*The New Civic Atlas* 1997; Salamon and Anheier 1997), while much further civil society activity is informal. According to the Union of International Associations, the number of active *transborder* civil society groups – that is, those that operate across several countries – multiplied more than tenfold in the last four decades of the twentieth century, to some 17,000 (UIA 1999: 2357; Anheier 2001: 221–230).[4] Much of this increased mobilisation has addressed global issues such as development, ecology, human rights and peace.[5]

The reasons for this rise of civil society and its greater attention to global affairs are complex and vary in the details between one case and another. However, at least half a dozen general developments in contemporary world history have created a context in which civil society can thrive. Several of these circumstances have been closely related to globalisation, understood here as the growing salience since the middle of the twentieth century of the world as a single place (Scholte 2000a: 41–61).

For one thing, the contemporary expansion of civil society has been a response to altered contours of governance in the wake of globalisation.[6] Traditional statist regulation has proved inadequate to govern transworld phenomena like air travel, telecommunications, transborder production, electronic finance, global markets and transboundary ecological degradation. To make up the deficits, countless sub-state, supra-state and private governance mechanisms have emerged alongside regulation through the state. Many civil society associations have formed as a means to promote the creation of these new sites of governance and/or to influence their policies once they are in place. Civil society organisations have offered citizens ways to engage bodies like the European Union (EU) and the Codex Alimentarius Commission directly, rather than at several steps removed via their states and national parliaments. Indeed, some citizens have turned to civil society engagement of other – especially supra-state – authorities as an indirect way to exert pressure on their national governments. In short, civil society has grown in tandem with the emergence of more multi-layered and diffuse governance in a globalising world.

Globalisation has also promoted the expansion of civil society inasmuch as the spread of transworld relations has encouraged a diversification of collective bonds beyond a narrow fixation on states-nation.[7] By attenuating the previous tight interlinkage of territorial geography (country), territorial governance (state) and territorial community (nation), globalisation has opened room for the expression of alternative collective identities. These other bonds of solidarity derive *inter alia* from class, ethno-nationality, gender, race, religious faith and sexual orientation. Contemporary globalisation has also stimulated some growth in cosmopolitan commitments, as witnessed for example in global human rights campaigns, transworld relief operations and transborder environmental advocacy. These various drives to express social solidarity on non-state lines have drawn many people into civil society associations.

The rise of non-state governance and the growth of non-state communities have both reinforced a third impetus to the recent expansion of civil society, namely, widespread dissatisfaction with party politics as the principal formal channel of political mobilisation. Political parties aim to shape governance mainly by occupying legislative seats at local, national and (exceptionally) regional levels. Thus party politics has little direct bearing on much contemporary governance, especially regional, global and private regulatory mechanisms. In addition, party politics has often not proved a very effective way to pursue non-national interests (for example, connected with gender or race). Moreover, across the world large sections of the public have lost trust in political parties and what are perceived to be largely insincere and corrupt career politicians. The search for alternative means of political action – in place of, or supplementary to, traditional party structures – has taken many citizens to civil society.

Although civil society has exhibited the aforementioned tendencies to deviate from and challenge traditional patterns of politics, its recent growth has also depended in part on sympathetic dispositions in established official agencies. For example, the spread of liberal, pluralist democracy and the decline of colonial rule and one-party states have created an environment that is conducive to the growth of formally organised civil society. From Japan to Romania, many (though by no means all) governments have in recent years enacted legislation that legalises civil society activity and/or establishes fiscal arrangements that facilitate civil society operations. In addition, many supra-state agencies (including most United Nations bodies and multilateral development banks) have instituted procedures for the direct involvement of civil society associations in their work. Cf. Weiss and Gordenker (1996), Willetts (1996), Knight (1999), O'Brien *et al.* (2000), Scholte with Schnabel (2002, Part 3).

The development of new communications technologies has further facilitated an expansion of civil society activities, especially through transworld associations. Cheap telecommunications and the Internet have enabled people with shared concerns and values to mobilise together over whatever distances and across whatever borders.[8] Likewise, messages spread through electronic mass media have allowed civil society associations to attract sympathisers on an unprecedented scale. Camera-friendly Greenpeace stunts and headline-grabbing so-called 'anti-globalisation' protests offer prime examples in this regard.

Finally, at a deeper structural level, civil society's current prominence reflects the emergence in contemporary history of a more reflexive modernity. With reflexivity, people have heightened awareness of the limitations – if not fundamental flaws – of the cornerstones of modern society, such as rationalist knowledge, capitalist production, bureaucratic administration and mass urban life (Beck *et al.* 1994; Smart 1999). Gone is the self-confidence that generally marked modernity prior to the mid-twentieth century. Instead, many contemporary modern people are gripped with concerns about ecological degradation, runaway markets, persistent social injustices, democratic deficits, the deterioration of community, and the loss of spirituality. Civil society has offered many reflexive modernists an arena to pursue their determination to repair – or perhaps transcend – modern social structures.

In spite of these powerful spurs to civil society activity, we must of course not exaggerate the scale of its growth. Some countries have experienced far more civil society development than others: for example, the Philippines as compared with China; France as compared with Russia. And everywhere in the world, public-sector and market operations have generally continued to dwarf those of civil society. Indeed, most people are not actively engaged in civil society initiatives, or participate only occasionally and peripherally.

Nevertheless, the recent growth of civil society and some of its impacts on global governance are striking. We need only think of the sorts of scenarios mentioned at the beginning of this chapter. The rise of civil society has at a minimum given world politics new actors. Have the impacts on global governance also extended further?

Impacts on global governance

Establishing the *precise* influence of civil society on *specific* outcomes in global governance is no easy matter. For one thing, questions of causality raise complex methodological problems. In particular, it is difficult – if not impossible – to disentangle the role of civil society in a given global governance scenario from the impacts of the many other forces in play: numerous actors, multiple social structures, and various historical trends. Thus, for example, some researchers have affirmed that NGOs were crucial to blocking the Multilateral Agreement on Investment (MAI) (Goodman 2000; Smythe 2000), while others have downplayed civil society's importance in this affair (Henderson 1999). It is even harder to determine whether certain organisational forms, capacities, objectives or tactics have allowed civil society to exert more influence than others, and under what circumstances. In any case, each claim of civil society's causal significance requires painstaking empirical verification. Such detailed research goes well beyond the scope of the present chapter.[9]

Thus, instead of reporting definitive findings about impacts, the following paragraphs advance more general and modest suggestions that civil society has become one of the important forces that shape contemporary global governance. The cumulative evidence is compelling, particularly when one invokes the counterfactual principle: that is, asking whether a given development would have occurred – or would have taken the particular turn that it did – if civil society had been absent. With considerable frequency, civil society initiatives have been followed by policy shifts, a correlation that has happened too often to be wholly coincidental. Furthermore, time after time governance authorities have ascribed their policy decisions at least partly, and sometimes largely, to civil society interventions. This is not to make exaggerated claims that civil society associations have emerged as 'new global potentates' following a wholesale 'power shift' in world politics (Spiro 1996; Matthews 1997). But it is to say that civil society has made a difference in contemporary global governance.

Civil society impact on rules in the global polity can be discussed under four general headings: discourse, institutional processes, policy content, and social structure. In other words, civil society has had effects in terms of language, decision-taking processes, substantive measures, and the overall shape of world order. These points are elaborated in turn below.

Discourse

First, then, civil society has had impacts on discourse in global governance. Language matters. The way that issues are thought about and talked about is crucial to shaping action. Civil society is important in the global polity in one sense because it has moulded governing ideas and mindsets.

Indeed, a number of key notions in contemporary world politics have achieved wide circulation in good part owing to their dissemination through civil society. Major examples include 'human rights', 'sustainable development', 'gender', 'corporate citizenship' and 'globalisation'. It seems highly doubtful that political parties, official agencies, market players and the mass media would have given these ideas the sort of prominence they have gained in recent history without their promotion through civil society channels.

Of course, given the previously mentioned divisions between con-formists, reformists and transformists, civil society actors have not spoken one and the same discourse regarding global governance. In respect of 'sustainable development', for example, conformists in mainstream economic research institutes have reinforced the prevailing tendency in official and business circles to approach this concept in terms of redressing the environmental externalities of market forces. In contrast, transformists in some NGOs, community associations and underground movements have promoted critical conceptions of 'sustainable development' as a touchstone for wholesale social change.

Likewise, civil society associations have promoted sharply contrasting discourses of 'globalisation'. On the one hand, many academic institutions, business fora and foundations have been instrumental since the late 1970s in spreading neo-liberal conceptions of globalisation, centred on a *laissez-faire* approach to market capitalism. In contrast, other research bodies, NGOs, religious associations and trade unions have figured significantly in spreading critiques of the so-called 'Washington Consensus' on neo-liberal globalisation. Some of these critics have advanced reformist discourses, which advocate that deliberate public policy interventions be used to steer globalisation in desired directions. Other civil society opponents of neo-liberalism have spread radical discourses that characterise globalisation as imperialism. These circles have popularised the language of 'de-globalisation'. From these different angles, civil society has helped to put debates about globalisation in the spotlight of public discussion. It seems most unlikely that we would have heard so much – and so much argument – about globalisation in the absence of civil society inputs to contemporary political discourse.

Institutional processes

A second area of important civil society impacts on global governance relates to institutional processes. Civil society has affected the procedures by which policies on global issues are made. This is no small matter, inasmuch as *the ways* that decisions are taken often significantly shapes *the substance* of the resulting measures.

For example, civil society mobilisation has sometimes been an important force behind the establishment of new organisations and offices in global governance. The World Economic Forum (WEF) provided significant impetus to the formation of the World Trade Organisation (WTO). Other business associations have promoted the creation of regional trade arrangements such as the Single European Market, the North American Free Trade Area (NAFTA), and the Southern Common Market (MERCO-SUR). Civil society mobilisation on gender issues in global governance has encouraged the introduction of a number of positions, departments and consultative bodies that focus on the status of women (Stienstra 1994; O'Brien *et al.* 2000: 24–67). Human rights NGOs have spurred the expansion of official human rights regimes since the 1960s (Risse 2000b). Outside official channels, civil society campaigners set up an Unrepresented Nations and Peoples Organisation in 1991 as a 'UN' for indigenous peoples, now with fifty-two members.[10] Regarding the environment, civil society urgings have helped to institute environmental impact assessments of multilateral development bank projects and to establish a Trade and Environment Committee and a Trade and Environment Division at the WTO (O'Brien *et al.* 2000: 109–158). On the other hand, persistent civil society calls for a new global financial architecture have to date yielded only modest rewiring rather than major institutional refurbishment (Scholte with Schnabel 2002).

In another shift of policy processes, many civil society actors have become direct participants in global governance decision-taking. As early as the 1920s, business confederations and trade unions were incorporated with governments into a tripartite arrangement at the International Labour Organisation (ILO). More recently, most major supra-state regulatory bodies have adopted formal procedures for communicating with civil society groups on policy matters, *inter alia* by installing specifically designated liaison officers and consultation committees.[11] Some institutions like the World Bank have developed quite extensive civil society participation in policy formulation (Nelson 1995; Fox and Brown 1998; O'Brien *et al.* 2000). Civil society actors have also become substantially integrated into global issue conferences through large NGO fora that parallel the official meetings (Clarke *et al.* 1998). A few activists have, moreover, joined certain national government delegations for these events.

In addition to their roles in policy formulation, civil society organisations have also in some cases been instrumental in the implementation of global governance measures. For example, national aid agencies, multilateral banks, and UN humanitarian assistance organisations have all made substantial use of NGOs to operate their relief and development programmes (Edwards and Hulme 1996; Van Rooy 1998; Smillie and Helmich 1999). Community-based associations have figured importantly in global policies to combat HIV/AIDS (Kenis 2000). In respect of multilateral ecological agreements, civil society bodies have played an active part in executing the World Conservation Strategy and the Biodiversity Conservation Strategy of the United Nations Environment Programme (UNEP). Environmental NGOs have likewise been integrated into the administration of the Tropical Forestry Action Plan of the Food and Agriculture Organisation (FAO) and the Convention on International Trade in Endangered Species of Wild Fauna and Flora (CITES).

Finally, civil society activism on global governance has had an impact on institutional processes by urging official agencies to become more publicly transparent. Many civil society strivings for reform of global governance (especially on economic matters) have urged greater openness about how regulatory authorities formulate, implement, monitor and enforce their policies. Thanks in part to this pressure, the Bank for International Settlements (BIS), the Bretton Woods institutions, the EU, the UN, the WTO and other supra-state bodies have taken substantial steps to produce more public information, to disclose more policy documents, to release more data, and to increase access to their archives. This transparency continues to have limits, but the governance agencies are now far less obscure and secretive than they were before they became a target of concerted civil society mobilisation.

Policy content

Important though shifts in discourse and institutional procedure may be, has civil society activism also yielded changes in policy substance? Countless specific instances show that civil society interventions have helped to initiate, propel, amend or block global policy measures. For example, campaigns by NGOs and community associations have prompted multilateral development banks to revise or abandon various infrastructure projects, including a number of pipelines, roads and big dams (Fisher 1995; Sen 1999; Khagram 2000). Disarmament movements have shaped policies on nuclear proliferation, biological and chemical weapons and – perhaps most prominently – landmines (Price 1998; Mekata 2000). Civil society pressure has been vital in the Heavily Indebted Poor Countries (HIPC) Initiative for debt relief: both for its launch by the International Monetary Fund (IMF) and the World Bank in 1996 and for the enhancement of its terms in 1999.[12] A contest between religious organisations and women's associations figured centrally in shaping the 1995 UN Conference on Population and Development in Cairo. Human rights groups have been a principal force behind *ad hoc* international tribunals for Rwanda and the former Yugoslavia and in the movement to establish a permanent International Criminal Court.[13] And so one could compile a very long list indeed of individual cases of civil society influence on particular policy outcomes.

In terms of effects on general policy directions, civil society activity has undeniably figured centrally in the growth of global environmental governance since the 1970s (Princen and Finger 1994; Conca *et al.* 1995; Newell 2000). It is inconceivable that several hundred multilateral environmental agreements would have appeared in recent decades without specific campaigns and general ecological consciousness-raising by thousands of NGOs as well as various think tanks and certain business associations. Official agencies and market actors have rarely picked up the environmental ball before civil society associations kicked it to them. To be sure, ecological security concerns have on the whole played a secondary part in global governance, but it is largely thanks to civil society that they have gained a notable part at all.

In addition, civil society initiatives on global governance have arguably played an important role in shifting the emphasis of macro-economic policy in more socially sensitive directions. Whereas neo-liberal *laissez-faire* doctrine held a firm grip on global economic governance from the early 1980s to the mid-1990s, pressure from large ranks of civil society associations has nurtured the growth in recent years of a limited global social policy. Trade unions, NGOs, religious organisations, various research bodies and certain business groups have persistently advocated deliberate policy interventions at state and supra-state levels to address questions of employment, poverty and social protection in the global economy. This cumulative pressure has helped, for example, to make so-called 'social safety nets' (to protect food security, basic education and primary health care) standard fare in IMF/World Bank-sponsored structural adjustment programmes. Also in line with many civil society urgings, the HIPC programme has incorporated social conditionalities that ring-fence debt relief for welfare expenditure. Both before and since the 'Battle of Seattle' disrupted a WTO Ministerial Conference in December 1999, civil society pressure has encouraged trade authorities to examine the effects of commercial rules on poverty, particularly in the so-called 'least developed countries' (Scholte with O'Brien and Williams 1999). A notable movement of 'socially responsible business' and 'corporate citizenship' – as recently expressed in the UN's Global Compact – has emerged in good part as a defensive response to civil society concerns about inadequate regulation of global firms (McIntosh 1998; Tesner 2000). Thus reformist and transformists elements in civil society have helped to make governance of the global economy a matter not just of efficiency and growth, but of social justice as well.

This is not to suggest that civil society has propelled global economic governance from neo-liberalism to some sort of fully-fledged world-scale social democracy. Moreover, significant sections of civil society such as business associations and research institutes of the 'new right' have done much to formulate and promote neo-liberal policies. Thus, for example, the International Chamber of Commerce has been an important champion of trade liberalisation, and the Institute of International Finance has promoted a global financial architecture that has market forces and private-sector self-regulation at its core.[14] The Adam Smith Institute and the Cato Institute have ranked among the more influential ultra-liberal think tanks, while countless other research bodies have promoted deregulation, liberalisation and privatisation with less evangelical fervour.[15]

To a smaller extent than environmental, social and economic policy impacts, civil society activism has also helped to generate some measures to promote cultural security in the global polity. Certain campaigns such as Survival International and the Movement for the Survival of the Ogoni People (MOSOP) have taken up causes of indigenous peoples that other political agents had thoroughly neglected.[16] This pressure has helped to bring the plight of these minorities to the attention of UN agencies, and several national governments have instituted corrective constitutional and social reforms. More generally, civil society associations have articulated a now fairly widespread concern that prevailing approaches to globalisation are undermining the cultural diversity of humanity.

Deeper social structures

As indicated so far, cumulative evidence suggests that civil society activism has on many occasions affected discourses, procedures and decisions in global governance. However, has civil society's impact also extended to the deeper social structures that constitute global order? As noted earlier, the contemporary rise of civil society has in good part *emanated from* certain structural shifts in the contemporary world system, including the emergence of post-statist governance, the growth of non-territorial communities, and the spread of more reflexive modernity. Yet has civil society also *contributed to* changes in social structure in a globalising world?

Certainly civil society engagement of global governance issues has not merely reflected, but also actively reinforced several major developments in social structure. For one thing, the rise of civil society has not only responded to, but also further encouraged, the trend away from statist governance. As indicated above, countless civil society associations have formed direct contacts with supra-state regulatory institutions, thereby adding to their relative autonomy from national states. As also noted earlier, many civil society associations have themselves become formulators and executors of global governance measures, thereby acquiring some tasks that were previously reserved to the state. In addition, many civil society associations – especially transborder groups – have encouraged people to nurture non-national identities and communities that direct at least some of their attention and loyalties away from the state. The growth of civil society under conditions of globalisation has by no means provided the sole impetus for the emergence of post-statist governance, but it has been an important aspect of this dynamic of change.

As just mentioned, contemporary (particularly transborder) civil society activity has reinforced as well as reflected an ongoing reconfiguration of structures of community. Although some civil society associations have engaged global issues from a national and in some cases even aggressively nationalist position, many other groups have – in contrast to most political parties – constructed their collective identity on class, faith, gender, race and other non-national, transborder lines. Civil society has thereby fuelled greater pluralism and cosmopolitanism in the ways that people form communal bonds. To the extent that contemporary history has witnessed the growth of global community within a nascent global polity, civil society has provided an important part of its glue.

Likewise, civil society activism of recent times has constituted both a cause and an effect of the emergence of a more reflexive modernity. Civil society has provided an important space to articulate – and by that process to intensify – unease with the downsides of modernity. Many (although by no means all) contemporary civil society activists who deal with global issues have maintained (implicitly if not explicitly) that modern rationalism, capitalism and urbanism lie at the root of current social problems. On the other hand, with the exception of certain radical circles, most civil society mobilisation on global governance has sought to repair modernity rather than transcend it.

In particular, the recent growth of civil society has generally proved to be readily compatible with a continuation of capitalism as the prevailing mode of production in a globalising world. Inasmuch as globalisation has altered processes of surplus accumulation – for example, with the rise of consumerism and the information economy – civil society actors have on the whole partaken rather than resisted. They eagerly employ computers and telecommunications, covet media attention, and – where their resources allow it – happily participate in global tourism. To be sure, some vociferous so-called 'anti-globalisation' protesters have articulated an anti-capitalist message. However, most business associations, NGOs, think tanks and indeed trade unions have argued either to retain the status quo or to institute reforms for a more 'humane' global capital. Mainstream contemporary civil society has not questioned capitalism itself and, on the contrary, has implicitly if not openly endorsed it. In this light neo-Gramscian theorists have seen cause to regard global civil society as – wittingly or otherwise – a hegemonic buttress for exploitative global capitalism (Gill 1990).

On the other hand, any conclusion regarding civil society impact on the underlying structures of a global polity may be premature. Large-scale civil society mobilisation on global governance issues is relatively new, whereas structural shifts generally only occur over a longer term. For the moment, civil society seems on the whole to be operating within the contours of modernity and capitalism rather than building some postmodern and post-capitalist world. However, recent developments in structures of governance and community have shown that civil society can contribute to significant shifts in the foundations of social order.

Legitimacy

So now to the final step in this summary analysis of civil society and the global polity: having established that civil society matters in respect of global governance, is this activity *legitimate*?[17] On what grounds, if any, do civil society associations have a right to exert authoritative influence in the politics of globalisation? Why, in normative terms, should civil society be accorded a role in global governance?

The present analysis does not take an *a priori* position on this question. Civil society engagement of global issues is not inherently legitimate or illegitimate. The assessment depends on whether the activities meet certain criteria. The task here is to specify such criteria – to suggest a conceptual framework for determining the legitimacy or otherwise of particular civil society initiatives.

The framework developed below highlights four principal grounds of legitimacy: morality, efficacy, democracy and social cohesion. Each of these (partly overlapping) standards can invite a lengthy philosophical treatise that the scope of the present discussion does not allow. Instead, the following paragraphs elaborate the general claim that civil society carries credibility when it promotes transcendent values, manifests competence, advances public participation and public accountability, and/or enhances community and social integration.

Some analysts might also invoke a fifth general criterion of legitimacy, namely, legality. In this case a civil society association would obtain credibility through recognition by and registration under the law with official agencies. However, this standard is too formalistic to be helpful in normative analysis. Moreover, legality can be a dubious basis when the legitimacy of the government that grants it is in doubt. Indeed, as many emancipation struggles over the ages have shown, certain illegal organisations can have morality, democracy and social cohesion on their side.

Morality

Civil society mobilisation on global governance secures moral legitimacy when the actors in question pursue noble objectives and fulfil the role of a social conscience. In some cases (such as movements against genocide), the campaign may have to subvert established authorities and oppose majority opinion in pursuit of its morally legitimate cause.

Civil society campaigns on global governance have often met the criterion of morality. For instance, many civil society initiatives on global ecological issues have appealed to transcendent values like the preservation of the planet's life-support systems and intergenerational ethics. In addition, many transborder civil society campaigns have met a moral standard of seeking to avert preventable human harm. Examples include programmes for disaster relief, poverty eradication, human rights guarantees, and the suppression of illicit traffic in arms, drugs and people. Recent civil society efforts to compel global pharmaceutical companies to relax patents on anti-AIDS treatments in poor countries have also had a powerful moral base.

Claims of moral legitimacy are not unproblematic, of course, since different individuals and cultures hold different conceptions of basic values. Some observers might even question apparently straightforward cases like those just described. A more common conflict of views has arisen when religious revivalists in civil society affirm their moral legitimacy in the eyes of a deity, while non-believers just as emphatically reject those claims. Pacifists condemn any civil society activity that involves social, psychological or bodily violence, while others concede the tactical necessity of some violence in certain situations in order to achieve a higher and longer-term good.

Then there are instances of civil society mobilisation on global governance that are widely agreed to be morally illegitimate. For example, most observers have rejected the violence of racism perpetrated through fascist civil society groups. Likewise, some civil society associations have promoted caste and class prejudice, homophobia, paedophilia, sexism, or oppression of the disabled. Meanwhile transborder criminal networks have sought to sustain morally dubious global arrangements like offshore finance and illegal narcotics trade.

In short, civil society does not *ipso facto* have morality on its side. Like any other political arena, it hosts the good and the bad, as well as many shades of ambiguity in between. Civil society associations have to demonstrate their moral credentials; their rectitude cannot be taken for granted.

Efficacy

Alongside morality, a second general basis for the legitimacy of civil society activity on global governance is the more mundane criterion of efficacy. Contemporary globalisation has generally outpaced effective regulation. Most regimes to govern global communications, global ecology, global investment, global migration and global trade have been wanting in some (often severe) ways. In meeting what might be called 'performance legitimacy', civil society associations have contributed to more workable global governance. They have demonstrated expertise, knowledge, information, or competence. In these cases civil society groups are legitimate because they 'do a good job'.

Much civil society work on global governance has met the efficacy standard. For example, many women's associations have produced detailed accounts of gender discrimination that have been used – or could be used – to bring positive reforms to global regimes. NGOs and community associations have frequently – though not always – proved to be more effective than official agencies and firms in executing humanitarian relief operations and poverty alleviation schemes. Business associations, NGOs, research institutes and trade unions have offered countless inputs to make structural adjustment programmes more economically, ecologically and socially viable. Environmental think tanks like the International Council of Scientific Unions, the World Conservation Union, and the World Resources Institute are widely credited with having contributed vital expertise to global ecological regimes. Consumer advocates have documented a number of health hazards in global business. Indigenous people's movements have provided insights into the circumstances of these populations that are not available from other quarters.

To be sure, as with morality, claims of efficacy are not uncontested. One person's insight can be another's ignorance. Knowledge is power, and claims of competence are secured through political struggle, be it overt or latent. In particular, currently ruling discourses of technocratic expertise have tended to promote 'scientific' knowledge above other epistemologies. Against this prevailing hierarchy of truths, civil society contributions of 'emotional', 'spiritual' and other non-rational expertise have been less appreciated, if not openly spurned. This is not to advocate a relativist position that all insight has equal merit, but merely to note that assertions of expertise are more problematic than those who uphold dominant forms of knowledge generally realise.

And civil society associations have on various occasions demonstrated considerable incompetence. For instance, many campaigners for global economic justice have had only limited knowledge of the mandates and *modus operandi* of the governance institutions involved. Some think tanks have promoted models of development that have little relevance to the circumstances that they are meant to address. Greenpeace lost considerable credibility – and some membership – after its 1995 campaign to prevent the deep-sea disposal of the Brent Spar oil platform proved to be scientifically flawed.

True, the vagaries of policy processes are such that ill-informed and misdirected civil society activities might sometimes inadvertently produce beneficial results. For instance, although many 'anti-globalisation' protesters of recent years have been economically illiterate, they have spurred official circles to make some improvements in global economic management. More usually, however, low-quality civil society inputs to global governance are either an unhelpful distraction or, at worst, a cause of actual harm.

So civil society activity in respect of global governance is not inherently able or wise. These inputs can shed light or generate confusion. They can improve or undermine the operation of regulatory regimes, sometimes ameliorating and sometimes exacerbating the governance deficits of globalisation. Like morality, the performance legitimacy of civil society cannot be assumed in advance, but must be demonstrated on a case-by-case basis.

Democracy

As well as morality and efficacy, civil society activism on global governance might be deemed legitimate on grounds of democracy. It is widely argued that contemporary globalisation has generated large democratic deficits (McGrew 1997; Scholte 2000a: 261–282; Hertz 2001). Established mechanisms of public participation and public accountability – mainly local and national representative assemblies – have provided many affected constituencies with little if any voice and control in the governance of global affairs. In these circumstances many people feel dispossessed, and civil society could be deemed legitimate inasmuch as it advances public involvement in global governance (Scholte 2002).

On many occasions it has indeed done so. For example, civil society associations have often given voice in global politics to certain publics that would otherwise be largely or completely excluded. In particular, civil society mobilisation has provided conduits of participation for marginalised circles like indigenous peoples, smallholder farmers, the urban poor and women. Civil society has also furthered democracy in global governance when it has encouraged open debate of plural views and provided spaces to express minority positions and dissent. In addition, civil society initiatives on public education have often enhanced the quality of popular involvement in global governance. Campaigners have in this regard prepared documentation, appeared on the mass media, organised workshops, and so on. Moreover, as noted in the earlier discussion of institutional impacts, pressure from civil society for transparency has induced many official circles to give more publicity to the workings of global governance. Civil society campaigns have also sometimes increased the public accountability of global governance, for example, with pressure that resulted in the establishment of independent policy review mechanisms at the World Bank in 1994 and the IMF in 2001 (Wood and Welch 1998; Fox 2000). In other cases civil society groups have goaded representative bodies like the French National Assembly, the Irish Dáil and (especially) the US Congress to subject global governance arrangements to greater scrutiny.

While the preceding remarks indicate that civil society initiatives have often enhanced democracy in global governance, in other respects they have limited public participation and public accountability. For instance, some civil society associations have offered their members little opportunity for participation beyond the payment of a subscription. Like government bureaucracies and corporate hierarchies, civil society organisations can be run with top-down managerial authoritarianism. In addition, many activists have inadequately consulted the publics whose interests they claim to promote. Moreover, policy-making in many civil society associations has been quite opaque to outsiders in terms of who takes decisions, by what procedures, on what grounds, and with what funding arrangements. Further question marks over democratic accountability have arisen when (as often occurs) civil society organisations have self-selected leaderships. And civil society activities can bypass and subvert other democratically legitimate authorities, for example, in local and national governments.

Yet some of the greatest shortfalls in civil society's democratic credentials have related to representation. In general, civil society activity on global governance issues has disproportionately involved residents of the North, propertied classes (North and South), urban dwellers, and white persons. Moreover, the leadership of these civil society associations has been predominantly middle-aged and male. Westo-centric higher education, computer literacy and English fluency have also generally provided greater access to 'global' civil society. In these ways the contours of civil society have largely mirrored the hierarchies of power and privilege in world politics at large. Even ardent civil society critics of current patterns of global governance have tended to be socially closer to the rulers than the disenfranchised.

In short – and contrary to the rosy assumptions of many enthusiasts – civil society is no more intrinsically democratic than the public sector or the market. Civil society holds considerable potential to democratise global governance, but it does not have this effect automatically and indeed in some cases can have detrimental consequences for public participation and public accountability. So, as with morality and efficacy, civil society legitimacy on the grounds of democracy cannot be proclaimed as given, but must be demonstrated through practice.

Social cohesion

The emergent global polity suffers not only from democratic deficits, but from a thin social fabric as well. As noted earlier, globalisation has often unsettled bonds of collective solidarity through the state and the nation. Community, social integration, the sense of belonging, and social guarantees of minimum welfare – as vital aspects of human security – have weakened in consequence. Civil society could thus obtain legitimacy to the extent that its activities further social cohesion in a nascent global polity.

Many such contributions have indeed occurred. For instance, many transborder civil society associations have created mutual support networks among previously distant people who share common experiences and values, e.g., related to a disability, an ideology or a profession. In addition, some civil society programmes have promoted mutual understanding across deep cultural divides, for example, with inter-religious dialogues, peace initiatives and efforts to protect endangered peoples. Meanwhile civil society actors like humanitarian relief organisations and development cooperation groups have contributed to incipient global social policy with transborder welfare support for the aged, children, the disabled, the infirm, the poor and the unemployed. Civil society advocacy for more equitable access to the opportunities of globalisation and a fairer distribution of its benefits – for example, between age groups, classes, countries, races and sexes – has likewise sought to consolidate social bonds.

However, not all civil society activity has had positive implications for social cohesion. On the contrary, heterosexists, racists, religious fundamentalists and ultra-nationalists in civil society have made it their business to exclude 'the other' from their polity. Meanwhile business associations, professional bodies and trade unions have sometimes focused on the narrow special interests of their members to the detriment of the larger collective welfare.

So in regard to social cohesion – as with morality, efficacy and democracy – civil society involvement in global affairs is not intrinsically legitimate. It can work either positively or negatively. The challenge is to nurture the beneficial possibilities and check the destructive potentials.

Taking all of the preceding points together, legitimacy shows itself to be as complex an issue for civil society as it is for any other political arena. None of the four main criteria suggested here is unproblematic; nor are the different standards always mutually reconcilable. For example, democratic conduct can in some cases produce immoral outcomes, and inept handling of an issue can sometimes be legitimised on other grounds if it promotes social cohesion. Hence the preceding remarks offer a framework for debates about civil society legitimacy rather than a formula for definitive assessments.

Conclusion

This chapter has offered little in the way of definitive findings about civil society in an emergent global polity. Indeed, indeterminacy has been the theme throughout. The manifestations and modalities of civil society engagement of global governance are so diverse as to inhibit precise pronouncements on – let alone predictions about – impacts and legitimacy.

Such a conclusion might be anticipated when, as in this analysis, one adopts a broad conception of civil society and a multi-causal explanation of its rise in respect of global governance. This looser account is appropriate to current conditions of globalisation, where multiple forces tug at history and different trajectories are possible. This chapter has indicated the various sorts of roles – both beneficial and negative – that civil society might play if, as seems likely, a global polity consolidates further in the decades to come. The conceptual map provided here might, one hopes, help civil society actors and those with whom they engage to create positive future scenarios.

Notes

1 This chapter builds on Scholte (2000b).
2 This category includes both industry lobbies (where market and civil society often overlap) and business associations like the World Economic Forum that address broad social and political issues.
3 These metaphors are adapted from Clark (2002).
4 The actual figure is likely to be higher, as the Union of International Associations often does not hear of a new association until several years after its formation. I am grateful to Joel Fischer of UIA for this advice.
5 Cf. Edwards and Gaventa (2001), Korten (1990), Lipschutz (1992), *Citizens Strengthening Global Civil Society* (1994), *Millennium* (1994), Smith *et al.* (1997), Keck and Sikkink (1998), Boli and Thomas (1999), Cohen and Rai (2000), Scholte (2000b).
6 The following points on globalisation and governance are drawn from Scholte (2000a: 132–158).
7 The following points on globalisation and community are drawn from Scholte (2000a: 159–180).
8 See Lee (1996), Hill and Hughes (1998), Harcourt (1999), Smith and Smythe (1999), and Deibert (2000). See also, for catalogues of web-mediated civil society activity, New Social Movement Network Resources (www.interweb-tech.com/nsmnet/resources/default.asp) and SocioSite Activism (www.pscw.uva.nl/sociosite/TOPICS/Activism.html).
9 For an excellent collection of detailed case studies of civil society impacts on global governance, see Florini (2000).
10 http://www.unpo.org.
11 Cf. Weiss and Gordenker (1996), Willetts (1996), Knight (1999), O'Brien *et al.* (2000), Scholte with Schnabel (2002, Part 3).
12 Author's interviews with over a hundred relevant officials and civil society campaigners.
13 See http://www.igc.apc.org/icc.
14 http://www.iccwbo.org/; http://www.iif.com.
15 http://www.adamsmith.org.uk/; http://www.adamsmithinstitute.com; http://www.cato.org/.
16 http://www.survival.org.uk/.
17 On this issue, see also Brown *et al.* (2001).

Part III

Prospects and agendas for the global polity in the twenty-first century

8 The historical processes of establishing institutions of global governance and the nature of the global polity

Craig N. Murphy

Introduction

I am interested in what the history of international institutions since the Industrial Revolution can tell us about the current prospects for creating a more egalitarian – a more substantively democratic – global polity (see Murphy 1994, 1998). This chapter summarizes some of those lessons in the context of the programs of political action in response to globalization that have interested many of my students over the last few years.

The most comprehensive layer of the global polity can be identified along three dimensions: the policy realms it affects, its institutions, and its social nature, that is, the social forces that it privileges or curtails. To be concerned with substantive democracy is to be concerned with helping shape a global polity without privilege. While I would not claim that this is the aim of my students, I do argue that they are representative of many relatively privileged people throughout the world who recognize a set of moral dilemmas that the late Susan Strange argued we all face, given the nature of contemporary, unregulated globalization.

Sadly, I believe that none of the different strategies that my students, and others, are following is likely to solve that moral problem. The middle of the chapter outlines a relevant historical argument about economic globalization and its co-evolution with systems of regulation. I argue there have been a series of stepwise changes in the scale of industrial economies from the sub-national economies of the early Industrial Revolution to the 'global' Information Age economy. Each transition to a more encompassing industrial order has initially been marked by a period of relatively slow economic growth in which rapid marketization takes place, the state seems to retreat, and uncompromising versions of *laissez-faire* liberalism triumph. A second phase has always followed, marked by the increasing role of a more socially-oriented liberalism, the rise of which has been linked to the growing success of egalitarian social movements, movements whose aims are similar to some of the political aims of my students today. This second phase has also been associated with the consolidation of the whole range of governance institutions – from the inter-state level down to the shop floor.

The late twentieth-century decades of relatively slow global economic growth, rapid marketization, and the relative retreat of the state may be a stage in the development of a wider, socially progressive, liberal world order. If the earlier pattern holds, the prospects for the next phase may, indeed, be linked to the relative success of the whole range of political practices that currently energize a generation of students who are often considered alienated and politically passive. Moreover, given the political opportunities open at this particular stage in the development of the global polity, it may very well be that the women's movements and human rights that attract many students will be the only egalitarian forces with significant influence on the shape of the emerging global order.

Pinocchio's problem

I teach at an elite college for women in the United States. Although we grant fewer than 600 bachelor's degrees each year, the College's graduates include a disproportionate percentage of the women in high public office in the USA, including the First Lady, the Secretary of State, and the US Executive Director of the World Bank, as well as the majority of female anchors and lead correspondents on national television and radio networks.

While the large majority of our students are middle-class or working-class women on scholarship, the rest tend to be unusually well connected politically. At the end of this semester, for example, when questions about the USA's off-again, on-again support of China's entry into the WTO came up in class, one student brought her father, White House Chief of Staff John Podesta, to 'clear things up'.

Increasingly, our students, whether already well connected or not, come from outside the United States; among the twenty women in the class to whom Podesta spoke were citizens of Bhutan, Bulgaria, China, Costa Rica, France, Korea, Pakistan, the Philippines, South Africa, Taiwan, and Thailand.

Given this background, it is surprising to many on the Wellesley faculty that our students' political attitudes and actions so closely mirror those of other young adults in the United States. Most are deeply alienated from contemporary politics and, at best, seem indifferent to many of the domestic social issues that interested their parents' generation. At Wellesley, as throughout the USA, the number of students majoring in political science or preparing for careers in social work, education, or even law has been declining for almost a decade.

Yet, in the last two years, students at Wellesley and at other American colleges have become energized by the anti-sweatshop movement and by the protests at the WTO meetings in Seattle and the recent joint World Bank–IMF meetings in Washington. Moreover, every year a very large number of our students seek out dangerous and poorly-paid jobs in refugee camps and relocation centers in Eastern Europe, Latin America and Africa. Even many of those who choose to climb the corporate ladder claim that similar moral convictions have led them to choose their own 60-hour workweeks and six-figure salaries.

On occasion faculty colleagues from outside of international relations ask me if there is anything that my fields can tell them about our students' political attitudes and actions. Lately I have provided an answer, taken from Susan Strange's reflections on the ethical dilemmas all of us confront in the current phase of the 'internationalization', 'globalization', or 'increasing paradigmatic scale' of industrial capitalism.[1] I argue that our students share the egalitarian goals honored by their baby-boom parents and teachers, but that the women in their twenties recognize better than most us do the sorts of things that Strange was trying to tell us about the changed world in which we now live.

In *The Retreat of the State* (Strange 1996) and her subsequent publications, Strange worried about a *specific*, and, I believe, incontestable way in which state institutions have become weaker in the face of processes of globalization. (Strange readily admitted that those processes were set in motion, in part, by powerful states themselves, but the consequences for all states remained.) What worried Strange was the increasing inability of all states – not just 'failed states' or 'new democracies' but also 'welfare states' and 'development states' – to do anything about the growing economic inequality across occupational classes, regions, races and ethnic groups, and even generations both within nations and across the world.

If there remained any question about the reality of increasing global inequality and about its connection to the weakening of state capacity, recent work completed by the World Bank's Development Research Group should put it to rest (Milanovic 1999). To put it in its starkest terms: income inequality between the world's households grew more in the twenty years that an average undergraduate student has lived than in the 200 years before. And, as most economic historians would argue, the two centuries of rising global income inequality since the Industrial Revolution were, themselves, unprecedented (Bairoch 1993).

The development state and the welfare state were created to slow or reverse that process. Until something like twenty years ago, they did. Now, as Strange argues, by themselves, individual states cannot. This gives us what Strange calls 'Pinocchio's problem'. Moral men and women of Strange's generation, the generation raised in the Depression, who fought for decolonization and against Fascism, knew the welfare state and the development state (for all their flaws) as moral agents. These states lessened the growing inequality that is an inherent product of industrial capitalism. Thus, moral women and men of Strange's generation and of the baby-boom generation had reason to be loyal to the state; we had the luxury of being able to rely on the welfare state and the development state as a moral compass (however biased). Now, when it seems that no state, by itself, is capable of confronting what was long called 'the social problem', none of us have that moral luxury. We are like Pinocchio at the end of the story: without strings; we have to make up our own minds about 'what to do and whose authority to respect and whose to challenge and resist' (Strange 1996: 199).

Strange insisted that *now* the responsibility for dealing with 'the social problem', the problem of reversing growing inequality, rested with all of us – in universities and private firms, as much as in philanthropic foundations and states. Our students' words and actions suggest that they agree. They try to act morally within the entire range of human institutions that have some impact on growing inequality. Their strategies can be summarized under three headings:

1   Creating stronger states.
2   Making private institutions more accountable.
3   Working for cosmopolitan democracy.

Each strategy has its limits.

Creating stronger states

In recent years I have been struck by the fact that the most frequently mentioned alumna hero of Wellesley's international relations majors is not Madeline Albright or Hillary Rodham Clinton, but Lori Wallach, the public-interest lawyer who masterminded the Seattle protests against the WTO after earlier working to remove the US President's ability to 'fast-track' trade liberalization and to scuttle the Multilateral Agreement on Investment (*Foreign Policy* interview 2000). Some American students strive to emulate her by working hard to promote the American labor agenda – taking active part in the AFL–CIO's training programs directed toward college students and supporting the union's legislative program: (i) limiting US involvement in multilateral and bilateral arrangements designed to foster ever freer trade and investment; and (ii) increasing public responsibility in support of nationally-oriented welfare and health policies. Similarly, some European students work for a more independent, and a more inwardly focused European Union. Both sets of students worry that the policies they support may serve to marginalize Third World economies even further. A stronger US or European state, their African, Asian, and Latin American friends tell them, is simply a stronger center of imperialism.

Some students from outside the OECD also try to overcome Pinocchio's problem by working for stronger states. Yet many accept the position articulated by Susan Strange and her collaborators that the successful contemporary development state, carefully following plans to improve 'human capital', is really just in the business of attracting global businesses, which, together, have much more of the social power than ever before.[2]

Making private institutions more accountable

Firms

The power of business deeply influences a group of students for whom another Wellesley alumna, Alice Tepper Marlin, is the hero. She is the inventor of socially responsible investment funds and founder and head of the Council on Economic Priorities, an organization that gives a series of awards for corporate responsibility. More recently, Marlin has successfully developed a set of monitored international private labor standards, SA8000, modeled on the environmental standards created by the ISO. The CEP describes this initiative as enabling 'organizations to be socially accountable by convening key stakeholders to develop voluntary standards, accrediting qualified organizations to verify compliance and promoting understanding and encouraging implementation of such standards worldwide'.[3] Students who champion the CEP's work see it as marshaling the power of firms that have decided to address Pinocchio's problem in the way that Strange believed that all firms should.

They, too, worry about their strategy. Despite the demonstrated impact of Marlin's earlier innovations that rely on the interest that firms that have made socially responsible bulky investments have in forcing others to make similar investments,[4] one can question whether it is sufficient to transform an institution – global capitalism – whose fundamental principle of profit maximization seems antithetical to the notion of universal corporate responsibility.

Non-governmental organizations

Matters of principle attract other students to organizations whose core principles seem to be closer to egalitarian norms, organizations like the Red Cross, Worldwatch, Oxfam, and the other charities who increasingly carry out the welfare work of the state in areas of humanitarian crisis.

Again, the flaws in a program to universalize that strategy are easy to find. As the charities themselves recognize, they have increasingly become merely conduits for funds from Northern governments trying to maintain international order on the cheap. The 1997 International Federation of Red Cross and Red Crescent Society Annual Report refers to the resulting 'NGO colonialism' and the 'pimp talk' that pervades NGOs seeking to satisfy the shifting charitable whims of Northern donors (IFRC 1997: 14–21).

Working for cosmopolitan democracy

Some more reflective students, including many of those who protested in Seattle and Washington, try to get beyond the moral dilemmas faced by the dependent NGOs by envisioning a world of international public institutions with greater power and with greater democratic accountability to their ultimate clients. For these students, David Held's (1997) theory of cosmopolitan democracy is the moral guide. Yet, even a student who has worked in the field with local activists trying to block one of the World Bank's massive dam projects, and who led a group from her country who actually had access to Bank decision-makers through its environmental review process,[5] complained about the excessive idealism of Held's approach, at least in the short-term. Pinocchio's problem may exist because states, by themselves, cannot reverse growing social inequalities. However, the same is even truer of today's international institutions, even the most powerful.

The double movement

We can make sense of the limits of these strategies by first recognizing that globalization takes place through the market/economic then social/political process that Karl Polanyi called the 'double movement'. By 'globalization' I mean here simply the tendency for successful industrial economies to outgrow their political boundaries. In Adam Smith's ([1776] 1981: 265–266, 630–634) terms, a successful economy is one in which there is an ever-increasing division of labor. This growth in the division of labor – not growth in the amount of money that is following through the market, but growth in the number of workers (or even more precisely the labor power) united within a single economy (a single 'market') – is a long-term requirement of a successful capitalist economy. Smith's insight ultimately is not one about markets, *per se*, it is one about the *technical* 'division of labor', as Polanyi (1957: 49) recognized: to have continuous economic growth requires constantly increasing the number of people across whom the division of labor takes place.

When Marx and Engels translated the same insight into their own terms, Smith's intuition became the basis for the Marxian image of the bourgeoisie progressively turning the entire world into a single productive machine (Marx and Engels [1848] 1932: 13–14). Marx's key idea, Kees van der Pijl (1998) writes, is that of the incremental, ultimately global, *socialization* of labor via the inherently asocial processes of the market. Capitalists need markets to expand beyond the social and political boundaries that once contained them and despite the support that any current set of bounded political entities might have given to industrial capitalism in the past.

Stepwise globalization

Globalization, understood in this sense, has never been smooth or continuous. It has occurred in a step-wise fashion in response to political changes, resulting in the periodic development of new, larger social orders. Political coalitions among capitalists are needed to support such 'new orders' since no individual capitalist industrial or financial sector reflects the general interest of capital *per se* and there are always more- or less-powerful sectors that benefit from the current, less-than-global, social order. Similarly, there always will be more- or less-powerful socially protected non-capitalist forces opposing the next phase of globalization.

The large steps in the step-wise process of globalization have occurred in conjunction with the periodic changes in lead industries. The beginning of each new era is initiated, in part, by large investments, which, in turn, have typically required market areas larger than those that typified the lead industries of the waning industrial era. The early nineteenth-century Industrial Revolution involved large, often public investments in the power systems for mills. The mid-century Railway Age involved large investments in railway networks. The turn-of-the-century Second Industrial Revolution required network investments in electrical power systems and telephone systems. The mid- to late twentieth-century Automobile Age involved even larger investments in roads, modern railway networks, airports, the modern mega-factories, and the marketing and research facilities typical of twentieth-century industry. The Information Age has required the even larger investments in the Internet and in the computerized design and factory systems, such as for the Boeing 777 or the planned new generation of Airbus super jumbo jets.[6]

As has been the case with the Internet (and as was the case with US railroads), these bulky investments sometimes can be made piecemeal. Nonetheless, since the Industrial Revolution, those network-building investments at the beginning of an industrial era always have taken place over a larger geographic scale than the network investments of the previous era. Other large investments, such as those needed to build power plants or to fund the costly research operations of a modern chemical firm, require a large market prior to the investment. This assures investors that enough of the product or service can be sold so that the investors can be confident that their investment will be paid back (Murphy 1994: 123–127, 229–231, 234).

In theory, the problem raised by the pressures toward globalization could be solved by means other than the geographic expansion of the fundamental political/economic units of industrial society. The size of the community over which the division of labor takes place could be achieved by natural growth in population, imperialism, or the progressive integration of industrial societies, but, in fact, integration has been an essential solution. Human populations cannot grow as rapidly as 'potential productivity' – that is to say, human invention of new ways to do things with seemingly less labor input – will allow economies to grow and imperialism is a relatively costly endeavor. To assure industrial growth via imperialism in less-industrialized societies (the British strategy of the late nineteenth century and the strategy of Italy and France in the first half of the twentieth century) adds the cost of political control to the cost of the investments in infrastructure and human capital needed to make the strategy successful. To assure industrial growth via imperial control of other core societies (the Nazi strategy in Europe) requires antagonizing other industrial powers, powers that, in combination, are likely to be able to defeat you. Figure 8.1 illustrates this perspective on globalization by highlighting the growth and integration of the market areas of lead industries since the Industrial Revolution.

Despite the fact that integration rather than imperialism is the characteristic mode of globalization, the process does not occur without conflict. Students of International Relations immediately recognize that many of the blank spaces in Figure 8.1 cover periods of great conflict: the American Civil War, the Franco-Prussian War, the World Wars. In *International Organization and Industrial Change* and in subsequent papers on the histories of the United Kingdom, Germany, the Northeastern United States, and Japan (Murphy 1994: 18–23; 1995), I argue that even successful industrial societies have had to deal with four types of fundamental social conflicts that are either inherent to industrial society or else inherent to the less-than-global stages of globalization that we have experienced so far. These are conflicts between those who benefit most from the emergence of new industrial eras and the following opponents:

1   Industrial *labor*, ultimately over democratic control of production.
2   All those who have received political-economic advantage from the current order, *older sectors* (i.e. agriculture and older lead sectors).
3   Citizens and local rulers of *'the third world'*, i.e., those regions within the market area that will not experience all the benefits of the new lead industries, regions whose economic roles will be limited to pro-

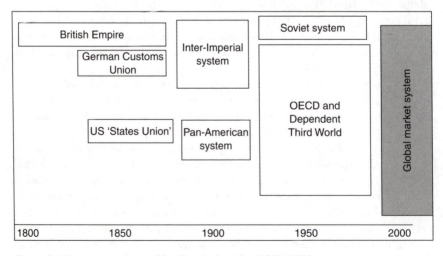

Figure 8.1 Economic areas of leading industries, 1800–2000

viding low-wage labor and resources (natural and agricultural) for the industrial core.

4   *Rival industrial centers* (other core powers within the same system) or *other industrial systems* especially those based on alternative forms of industrialism or proto-industrialism, i.e., the Southern slave system, German and Italian fascism, or Soviet socialism in contrast to what van der Pijl calls the 'Lockean' systems of the industrial powers that have so far been the most successful.

While managing these four types of conflict is the central, fundamental new task of modern statecraft, the fundamental conflicts of pre-industrial civilizations remain:

5   Conflicts between humanity and the rest of the living world, the '*environment*', that are rooted in our incomplete transition to a settled form of life.
6   Conflicts over *gender* inequality that are rooted in the gendered origin of the state.
7   Conflicts between privileged and less-privileged *ethnic groups* that are rooted in the characteristic response of settled societies to their vulnerability to raiding/warrior societies.

(Murphy 2001a)

The intensity of all of these conflicts changes over time and is linked to the regular pattern of transition from one industrial era to the next in what can be summarized as a *build, thrive, clash-grab-hoard cycle* (Murphy 1994: 26–46, 261).

The *build* phase is characterized by the temporary resolution of most of the conflicts. Scholars who base their analysis on the insights of Antonio Gramsci write about the formation of a new *historical bloc*, reflected in a mix of governance strategies of firms, states, international institutions, and popular social forces. The social calm thus established encourages and is reciprocally encouraged by relatively large fixed investments that fuel the take-off of new leading industries.

These lead to a period of relative prosperity (*thrive*), also characterized by the mitigation of the social conflicts inherent to capitalist industrialism. The last years of this period are apt to be marked by a kind of high cosmopolitanism, a widespread willingness of governments to risk resources in new liberal internationalist projects. This is the phase in which the first of the new market-expanding international institutions that become relevant to the *next* phase of industrial growth are established. The International Telegraph Union of 1865 helped create the infrastructure of the extended national markets of the Second Industrial Revolution take off in the 1890s. The Radiotelegraph Union of 1906 helped link the intercontinental markets of the Automobile and Jet Age. Intelsat, established in

1965, provides essential infrastructure for today's Information Age (Murphy 1994: 6).

However, almost simultaneously with this high cosmopolitanism, some of the inherent conflicts re-emerge: conflicts with labor, conflicts with those on the periphery of the privileged capitalist core, conflicts between different industrial centers of the core, especially conflicts with other social models governing parts of the world economy.

These *clash*es mark the beginning of a long period of reduced prosperity, the next phase of which begins with the reassertion of capitalist power in a profit-*grab*bing mode that may include cost-cutting globalization.

The temporary triumph of finance and the transience of Pinocchio's problem

As Henk Overbeek (1990: 28) argues, this clash-grab-hoard period is one in which productive capital is in crisis and the 'concept of money capital "presents itself" as the obvious, rational solution'. Governments adopt cost-cutting policies and begin to focus on issues of international competitiveness, and the institutions responsible for the stability of the international financial system begin to impose liberal fundamentalist policies on states that are increasingly desperate for such international or transnational support.

While this phase of reassertion by financial capital may be marked by significant economic activity, much of it is apt to be speculative, and of little lasting importance. Moreover, when speculative bubbles burst, the habit of under-investment in production is apt to continue, leading to the stagnation of the *hoard* phase of even more defensive strategies and greater political parochialism.

In slightly different ways Robert W. Cox (1992), Kees van der Pijl (1990), and I have described the transitions that take place at this point as involving the second half of Polanyi's double movement against the extreme market logic of the liberal fundamentalism that becomes so predominant in the grab phase. That movement involves the intellectual leadership of the *cadre class*, usually *critical* liberals who see a larger role for government. These intellectual leaders have marshaled both political leaders and industrial leaders (most often, of the new potential leading sectors) in what Gramsci called *passive revolutions*, comprehensive reformist projects that, nonetheless, require no 'fundamental reordering of social relations'.[7]

Historical sociologists of the world polity perspective connected with the Stanford Department of Sociology tend to argue that the liberal internationalism that has characterized a wider and wider sphere of state and civil society institutions, is, itself, the force propelling the development of the global polity (Boli and Thomas 1999; Luo 2000). I would argue that this *reformism* of international capital was behind many, but not all, of the 'new world orders' that have emerged from periods of crisis. There certainly have been non-liberal experiments – fascist Italy, Nazi Germany – that Polanyi understood as part of the double movement. Some – the Soviet and Communist Chinese systems – lasted throughout an entire long cycle. Nonetheless, the power of international capital has always ended up behind the liberal reformism, hence, perhaps, its triumph.

Excluded social forces and the political space created by crises of governance

As the sequence of bursting bubbles (perhaps, in recent years: the Japanese real estate and banking crisis, the East Asian and Russian financial crises) increases, the political space for egalitarian social forces increases. It is this political potential that, I believe, many people with egalitarian urges sense today. They hope to be part of the creators of a double movement, a move back toward a reformed social order. Yet, although history tells us that such a potential exists, history also tells us that it probably exists only for some social forces. In particular, it may exist for social forces that have not been implicated or blamed by the powerful for the economic doldrums of the last quarter of the twentieth century.

In similar periods in the past, the increasing inequality engendered by unregulated capitalism (under the hegemony of finance) began to become more tractable as new forms of social regulation emerged. These were, most often, forms consistent with the long-term liberal internationalist project.

Some popular social forces do not get to be innovators

When one thinks of the historical links between egalitarian social movements and industrial cycles what immediately comes to mind is not this hypothesized link to the construction of new industrial orders, but the clear connection between egalitarian politics and the social conflicts that mark periods of relatively slow economic growth. Labor movements, anti-colonial movements, development movements, women's movements, movements for ethnic and racial equality, and more comprehensive movements for democracy and human rights all serve to identify and articulate the fundamental conflicts that emerge within industrial societies.

Much of the most persuasive literature on social movements has emphasized the modernity of social movements, their 'modular' (replicable and replicated) character, and the way in which they are facilitated and limited by the political opportunities created by modern nation-states.[8] Nonetheless, these findings should not serve to obscure the connection between economic and social conditions and the likelihood that egalitarian movements will form and act. Eighteenth-century settlers in Britain's American colonies organized their anti-colonial republican movement in response to the increasingly harsh direct rule necessitated by the long (if successful) British hegemonic conflict with France as well as to the political opening created by an increasingly distracted imperial power. The British Chartist and factory hours movements responded both to the harshness of the labor regime in the early mills as well as to the political opportunities created by proximity and by the opportunity for alliances with embattled Tory interests. Turn-of-the-century labor and anti-colonial movements tried to expand the limits of the possible in an era when unprecedented prosperity and relative peace promised a more fundamentally democratic future. Similar economic and social conditions influenced the civil rights movements, development movements, and new social movements of the 1950s and 1960s.

Standard arguments about the frequency and intensity of domestic conflict should lead us to expect that social movements will become active during periods of relative peace and prosperity. We should also expect that they will become intensely contentious if the high expectations that they have during those 'good times' are frustrated by more powerful social forces bent on maintaining the inegalitarian status quo. My earlier study of the United Kingdom, the USA, Germany, and Japan revealed the role of specific egalitarian movements in the early clashes that marked each of the ends of periods of relative prosperity.

At a more inclusive level of analysis – that is not at nation-states or sub-national units but at the level of the geographic units in which the leading industries of industrial economies have developed (as outlined in Figure 8.1) – the dominant conflicts of each clash period have often been between alternative economic centers and alternative social orders. These include the conflict between industrial North and slave South in the United States, the series of brief wars between Prussia and Denmark, Austria, and France that helped unify the German Empire while securing its specific geographic class structure, and the World Wars that bracketed thirty years of this century.

It is commonplace, and relatively accurate, to conclude that the political–economic models of the social forces that lost these 'international' conflicts bridging the periods between industrial eras played no role in the historical blocs (the combination of ruling social forces, ideas, and institutions) that defined the new industrial era. The social model of the American slave Confederacy played little part in the social order of the Gilded Age and Progressive Era United States and its new empire in the Caribbean and Central American 'near abroad' and in the Pacific. The Austro-Hungarian vision of Germany and Napoleon III's vision of Europe played little role in the new Prussian German Empire or in the European Inter-Imperial System that provided German firms with the market area needed to be part of the Second Industrial Revolution. The Fascist vision of Eurasia and Africa and the idea of an Asian Co-Prosperity Sphere played little role in the 'Free World' order established under US hegemony after World War II.

Something similar may be the case when the dominant conflict preceding an industrial era is 'domestic', or, at least one contained within the older economic unit. The social forces that 'lose' play little role in the next world order. For example, when Chartists and early industrial labor movements challenged the early nineteenth-century social orders of Britain and New England, that may have helped assure that the Railway Age would, in both regions, remain a period of little concrete improvement for wage workers. When the Indian revolutionaries of 1857 failed, they nonetheless raised the perceived long-term costs of maintaining the economically crucial empire, and that may have contributed to Britain's commitment to an increasingly coercive imperialism throughout the rest of the century. When Vietnamese Communists, OPEC oil barons, and other elements of the diverse Third World reaction to American hegemony contributed mightily to the end of the post-World War II 'Golden Years', but failed to create a New International Economic Order, they may have helped assure that the Information Age would be particularly harsh on the societies condemned to be providers of resources, low-wage products, and cheap labor (see Augelli and Murphy 1988, 1993, 1995).

But some popular social forces do

Some may find this thesis neither interesting nor surprising. Why should we find it remarkable that social movements of those who suffer from persistent structures of inequality play no role in the development of new social orders? It is only surprising when we recognize that *some* movements of that sort have played such a role as part of the double movements that have marked the transitions from one industrial era to the next.

For the most part, the relevant movements have been 'domestic', labor and progressive parties, suffragists, anti-slavery movements in the USA and the UK, and anti-colonial movements within empires. Yet there has long been a transnational character to many of the most successful egalitarian movements. The anti-slavery movement in the USA originated in transnational (often Quaker or Jacobin, i.e., French-Revolution-inspired) associations, was fostered and transformed by world associations of the African Diaspora who opposed the Anglo-American 'progressive' solution of resettling all black slaves in Africa, and helped nurture and maintain the social movements that fought for the end to slavery in Latin America (Charnovitz 1997: 192–193; Goodman 1998; Keck and Sikkink 1998: 41–51). Anti-colonial movements have relied upon strong transnational links that transcended the realms of individual colonial powers, throughout this century (Nyerere 1980; MacFarlane 1985; Ansprenger 1989). The modern movements for women's suffrage and women's rights have always been transnational (Keck and Sikkink 1998: 51–72). In addition, of course, in the beginning 'internationalism' was simply 'labor internationalism' (Waterman 1998: 14–44; Lynch 1999).

In the current period of transition, egalitarian social movements, now almost always involving transnational links, have played demonstrably significant roles in the development of the social order connecting the industrialized OECD core to the dependent Third World and to semi-peripheral societies in Latin America, Eastern Europe, the Middle East, and Southeast Asia. Democracy movements and human rights movements, transnationally linked and often supported by core governments (especially since the mid-1980s) have played a central role in the transformation of Latin American, African, and East European societies, and continue to play significant roles in the remaining large states that have not made movement toward liberal democracy (Chilton 1995; Gaer 1995; Robinson 1996).

Similarly, transnationally linked women's movements have been instrumental in transforming the 'development' agenda of inter-governmental agencies to one that emphasizes the empowerment of women. At the same time women's movements have linked national struggles for gender equity allowing lessons learned in one area to be applied in others and contributing to the rapid diminution of legal gender discrimination as well as to substantive gains in women's access to income, wealth, job opportunities, and political positions (Chen 1995; Higer 1997).

The 'Information Age' double movement has not yet happened

The influence of these social movements on the verbal commitments of governments and inter-governmental agencies, on the allocation of international aid funds, and on domestic legislation (whether enforced or not) is clear from a number of regional studies. However, it is equally clear that neither these movements, nor the less successful movements promoting the interests of labor and the Third World have been able to reverse trends toward widening income gaps within and across societies. Moreover, as the current global financial crisis demonstrates, outside the United States and the European Union conditions hardly encourage the pattern of bulky investments needed to build the Information Age global economy. In large parts of the semi-periphery and the periphery, the Former Soviet Union, parts of Latin America and South Asia, and much of Sub-Saharan Africa, a kind of kleptocratic anarchy remains (Murphy 2001b).

Nonetheless, even today the outlines of the social compromises at the center of the next world order may be visible. Temporary resolutions of the fundamental conflicts of industrial societies may emerge from the small victories of the egalitarian social movements that have found political opportunities in the 1980s and 1990s. Many of us who live in industrialized societies are, for example, aware of the way in which the massive entrance of women into the wage labor force has allowed household incomes for most families to remain stable or shrink less dramatically despite the fact that most of the economic growth of the past decades has gone to the top 5 percent of wage earners (Larin and McNichol 1997). In this context the slightly rising incomes and protections for dual income working families associated with the 'third way' economic policies of Bill Clinton, Tony Blair, and Italy's post-1996 center-left governments have created a surprisingly strong and broad sense of social legitimacy that has extended even to the business elites regularly interviewed by the International Institute of Management Development and the World Economic Forum (Murphy 1999). As a result we someday may look back on this period as one in which the victories of women's movements in the industrialized world helped temporarily resolve the fundamental labor conflicts that would otherwise have impeded the complete emergence of the Information Age.

Similarly, empirical studies of the massive impact of gender-based small-scale lending, primary education for girls, and other elements of the emerging global consensus on development that have been fostered by transnationally connected women's movements suggest that some aspects of 'the Third World problem' may, without conscious strategic decision, end up being managed by seemingly marginal and low-cost gender-related changes in North–South relations (Evans 1998; Mayoux 1998). The recent wave of 'democratization without development' in Latin America, Africa, and Eastern Europe has been more self-consciously supported by some Northern governments (especially the Reagan administration) as a strategy to manage the increasingly fraught North–South relationship, and we may someday also look back on it as part of the historical bloc that maintained the period of relative peace and prosperity associated with the Information Age (Augelli and Murphy 1993; Robinson 1996).

Lessons for today's egalitarian social movements

The previous section argues that one important constraint on the influence of transnational egalitarian social movements may be their perceived role as a primary source of the conflicts that destabilized the earlier period of relative peace and prosperity. The relevant perception is, of course, that of the more powerful social forces – the ruling classes and ruling states – or, to be more operationally specific, the groups that serve as 'political parties' (in Gramsci's sense) for the dominant economic interests and states, the groups that effectively articulate the world-views and political programs followed by powerful nations, international institutions, and individuals. The relevant perception is that of the political movements of the powerful. Table 8.1 takes each of the industrial systems that are precursors to the emerging 'Global' Market System of the Information Age and gives a shorthand reference to the political movements, or Gramscian 'parties' of the powerful who provided the primary set of innovations for each era. The sources of Table 8.1 include my own work on the major

Table 8.1 Innovators associated with industrial orders

Industrial system ('world order')	Primary innovators
Late Industrial Revolution Britain	William Pitt the Younger's Conservatives
Railway Age British Empire	Disraeli's Conservatives
Railway Age German Customs Union	List's German Nationalists
Railway Age American 'States Union'	'Hamiltonian' Jeffersonians (*à la* Tickner)
Second Industrial Revolution	Large-enterprise German liberals, Cecil
Inter-Imperial System	Rhodes's liberal imperialists
Second Industrial Revolution	American 'Progressives', McKinley,
Pan-American System	Theodore Roosevelt
Automobile Age 'Free World' System	New Deal Liberals, Ford, Keynes,
(OECD and dependent Third World)	Monnet, Schuman
Soviet Industrial System	Lenin, Stalin, Bolsheviks

powers and on the international organization system (Murphy 1994, 1998), J. Ann Tickner's (1987) and Daniel Duedney's (1996) analyses of the antebellum United States, and Amsterdam School analysts Henk Overbeek (1990) and Kees van der Pijl's (1998) accounts of British, European, and trans-Atlantic social movements in relation to the emergence of industrial orders.

In many of these cases the social movements of the powerful acted as political leaders, promoting institutional innovations that had earlier been articulated by 'cadre class' civil servants and their political parties or party factions of the democratic left. The forces that maintain this class that is dedicated to resolving social conflicts assure that there is at least one source of the innovations needed to resolve the periodic crises of a conflict-ridden, globalizing industrial capitalism, just as the ever-growing relative power of the capitalist class (partially as mediated through powerful states), provides the 'selection mechanism' that determines which innovations will be institutionalized, thus providing the two necessary parts of any evolutionary explanation (Murphy 1994: 35–37).

However, the periodic need for social conflict-resolving and globalizing institutional innovation also creates political opportunities for social movements that are more firmly connected to egalitarian goals than the left-sympathetic 'experts in government' may be. To act effectively within this arena the history of successful egalitarian social movements suggest that they need to include at least five elements in their strategic mix:

1   Model mongering.
2   Elite-radical cooperation.
3   Transnational leadership cadre.
4   Cross-regional learning.
5   Using international institutions.

Model mongering

First, a dedication to what John Braithwaite and Peter Drahos (2000: 588–590) call model mongering, meaning the constant, experimental promotion of an ever-growing array of possible (egalitarian) solutions to the conflicts and globalization problems faced by governments and powerful social forces. For example, small-scale gender-based lending, reproductive freedom, primary education for women, and other elements of a quarter-century old Women in Development agenda have been well 'mongered' across a host of institutions whose primary concerns are not gender equality, but who have become convinced that these programs will reduce poverty, minimize costs of development assistance, placate an increasingly powerful Northern women's constituency, help clean up the environment, etc.

Elite-radical cooperation

Second, to be able to both successfully innovate in the interests of less-advantaged groups and to sell those innovations to status quo-oriented institutions requires a division of labor within the social movement into more and less radical elements *that maintain active cooperation with one another.* Amy Higer (1997) notes the importance of this element in the success of the International Women's Health Movement and similar conclusions have been drawn about nineteenth-century anti-slavery movements (Goodman 1998).

Transnational leadership cadre

Third, a unified central cadre of activists operating across the regional lines separating the emerging, more global industrial system. Again Higer's (1997) account of the International Women's Health Movement, historical accounts of anti-slavery movements, and the experience of nineteenth-century labor internationalism and twentieth-century anticolonialism make this point. To go back even further to the very beginning of the social movement era, one might argue that any successful movement needs its Thomas Paines, i.e. men and women who act in relation to a number of states and who can temporarily help protect the egalitarian activists of one society by offering sanctuary or marshaling diplomatic pressure from another.

Cross-regional learning

Fourth, a willingness and ability of local movements in one part of the new 'globalized' region to learn from the experience of local movements in other regions. Again, this seems to be a key element of the success of contemporary women's, democracy, and human rights movements, perhaps in sharp contrast to labor and Third World movements which have been riven by regional differences and perceptions that fundamental differences in interests (say, between industrial workers in Bangladesh and industrial workers in the USA or between Africa and Latin America) make cooperative learning impossible.

One of the strongest pieces of evidence supporting both the third and fourth points comes from the response of status-quo powers to the international conference system and especially to the NGO fora that now regularly take place alongside the inter-governmental meetings on the rotating list of major topics (e.g., human rights, the environment, women, population, social development). There is a widespread belief among NGO participants that the NGO fora serve as a major venue for inter-regional learning as well as the primary locus for the development of a transnational cadre linking various regional social movements. And, in fact, the belief in the efficacy of the NGO conferences for exactly that purpose has been a primary motivation for the work of conservative forces within the United States to end the global conference system (Fomerand 1996).

Using international organizations

The fifth and final issue is related: successful egalitarian social movements have been those willing to marshal the albeit limited powers of inter-governmental organizations to promote and test the movements' proposed institutional reforms. Again, contemporary democracy and human rights movements, which have added forms of political conditionality to inter-governmental development assistance and have convinced the central organs of the UN to be service providers to almost every state involved in a democratic transition, illustrate the point (Joyner 1999).

Lessons for my students

Returning to the small group of the world's seemingly alienated and politically disengaged students that I know, I am struck by the degree to which the political actions that *do* engage them are consistent with the lessons of the longer history of the development of the global polity. I do not think that it is simply displaced hubris or wishful thinking to say that I see among Wellesley students and alumna a part of a transnational leadership cadre of women concerned with what is ultimately a reformist project of developing a more socially accountable system of international governance to accord with the larger market area of the Information Age.

To promote that project some have become familiar with the political spaces offered by existing international organizations, and they have worked to both strengthen and democratize those institutions. Other women have become mass organizers and model mongers, like Lori

Wallach.[9] Others have become corporate executives or advocates of innovative forms of business self-regulation.

What they – and the other creators of the next world order – have, perhaps, not yet learned is the importance of cooperation across those two groups of organizers (elite and mass). Nor, perhaps, have they come to understand the significance of constantly passing the lessons of state strengthening strategies in one part of the world to another.

Finally, let me reiterate the possible significance of the links between this part of the emergent leadership cadre and the modern international women's movement. Recall that prior eras of a more socially responsible international liberal order have to pass as a coalition between privileged capitalist social forces and *some* of those that have not been privileged: (1) industrial labor; (2) groups and regions relying on older sectors; (3) the Third World; (4) states championing other industrial systems; (5) champions of the environment; (6) women; and (7) less-privileged ethnic groups. In the past, groups that the privileged have considered 'responsible' for the breakdown of the last era of 'peace and prosperity' rarely have become allies in the creation of the new.

A recent in-depth study of the perceptions and attitudes of a small sample of highly privileged but 'socially responsible' American men revealed a tendency to consider the demands of industrial workers, the Third World, and American minorities, and the costs of fighting the former Soviet system as responsible for the economic doldrums of the mid-1970s through the mid-1990s. Despite the relative gains of women and environmentalists over the same period, they were seen more as allies or as justified claimants rather than as enemies (Kelley 2000). There may be no better place to look for the outlines of the emerging world polity than among activist women.

Unfortunately, given those who are still perceived as 'to blame' for the world's economic problems, it is unlikely that the global polity will be able to resolve the social issue at the core of Pinocchio's problem. The 'best' global governance we can expect may well remain inefficient, incapable of shifting resources from the world's wealthy to the world's poor, pro-market, and relatively insensitive to the concerns of labor and the rural poor, despite the progressive role that these institutions may play in gender relations.

Notes

1 The last of the three phrases has, I believe, the greatest surface validity. It was suggested by Henk Overbeek, Kees van der Pijl (1998), and others of the 'Amsterdam School'.
2 See John S. Henley's contribution to Stopford and Strange (1992).
3 Mission of the Council on Economic Priorities Accreditation Agency; found on the web at http://www.cepaa.org/.
4 The strategy is described in Murphy (1997).

5 Jonathan A. Fox (2000) outlines the limitations of this democratic opening in the procedures of the Bank.
6 This perspective on the connection between large or 'bulky' investments and the beginnings of new industrial eras is consistent with Systems Dynamics arguments about the long wave, see Sterman and Mosekilde (1994) as well as Modelski and Thompson (1995).
7 'The "dialectic of conservation and innovation" which constitutes passive revolution is called "reformism" in modern terminology', Gramsci (1988: 428).
8 Most significantly, Sidney Tarrow (1998). For a review of the well-developed *theoretical* work in comparative politics and a discussion of the underdevelopment of empirical theory on transnational social movements, see Joel Krieger and Craig N. Murphy (1998).
9 It is interesting to compare Wallach's own account of her work in Geneva in the early 1990s ('There was no openness, and the level of arrogance was amazing. As disheartening as it was, it was also a motivating factor for an enormous amount of political organizing' (*Foreign Policy* interview 2000: 32) with Braithwaite and Drahos's (2000: 31) empirical conclusion, based on hundreds of interviews in Geneva, that Wallach's (and Ralph Nader's) organization was the most effective of the international model mongers during those years.

9 Europe

Regional laboratory for a global polity?

Knud Erik Jørgensen and Ben Rosamond

Our European model of integration is the most developed in the world. Imperfect though it still is, it nevertheless works on a continental scale. Given the necessary institutional reforms it should continue to work well after enlargement, and I believe we can make a convincing case that it would also work globally

(Romano Prodi, 31 March 2000)

There is in effect now more of 'the world' in Europe than of Europe in the world.

(Zaki Laïdi 1998: 82–83)

Does Europe really have any collective sense of how it can and should stand up for the principles and ideas that (with American help) shaped our current destiny? Do we have in Europe any remaining value driven vision of the world?

(Chris Patten 1998: 324–325)

Introduction

This chapter is about the European Union *and* or perhaps *in* the global polity. The choice of 'in' rather than 'and' promises to take the argument in a very particular direction. At the risk of indulging in semantic excess, the idea of the European Union (EU) *in* the global polity invites us to think outwards from the EU. It invites us to contemplate issues such as the role of regional integration schemes in an evolving system of global governance or the capacity of organisations such as the EU to exercise 'actorness' in world politics. It might involve inverting the problem and thinking about how the development of a global polity might influence European integration or shape patterns of European governance within and among the member-states of the EU. *In* carries the connotation that we are dealing with separate spheres of action when we discuss the global polity and the EU – that one impacts upon the other or that the latter constitutes itself within the former.

And, we suggest, connotes something rather different. The emphasis here is on the evolving EU as part of the emerging global polity. So rather than seeing 'the global polity' or 'globalisation' as exogenous stimuli, the EU's complex system of governance might be thought of as an expression of these phenomena, albeit mediated through the relatively long-standing institutions of European integration. Instead of looking outwards, the use of *and* invites us to look inwards at the EU and to think about the shape and scope of its regime(s) of governance. The danger of not looking inwards is bound up with the peculiarly complex and *sui generis* character of the EU, something that can go missing in attempts to view the EU through an IPE-like lens (Wallace 1994). While there are interesting and important parallels between the reinvigoration of European integration from the mid-1980s and the growth of the so-called 'new regionalism' from the same period, it is important to remember that the EU remains formally and informally rather distinct. In formal terms the EU has greater longevity. It arose within a specific set of historical circumstances that help to account for a second aspect of its formal distinctiveness: its distinct legal-institutional design. Informally, and perhaps because of the path-dependent consequences of those formal acts of legal-institutional creativity, the EU has developed into a quite distinctive regime of economic and political governance.

In our exploration of Europe's potentials as a regional laboratory for a global polity we approach the issue from two perspectives. We begin by looking 'inwards' at the EU polity comparing it with the global polity and examining Europe's 'balance of trade' in terms of modes of governance. In the subsequent section we think 'outwards' from the EU, analysing projections of the EU as a new type of actor in a potentially new type of world order. Our analysis addresses issues like the EU's actorness, recognition politics and changing spheres of political action in a globalised world.

The EU polity and its modes of governance

To what extent does the EU supply analysts with guidelines about the evolving nature of the global polity? Is it – in essence – an advance indication of the ways in which patterns of governance will change? Does the EU's complex system of governance offer a model for a putative global 'neomedievalism'? More dynamically, does the EU represent a source of ideas about complex post-national governance in a globalised era? Nowadays there seems to be widespread acknowledgement among Europeanists that the EU is better studied as an instance of a political system than as an experiment in regional integration or as an international organisation traditionally conceived. The insight here is not new (cf. Lindberg 1967; Puchala 1972), but it is a view that has come to prominence in EU studies in the past decade. To study the EU as 'integration' implied that the principal line of political cleavage within the EU could be captured by oppositions such as 'more or less integration', 'inter-governmentalism versus supra-nationalism' or 'nation-state versus super-state'. However, the depth of the EU's institutionalisation and its wide-ranging issue coverage make it clear that politics within the EU is about much else besides and that not every actor engaged in this politics has a concern with *integration* outcomes.

Beyond this basic acknowledgement that the EU is a polity of sorts lies considerable disagreement. One strategy is to argue that EU politics conforms to the timeless Lasswellian notion of politics as 'who gets what, when, how?' (Hix 1999). Consequently, the tools required for the study of the EU are more or less the tools of normal political science. This view regards the discipline of International Relations as largely moribund in this regard because it cannot conceive of the EU as a polity and is, at best, useful for the investigation of the international or systemic stimuli that impact upon actors within the EU system. Alternatively the EU can be thought of as occupying several distinct levels of action at which different sorts of politics occur. Alternative disciplinary homelands will be appropriate to the analysis of each of these levels. A final view is that the 'Political Science'-'International-Relations' distinction relies on caricatures of both that miss commonalities in terms of the sociology of knowledge (Hix 1994, 1996, 1998; Peterson 1995; Hurrell and Menon 1996; Ebbinghaus 1998; Rosamond 1999b, 2000: Chapter 7). Most agree though that 'EU Studies' traditionally conceived gets stuck in an insoluble *sui generis*/$n = 1$ problem which cannot generate anything other than primitive, descriptive social science.

These are not just squabbles among particular sub-disciplines. They cut to the heart of the issue of what the EU is and the extent to which it signifies something distinctive or generalisable in the global era. There is no shortage of attempts to encapsulate what the EU is. It has been variously described as a 'system of multi-level governance' (Marks *et al.* 1996), a 'confederation' (Warleigh 1998), a 'confederal consociation' (Chryssochoou 1994), a 'regime' (Breckenridge 1997), a 'political system, but not a state' (Hix 1999), 'post-sovereign, polycentric, incongruent [and] neomedieval' (Schmitter 1996), 'part of a reconfigured pattern of European governance' (Wallace 2000: 9), a 'policy-making state' (Richardson 1996), a 'regulatory state' (Majone 1996) and a system of 'liberal intergovernmentalism' (Moravcsik 1998).

Helpful as these characterisations are, any attempt to capture the essence of the EU is likely to be partial. The EU has a formal set of institutions and decision-making procedures, but the implications of action within that framework reach profoundly into the diverse national political systems of the member states. It is fair to say, moreover, that the EU has become recently more 'multi-actor', 'multi-level' and multi-process (Cram *et al.* 1999). Formal mechanisms have been colonised by an array of governmental and non-state actors and patterns of informal interaction have become institutionalised. New procedures have been devised to take account of the EU's reach into new areas such as foreign and security policy and coordination in justice and home affairs, not to mention the realisation of monetary union among the majority of member states. It has been argued that the existence of informalism and 'subterfuge' within the EU is the very reason why it is able to escape from the gridlock one might expect a fifteenth-country polity to possess (Héritier 1999).

With this in mind and with characteristic clarity, Helen Wallace has recently identified five distinctive 'beasts' with a 'shared ecology' that together make up the EU policy-making process (Wallace 2000: 28–35). The first of these is the classical 'Monnet method' of supra-national–inter-governmental partnership as described at length in most orthodox textbooks on the EU. The second is the European regulatory model of 'negative' market integration and harmonisation through mutual recognition rather than active (interventionist) regime-building found most obviously in the construction of the single market. The third is the game of distribution and redistribution found in EU policy areas like agriculture and structural funding, often captured by the phrase 'multi-level governance'. The fourth is the accumulation of technical expertise to produce agreed standards and policy norms (benchmarking). The fifth Wallace labels 'intensive transgovernmentalism' and is found in areas of high politics that the EU has increasingly colonised. From the point of view of this chapter, perhaps the most interesting issue arising out of Wallace's classification is the relationship between the various co-existent EU policy modes and patterns of governance exhibited elsewhere.

Quite clearly, the Monnet or community method is very much a creation of post-war *European* integration. Furthermore, it is a policy mode that finds little obvious application elsewhere in the world. Indeed, the classical supra-national–inter-governmental model of partnership and balance was an idea that came under strain within the Communities from the mid-1960s (Wallace 1996). Nevertheless, the classical community method provides the EU with its core institutions, ascribes to each powers and functions, and provides mechanisms for decision-making. It reflects, in a fundamental way, the institutional choices made in Western Europe during the 1950s. Although subsequent treaty revisions have embellished and revised the basic formulae of the Treaties of Paris (1950) and Rome (1957) in significant ways, the basic template for formal decision-making over the vast majority of policy areas covered by the EU remains intact. This has at least two implications. The first, following a historical institutionalist line of argument, is that the consequences of these institutional choices are reflected in path dependencies. Institutional purposes 'lock in', especially in situations where the institutions concerned are granted autonomy – and this often induces a divergence between institutional outcomes and the founding motivations of their authoritative designers. But the range of possible pathways and outcomes is circumscribed by the conditions of institutional choice. This means that new challenges or circumstances are not engaged in terms of an institutional *tabula rasa* (Pierson 1996). Moreover, second, the formalities built into the chosen institutional pattern have spawned around them complex and sophisticated processes, which although strictly informal have become institutionalised and thus in turn help to contribute to the longevity of the basic institutional framework (Sherrington 2000a). As Peterson and Bomberg note, the EU has developed a series of decision-making norms over time that 'govern exchanges within and between EU institutions, and define the acceptable parameters for political action by agents in decision-making' (1999: 53).[1]

Thus, from the viewpoint of the EU, one conclusion to draw is that the institutional conditions under which Europeans have encountered the challenge of 'globalisation' have been very distinctive and quite unlike those faced by other regions. The Monnet/community model arose out of institutional choices made in quite specific temporal, strategic and epistemic contexts. So while it is perfectly possible to argue that much recent policy innovation and formal integration have represented some sort of adjustment to global market imperatives, it is equally important to understand that European integration and the Europeanisation of economic governance might equally be thought of as playing out a set of decidedly internal logics.

For example, the initiative to complete the single market among the member states that arose in the mid-1980s was, in many ways, a clear attempt to realise the aspirations of the Treaty of Rome to create a common market after years of relative stagnation. To an extent the Single European Act can be read as an attempt to fulfil some of the functionalist calculus of the Communities' founders (where the achievement of a common market would be the latest stage along a route to full economic and thus political integration).[2] Moreover, the institutional methodology chosen was a more efficient version of the classical community method. Finally, there is a good deal of evidence to back the view that the single market programme had much to do with a renewed sense of institutional purpose within the European Commission under Jacques Delors.[3]

Also the encroachment of the EU into many new areas of regulation and policy competence can be explained less by the impact of external stimuli and more by the playing out of the EU's 'everyday politics'. The accumulating jurisprudence and judicial activism of the European Court of Justice are important here, as is the adroit use of Treaty provisions by the Commission to colonise new policy areas such as the environment and to gain a toe-hold in others such as social policy.

All of this suggests that the EU's development and present trajectory have much to do with the resolution of internal games and the playing out of institutionally embedded logics. It is quite clear, moreover, that the model of institutionalised integration represented by the EU has been deliberately avoided by designers of regional orders elsewhere. Even if

European integration has been a stimulus to other collective endeavours both during the 1960s and in the present period (Mattli 1999), there has been little inclination globally to either (i) go beyond the construction of free trade zones or (ii) create active supra-national institutions. The Community method has not been a successful European export to the global polity, but it remains a significant reference point for more or less any discussion about regional integration (if only in a negative sense).

In contrast, Wallace's second policy mode, the EU regulatory model, is widely imitated. This involves the achievement of 'negative integration', that is the removal of barriers to market efficiency and factor mobility combined with the management of economic interaction through regulation rather than traditional command and control mechanisms. The literature on the regulatory state suggests that this policy mode has been historically most embedded in the governance of the American economy (Majone 1991, 1994, 1996). In contrast, twentieth-century Western Europe has been characterised by an emphasis on the redistribution and stabilisation functions of the state. The growth of regulation as a policy mode in Europe coincides with (i) the growth of the EU; and (ii) perceptions of the need to rectify market failures in light of international competitive threats. Regulation has two primary attractions in the EU context. First, it is cheap. The EU's budget accounts for about 1.2 per cent of total Community gross national product (GNP) and vast swathes of the budget are used to finance the Common Agricultural Policy and structural funding – both more obviously redistributive than regulatory policies (Laffan and Shackleton 2000).[4] Second, regulation fits well with the dominant neo-liberal ideational framework of most European policy-makers. Also, as both Wallace and Majone note, Europeanising regulation is a potentially useful way for national policy-makers to escape rigidities in their domestic contexts.

The Communities were well suited to developing a regulatory policy mode. The single market agenda of the mid-1980s required the creation of a common market without fiscal, physical, technical or other barriers to the free movement of factors of production. This was largely an exercise in negative integration, a tendency reinforced by the establishment of the principle of 'mutual recognition'. This meant that EC-wide standardisation would not be required. Instead, the reciprocal acceptance of existing national standards legislation would in itself prevent the erection of barriers to the free movement of goods (Alter and Meunier-Aitsahalia 1994). Of course, this relies upon the intercession and effective jurisdiction of the European Court of Justice and, in the case of creating the momentum for the spread of regulation, an active and strategically inclined supra-national agent (the Commission) (Peterson and Bomberg 1999: 69).

In addition to these attractions, Armstrong and Bulmer argue that regulation forced its way onto the Communities' policy-making agenda in the 1980s as a consequence of 'contagion'. This has two senses. The first is the spread of neo-liberal notions of regulation (i.e. 'deregulation' in the sense of dismantling command and control mechanisms and 're-regulation' in terms of liberalisation under the rule of law). Most obviously this aspect has a transatlantic dimension, but it is also clear that – ironically perhaps – the British Conservative government under Margaret Thatcher was the most active and aggressive proponent among the member states of this new regulatory style.[5] The second sense of contagion relates to the global impact of deregulation in the United States from the late 1970s (Armstrong and Bulmer 1998: 9). This might be seen as an explanation why public authorities in the West began to sponsor economic policies consistent with neo-liberal globalisation, but it cannot of itself account for why in Europe regulation came to be undertaken significantly and increasingly at the macro-regional level.

Three sorts of explanation seem to prevail, two 'rationalist', one broadly 'constructivist'. The first looks to the preferences of member states and to the domestic context within which those preferences were formulated. Demands for supra-national regulation come from powerful economic groups. Governments conscious of the need to maintain the support of these groups and sensitive to the benefits (in terms of autonomy) to be gained from upward delegation tend to accede to their demands. Alternatively, economic actors operating in an emergent transnational space seek rule-bound orders from pre-existing supra-national authorities (Sandholz and Stone Sweet 1998). The third view argues that Europeanisation requires the discursive construction of the idea of a European economic space and of discernible 'European' economic agents. This is accomplished more often than not through the invocation of external economic imperatives that (i) render national modes of economic governance obsolescent; and (ii) require neo-liberal deregulatory responses (Rosamond 1999a).

Wallace's third policy mode is multi-level governance (MLG). She uses the term in its original and narrow sense to describe the redistributive politics that have emerged in the context of the EU. There has always been a redistributive aspect to the activities of the Communities. The Common Agricultural Policy (CAP) as a system of agricultural support might be best thought of as a sort of 'welfare state for farmers' and so-called structural funding is the second most expensive line item on the EU's budget. MLG in this sense describes the breakdown of national governments' capacity to 'gatekeep' the interactions between their domestic polities and supra-national institutions as well as the growing politics of sub-national regionalism that emerges in this context (Marks 1993; Hooghe 1996). We are forced to expand our conception of the EU polity rather well beyond the institutional fora of Brussels and Strasbourg. This conception of MLG draws attention not simply to the role in Europeanisation played by strategic elements in the Commission, but also to their equivalents working in sub-national contexts. It gives us a very firm sense of tiered or layered governance.

In the above sense MLG would seem to be a very European creation – a consequence of particular policy innovations and the need to ensure cohesion in the context of deepening (and thus potentially displacing) market integration with little application elsewhere. However, MLG has come to be used in a more broad-ranging sense as a way of describing the EU polity as a whole. Here MLG is used as a metaphor for the non-state-centric, multi-actor and rather fluid system of governance characterised by multiple *loci* of public and private authority currently evolving in Europe (Marks *et al.* 1996; Ebbinghaus 1998; Rosamond 2001a). It has been used to depict the EU as 'a horizontally as well as vertically asymmetrical negotiating system' (Christiansen 1997). Gary Marks and his colleagues define their approach thus:

> The point of departure for this multi-level governance (MLG) approach is the existence of overlapping competencies among multiple levels of governments and the interaction of political actors across those levels. Member state executives, while powerful, are only one set among a variety of actors in the European polity. States are not an exclusive link between domestic politics and inter-governmental bargaining in the EU. Instead of the two level game assumptions adopted by state, MLG theorists posit a set of overarching, multi-level policy networks. The structure of political control is variable, not constant, across policy areas.
>
> (Marks *et al.* 1996: 41)

Note how MLG in this sense is not so much a description of the EU as a rival perspective to the dominant inter-governmental theories. Not only is MLG a less-state centric approach than, say, Moravcsik's liberal inter-governmentalism (Moravcsik 1998), but it also draws on a rather more pluralistic and organisational conception of the state. This in turn resonates with the idea of the state as partially internationalised and permeated in the context of globalisation. In that sense MLG might be less EU-specific than at first sight.

The fourth policy mode Wallace describes as 'policy co-ordination and benchmarking' which she explicitly identifies as an import from the OECD. This technique aims to spread 'best practice' in policy-making through the accumulation of specialist expertise. In the EU this takes place within and beyond the formal institutions where the statistical auditing of various aspects of the European economy is now a routine exercise (Lee 2002). Benchmarking is built on the idea that it is possible to isolate those variables that contribute to the under-performance of the European economy in relation to (particularly) the United States. According to the Commission's Competitiveness Advisory Group, the technique also aspires to find ways of transferring 'positive' experiences (Jacquemin and Pench 1997). Benchmarking can operate at the macro-level by exploring the issue of European competitiveness, but it is also used at the sectoral level.

The EU is well suited to this policy mode. The need for technocratic legitimacy is arguably a precondition for the development of European-level action and regulation through expertise might be thought of as a function of a pillarised, bureaucratic system (Radaelli 1999). The key issue with benchmarking concerns its lack of formal interventionist or regulatory character. It is a policy methodology that operates at the level of the dissemination of knowledge and builds on the idea that particular deficiencies in European capitalism can be overcome through the reform of practices at both policy and enterprise level. This may indicate a broader preference for the Americanisation of the European economy and the inculcation of neo-liberal practices that displace elements of the European social model, though it might also reflect the dominance of the policy style of a particular member state – the UK – in the development of EU-level industrial policy (Lee 2002).

The final policy mode is 'intensive transgovernmentalism'. At first sight this would appear to be another phenomenon distinctive to the EU. Wallace coins the term to describe the sort of politics arising in the context of the EU's incursion into areas of traditional high politics, particularly monetary union, the Common Foreign and Security Policy (CFSP) and cooperation in justice and home affairs (JHA). Regardless of the formal provisions of the TEU, the development of Economic and Monetary Union (EMU) and its subsequent enactment have relied on a delicate set of negotiating arrangements involving national governments, finance ministries, central banks and the Commission (Dyson 1994; Dyson and Featherstone 1999). CFSP and JHA occupy separate 'pillars' of the European Union and were constructed to be altogether more inter-governmental in character than the 'core' areas of economic governance colonised by the Communities. Thus the Commission's wings are severely clipped and neither the European Parliament nor the European Court of Justice have significant input into policy-making in these areas.

Yet characterising the interactions in these areas as 'inter-governmental' in the traditional sense is rather misleading. The term suggests that the EU is best conceived of as a forum for inter-state bargaining or for the 'practice of ordinary diplomacy under conditions creating unusual opportunities for providing collective goods through highly institutionalised exchange' (Pierson 1996: 124). But close scrutiny of these policy areas reveals something rather more complex. For example, a straightforward inter-governmentalist analysis would miss the emergent rules of the game in the CFSP that underwrite notable processes of organisation adaptation and socialisation (Jørgensen 1997). An intensive and complex foreign and security policy network seems to have arisen involving substantial cross-fertilisation of officials from foreign and defence ministries. Interest groups and supra-national institutions do not figure, but as Forster and Wallace observe:

> Some of the classic characteristics of European integration have ... been evident in this field: the importance of socialisation through working together, the proliferation of working groups as a basis for policy-making and policy implementation, the hierarchy of committees through which ministers and prime ministers set general objectives and officials struggle to translate these into detailed policies
>
> (2000: 489–490).

If anything, cooperative activity in JHA has been rather more sluggish, but the tell-tale signs of intensive transgovernmentalism have begun to emerge through innovations such as the European Judicial Network (1998) and a developing policy network among member states' interior and justice ministries (den Boer and Wallace 2000). The potential significance of intensive transgovernmentalism may go beyond its present European homeland. True, it has arisen in policy areas associated with deep integration, but the obvious lack of supra-nationalism makes this a rather more readily exportable model.[6]

Global projections of the EU

The acceleration in formal European integration can usually be dated to the mid-1980s and the conscious attempt to create the regulatory conditions and a timetable for the establishment of a genuine common market among the member states. This was followed by the provisions on Economic and Monetary Union (EMU) contained in the 1992 (Maastricht) Treaty on European Union. Both of these initiatives required and were accompanied by significant growth in supra-national policy competence. The idea that these recent spurts of European integration emerged in response to similar stimuli to NAFTA, etc. is tempting and – to a degree at least – plausible, but any suggestion of this sort has to confront the institutional longevity of what is now known as the EU. Conventional 'regionalist' explanations of the EU perhaps also place too great an emphasis on *external* stimuli for state action.

On the other hand, the literature on the EU addresses significant questions about the extent to which regional orders are capable of becoming coherent, actor-like entities within an emergent global polity. The question is again one that might only be applicable to the EU for similar reasons to those cited in the previous sections. However, the idea that 'the region' might emerge as a significant type of authoritative unit in world politics is an idea that offers a compelling challenge to a number of well-known post-Westphalian world order scenarios.

This runs into the serious question of what might constitute 'actorness' in the global polity. If our initial presumption that the criterion for significance as an actor is bound up with those authoritative features traditionally associated with the nation-state, then we are in danger of falling into the trap of thinking that the states system can only be replaced or undermined by a system populated with entities that are institutionally substitutable for the state (Ruggie 1998: 172–192). The problem is that 'the notion of an international actor is wedded, as least historically to the concept of the nation, sovereignty and the broad tenets of *realpolitik*' (Holland 1996). In that light, it is interesting to note how Europeanists have contributed to the idea of what a significant post-national or supra-national actor might look like. For example, Hill has attempted to conceptualise the EU's world role by making a distinction between 'actorness' and 'presence'. Presence requires a discernible EU impact upon international relations (Hill's choice of term) while the former is accomplished where a unit is clearly delimited from others, has a legal personality and possesses various structural prerequisites for action in the international arena.[7] This distinguishes the EU from the conventional state and its foreign policy apparatus, but leaves largely unquestioned the nature of the polity it inhabits.

This can be thought of as being analytically conservative because if the EU is thought to be a manifestation of something new or distinct, then its presence within international society should not be assessed according to the norms of the status quo. On the other hand, 'actorness' is not only about the objective existence of dimensions of external presence, but also about the subjective aspects embodied in the validation of a collective self by significant others (Allen and Smith 1990; Smith 1996; Rosamond 2000: 177). The importance of the subjective dimensions of the global polity serve to remind us that the conventional discourse of world politics among practitioners remains wedded very much to the diplomatic norms of the states system. Thus interlopers into the system, such as the EU, seeking legitimacy within that system have obvious incentives to present themselves in terms comprehensible by other units.[8]

Writing about developing an 'organisational approach' to the study of world politics, Friedrich Kratochwil argued that '[o]ne implication ... is that we must pay attention to the way in which the system and the units are co-constitutive of each other. For example the emergence of the territorial state and the creation of the European state system occurred simultaneously. Sovereignty thus became the most important notion for both domestic and international politics' (1994: xi). Thus in many ways the EU may present itself as a challenge to the prevailing norms of the international system, but its relationship with that system will be complex and dialectical. Important questions to ask include whether the EU as a 'presence' simultaneously reflects the emergence of new systemic norms and/or contributes to the normalisation of a new form of global polity.

Among these complex and dialectical relations, the issue of recognition belongs to the most fundamental. While it is an undeniable fact that the European Union has not been formally and fully recognised as a constituent entity of international society, it is equally true that the issue is much more complicated than that. Despite the lack of formal *de jure* recognition, the Union is nevertheless playing a prime role in a number of policy areas and in other policy areas a considerable role, thus enjoying *de facto* recognition across a wide spectrum of activities in the global polity. Were the European Union to become a state like other states in international society, then it is likely that recognition would follow immediately. Yet member states of the EU have been very reluctant to give up representation, resulting in several cases of 'mixed competence'. Thus while the United States need not (any more) engage in international recognition politics (concerning itself) – the European Union does. However, most studies of the European Union in world politics neglect issues of recognition or register them without attributing too much importance to them (for exceptions, see Jupille and Caporaso 1996: 214–216; Bretherton and Vogler 1999). In our view this is unfortunate because recognition politics constitutes a key dimension of the EU's presence – and problems – in the global polity.

International recognition politics concerns status, symbolic or ceremonial politics, identity and, in a word, *being* an international actor. In a sense, the defining moment of a state is the moment when it is recognised by other states and thus becomes a unit in international society, consisting simply of the units of the system recognised as states by other states. When the European Union is brought into the equation, the increase of complexity is considerable. Partly because the European Union requires both 'internal' and 'external' recognition. The Union has to be recognised by its member states and, without 'domestic' recognition, the Union will obviously have a hard time being recognised by others. The varying degree of domestic recognition results in a spectrum from fully recognised (for instance, trade negotiations) to not at all recognised (UN Security Council). Furthermore, recognition has both a formal *de jure* dimension and a *de facto* dimension. The *de jure* dimension of recognition is of crucial importance. In Charles Taylor's words, 'the formal trappings of sovereignty – the exchange of ambassadors, a seat in the United Nations, and so on – are the paramount form of international recognition today' (1993: 53). Yet, precisely formal recognition has proved very difficult for the European Union to achieve, in part because member states have been reluctant to legally transfer competence to the European Commission. Without *de jure* recognition, the Union cannot vote in international fora or sign international agreements. In turn, the Union is unable to engage in follow-up activities, including compliance or non-compliance. Consequently, European institutions lack good reasons to establish capacities to handle international affairs. Nevertheless, the Commission has been very active in promoting itself as a European player, reaching a possible zenith at the UN Earth Summit in Rio when the then President of the European Commission, Jacques Delors, wished to 'sit at the top table in Rio ... as the leader of an essentially sovereign entity during the formal signing and concluding ceremonies' (Jupille and Caporaso 1996: 222). Concerning informal recognition, Jupille and Caporaso argue that, 'De facto recognition of the EU can result from its instrumentality for third states and from the sociality of global politics. Third parties that decided to interact with the EU implicitly confer recognition upon it' (ibid.: 215). One significant example of active mutual constitution at play is the 'rush to Brussels' when the Single Market project had been launched, i.e. the choice of most third states to accredit their delegation also to the European Community and not only to Belgium.

International recognition is sometimes more than an issue of formality. It can just as well be linked to identity. In Taylor's words, 'it becomes very important that we be recognised for what we are' (1993: 52). So what does the European Union want to be recognised as? We begin in an *ex negativo* mode, noting that the European Union does not want to be regarded as merely a regime or simply an international organisation. In attempting to arrive at a more positive answer, we note that the Union has built up an impressive network of external representation. At the European regional level, the EU is cultivating relations with several international organisations including the Western European Union, the OSCE, NATO and the Council of Europe. This is most unusual for an international organisation and hints at the Union's qualities as an international actor. At the inter-regional level, the EU is conducting dialogue-diplomacy with other regional integration organisations, including ASEAN, the GCC and the MERCOSUR, and a network of intercontinental dialogues like the Asia–Europe and Europe–Africa Summits has been established (Edwards and Regelsberger 1990; Piening 1997). Such bilateral relations on a continental scale hint at new forms of global politics, though it is fair to say that the significance of this new form of politics remains largely uncharted. At the global level, the EU has observer status in most UN bodies and belongs to the G8 circle. Furthermore, it is indicative that the EU has considerable shares in the creation of the WTO, is a full member of FAO, and has a *sui generis* status in the OECD. Besides these links with international organisations, the European Commission has delegations in some 120+ third countries.[9] The Union thus aspires to be or become a major international player, acting on arenas provided by international organisations and, crucially in the present context, the EU has in numerous areas been *de facto* recognised as such a player.

Given that the Union has been *de facto* recognised by other actors in the international society and that the Union has a significant international presence, what does the Union attempt to promote internationally? Should the Union be seen as a model? Does the Union have 'domestic' institutions that can be projected globally? Which key principles, values or visions does the Union use to inform its foreign policies? These questions can only be touched upon briefly yet hopefully sufficiently to suggest directions for further research. Reflecting on these matters, the present Commissioner for EU External Relations, Chris Patten, does not provide any clear answers yet sounds somewhat doubtful about the likelihood of European leadership. He takes his point of departure in Europe's aspirations 'because of our history, our civilisation and our self-approbation we aspire to play some role in the world. But what are we for, what do we believe, what are we prepared to do', continuing, 'what are we prepared as a whole in Europe today to risk for the sake of decency and liberty elsewhere?' (Patten 1998: 324).

There are good reasons for Patten's agnosticism. After all, even if references to the EU as a model for the global polity are legion, they have more often than not been rather vague, hinting at Europe's status as a security community (forgetting about Cold War security dynamics), Europe's achievements in terms of regional integration (neglecting their perhaps distinct European relevance) or under-specified European values and principles. During the Cold War, 'Europe' was often presented as a 'mediator' or 'third force', more responsible and 'civilian' than the superpowers. Plausible or not, it is in any case not a model that is relevant for the post-Cold War world. In terms of institutional projection, we have at best a mixed picture. Thus, the EU has been unable to impact upon institutional designs of international organisations like the G8, unable to influence the design of regional organisations like MERCOSUR, the GCC or NAFTA and similarly unable to influence key processes of regional integration such as in South East Asia. On the other hand, in terms of developing development aid policies (the entire development aid complex), or conducting UN peacekeeping operations, Europe has contributed a distinct approach and thus informed the part of the global polity that is the UN.

The EU and politics in the global polity

The final issue to consider is what all this means for the form of politics we should expect in a global polity. The image of changing boundaries of the political seems highly relevant for an adequate understanding of processes of globalisation of politics. At least three options seem relevant:

- the disappearance of politics;
- the reappearance of politics;
- the appearance of global politics.

It should be remembered that European integration for decades was a political project that attempted strenuously to dissociate itself from traditional (power) politics. Due to extremely bad experiences with unbound political forces during the 1920s, 1930s and 1940s, the launch of the integration process was informed by a desire to transform politics into 'non-politics'. Hence David Mitrany's plea for 'functional' agencies and the technocratic character of the Monnet method. In Kahler's apt words, 'For the functionalists, the enemy *was* high politics – source of Europe's bloody civil wars in this century – and the goal was political federation' (1987: 299–300). The emphasis of Monnet and Haas (1958) on processes of *engrenage* or functional spillover points in the same direction, though with some space left for politics. Hence the specific design of the political superstructure of the Euro-polity: a relatively weak parliament, an intended strong supra-national (read *a*-political) institution like the European Commission, and, originally, a modest role for the Council of Ministers. The European project has thus always been political yet presented as apolitical and employing (neo-)functional means.

When analysing the possible disappearance of politics, we note the argument that international organisations and also the European Union, intended or unintended, represent de-politicised national politics. According to Kahler, 'High politics ceased to be politics ... [S]trategic policy was sterilised politically and insulated bureaucratically. Ironically, that triumph of technocracy sought by many in the construction of a United Europe could be discovered instead in the reduced sphere of high politics' (1987: 289). Thus, politics has somehow become technocratic social action, limited to persons who represent states, corporate interests or other types of interest groups, meeting in global hubs for the purpose of social management. In the case of the European Union, this process has even become squared, in the sense that first we have the transfer of politics from national spheres to the European level and then, in turn, the Union represents the member states at the level of the global polity. With the growing role of international organisations in the global polity, politics has therefore not been globalised, politics has disappeared. Besides adding to complexity, the Union does not disturb the argument because both the Union and the global polity can be regarded as instances of a global process leading to de-politicisation of social action. Politics has declined if not disappeared. Instead of public politics, we see private or corporate actors or politics has been transferred to the structural forces of the economy, i.e. to the market.

Second, the disappearance of politics option may in some sense well be true but the political has not disappeared entirely. According to one version of the argument, there are 'pockets' of political activity around in the OECD world but this type of social action has become marginalised and squeezed into the streets of Seattle or Prague. Concern about marginalised political activity can be left with the police departments of major cities around the world, serving as meeting places for the de-territorialised global polity. According to another version of the argument, if the political ever disappeared, it has now reappeared, albeit in a new key. Only politics concerning socio-economic interests has disappeared, politics as such has survived or reappeared, yet because socio-economic politics has been taken off the political agenda, the political deals now with ethnic or cultural issues or, reappearing under the rubric of 'the national'. Because politics went global and became apolitical, the local and national have been left to somebody else. In this way the two first options are not necessarily mutually exclusive. Both images may well be very accurate descriptions of the current state of affairs.

According to the third option, politics has neither disappeared nor reappeared. Instead, through the process of going global, it has been dispersed and has definitely assumed new forms. Politics is not what it used to be. In the words of David Held *et al.*, 'Globalisation is not bringing about the death of politics. It is re-illuminating and reinvigorating the contemporary political terrain' (1999b: 496). The emergence of global politics is another way of saying that politics to some degree has left national boundaries behind and that also 'international politics' is no longer a fully adequate concept. In other words, politics is social action unfolding at several levels and including different kinds of actors. Politics is no more a domain reserved for national politicians or parties. Corporate actors engage in global politics just as well as global non-profit interest groups, epistemic communities, or officials employed by international organisations. In short, the increasingly important role of the global level of political deliberation is accompanied by new forms of politics, cultivated by new kinds of actors, using novel means of communication. This description is strikingly similar to one interpretation of what is going on inside the European Union, where the political has been differentiated into several levels, i.e. the multi-level governance model in which politics in the Euro-polity has been added to politics in existing polities, constituting simply European Union politics.

Conclusion

At the beginning of the chapter we claimed that any discussion of the EU in relation to the global polity would require a lengthy preface about the emergence of a putative 'EU polity'. Instead of arguing our case from just one perspective, we opted for two. One is to think about the EU as a polity and to explore, crudely, the 'balance of trade' of modes of governance. Drawing on Wallace's classification is helpful because we can think about the various policy modes in a global context and get some sense of what is going on within the EU polity in relation to developments in the wider world. The picture that emerges is far from one of the EU pursuing its own path-dependent logic in isolation from developments in governance elsewhere. The import and export of policy styles and modes of governance are evident. To argue that the EU provides nothing in the way of a model for the global polity relies upon a rather outdated conception of how the

EU operates. This view is rather distracted by the formal institutional manifestations of the EU and less attentive to the growth of less Treaty-bound and more informal policy developments. The in-route gives us a decent idea of the sheer complexity of how EU policy-making is adapting itself, to both exogenous and endogenous (or path-dependent) stimuli. But it also shows why the EU is a useful venue for the exploration of ideas about governance as well as the practice of governance in a globalised era. The second perspective is to explore the external projection of the EU as a new type of actor in a potentially new type of world order. The presence of the EU in the latter may be constitutive of the global polity, making it compulsory to include the EU in any serious discussion of the global polity. But equally, we should think about the ways in which the global polity (or for that matter the residue of the pre-global polity) impacts upon the EU.

The chapter has demonstrated how the development of both the EU polity and the global polity are closely intertwined. Yet the chapter also suggests that research on the global polity can benefit significantly from research on European integration. Indeed, if discussions about the global polity are largely about emergent 'post-national' forms of governance, then debates about European integration may have prefigured these by at least thirty years. On the other hand, any discussions of the European dimensions of the global polity need to take account of the awkward fact that the development of institutions of integration and economic governance have been in place and developing for a long period. So the various pressures that occasion the appearance of the 'global polity' do not strike the EU as a 'greenfield' site.

Finally, the appearance of both an EU polity and a 'global polity' is suggestive of change from established patterns of world order. It conveys a sense that world politics is becoming more 'organised' and, therefore, less anarchic. In terms of order this takes us away from the system of anarchy that formed the basis of the classical Westphalian system. In terms of units it implies a multiplication of numbers and types of significant actors in the system. In terms of processes, it suggests that world politics is as much about transnational, trans-societal and post-territorial relations as it is about international or inter-governmental forms of interaction. The latter continue to exist, but as part of a wider and more complex web of social relations. This also means that authority is more widely dispersed and more prone to reside beyond the grasp of formal public institutions, hence the phrase 'governance without government'. Analytically, this all suggests that we should be less state-centric and analytically more multidisciplinary. The global polity might be thought of as the political expression of economic globalisation, or, as perhaps a form of complex institutional adaptation or response where patterns of governance shift in response to changed structural realities, or, as a set of mechanisms designed to promote further globalisation or simply part and parcel of the new globalised political economy.

Notes

1 They identify the following norms as being particularly central: the use of 'soft law', 'negotiated enforcement', 'waiting for a policy window', 'punctuated equilibriums', 'package dealing', 'subsidiarity', 'informal decision-making' and 'consensus at (almost) any cost'.

2 If anything, this highlights the significance of the epistemic foundations of the Communities. There is quite a striking similarity between the strategies employed by the institutional designers of the Communities, the models of integration being developed by economists at the time and the growth of neo-functionalist theories of political integration (see Rosamond 2000: Chapter 3).

3 This argument should not be pushed too far though. Powerful arguments have also been advanced to suggest that the single market project was facilitated by a neo-liberal preference convergence among the key member states (Moravcsik 1991). Others look to the development of pressures from powerful non-state corporate actors increasingly operating in transnational economic space who came to make demands for a rule-bound transnational order and to forge alliances with strategically minded quarters of the European Commission (see Stone Sweet and Sandholtz 1998). Moreover, the governance of the single market conforms more readily to the regulatory policy mode.

4 Laffan and Shackleton cite figures from *Agenda 2000* showing that the Commission expects 'internal policies' (other than agriculture and structural funding) to continue to consume no more than around 6 per cent of the budget until 2006 (2000: 230).

5 This raises complex issues to do with policy transfer and lesson-drawing that cannot be dealt with here. See Dolowitz and Marsh (2000), Stone (1999). On policy transfer in the EU, see Radaelli (2000).

6 This would be especially true in a scenario where regional elites sought to embark upon a scheme of monetary integration rather than taking an orthodox free trade area-customs union-common market-monetary union model. See Dieter (2000).

7 Richard Whitman (1997) has gone some way to providing a detailed mapping of the realities of the EU's 'actorness' and presence in the international arena which together help to establish an international identity for the EU.

8 This does of course represent something of a radical analytical departure taking the emphasis away from the study of the objective reality of the international system towards the analysis of norms within that system and their capacity to sustain themselves (see Shaw and Wiener 2000).

9 Commission delegations in EU member states belong to a different category.

10 From global governance to good governance

Theories and prospects of democratizing the global polity

Anthony McGrew

Introduction

In a recent statement to the International Monetary and Financial Committee, Lawrence Summers called for the modernization of the IMF. Central to the achievement of this task, he argued, was a more representative, transparent and accountable organization (Summers 2000 (16 April)). Likewise, in the aftermath of the Battle of Seattle (1999) and Kofi Annan's prescriptions for better global governance – i.e. 'greater participation and accountability' – the rhetoric of democracy increasingly finds expression in official proposals to reinvent global institutions to meet the challenges of globalization (United Nations 2000: 13). Beyond the cosmocracy too, the language of democracy also informs the demands of many progressive social forces, such as Charter 99, in their campaigns for more representative and responsive global governance. For Robert Dahl, among others, such laudable aspirations are simply utopian in that 'we should openly recognize that international decision making will not be democratic' (1999: 23). Underlying Dahl's scepticism is a reasoned argument that, despite globalization and the diffusion of democratic values, the necessary preconditions for democracy remain largely absent in the international public domain: a domain which lacks the credentials of a properly functioning polity and in which might still trumps right. Herein lies a curious paradox: for in an era in which democracy has increasingly become a global standard of good governance it is judged inappropriate, by many of its strongest advocates, as a principle to be applied to international governance. Is such scepticism justified? Can the global polity be democratized? What might democracy mean in relation to structures of global governance?

In posing the questions in this way there is a presumption that the terms global polity and global governance in particular have some substantive meaning beyond mere political rhetoric. This is not secure conceptual territory since such terms are subject to serious disputation and qualification. Although this is not the appropriate place to rehearse those debates, some initial clarification is called for. As used here, the notion of the global polity refers to the constitution and organization of political authority among the political communities and associations which define the world system. By comparison, the concept of global governance refers to those diverse structures and processes of political coordination among governments, inter-governmental and transnational agencies – public and private – designed to realize a common purpose or collectively agreed goals through making or implementing global or transnational rules, and managing transborder problems. It differs dramatically from the concept of world government which presupposes the idea of one central, global, public authority which legislates for humanity. Instead the notion of global governance refers to the process by which individual governments, inter-governmental bodies, such as the UN, NGOs and transnational forces, from the World Wildlife Fund to Monsanto Corporation, come together to establish global rules, norms and standards or to regulate or resolve specific transborder problems, such as the global drugs trade.

Global democracy for global times?

Democratic theory (and practice), notes Shapiro, has always appeared 'impotent when faced with questions about its own scope' (1999: 1). Binary oppositions between the public and the private, the domestic and the international have been central to controversies concerning the boundaries of democratic political life. Radical critiques of modern liberal democracy, for instance, have advocated both the widening and deepening of the democratic order to embrace the private spheres of the household and the workplace (Held 1996). Yet, until recently, theories of democracy have presumed a strict separation of political life into the domestic and international realms: the bounded political community and the anarchical society respectively (Connolly 1991; Walker 1991). Theorists of modern democracy have tended to bracket the anarchical society while theorists of international relations have tended to bracket democracy. Of course, there have been exceptions to this. Liberal internationalism in its classical version, from Wilson's new world order to the early advocates of functionalism, such as Mitrany, sought to establish the normative and practical basis of a more democratic global polity (Mitrany 1975). In so far as critical theory sought to provide an alternative conception of democracy, it was imbued with cosmopolitan pretensions which challenged the inside/outside logic of orthodox accounts of the democratic political community (Linklater 1990; Hutchings 1999). But, for the most part, it is only in the post-Cold War era that global governance has come to figure seriously in the writings of democratic theorists and democracy on the agenda of international theory (Held 1995; Clark 1999).

This theoretical convergence has to be set in the context of several inter-related political developments: the recent intensification of globalization, the third wave of global democratization and the rise of transnational social movements. Economic globalization, many argue, has exacerbated the tension between democracy, as a territoriality rooted system of rule, and the operation of global markets and transnational networks of corporate power. In a world in which even the most powerful governments appear impotent when confronted by the gyrations of global markets or the activities of transnational corporations, the efficacy of national democracy is called into question. For if, as Sandel observes, governments have lost the capacity to manage transnational forces in accordance with the expressed preferences of their citizens, the very essence of democracy, namely self-governance, is decidedly compromised (Sandel 1996). Moreover, in seeking to promote or regulate the forces of globalization, through mechanisms of global and regional governance, states have created new layers of political authority which have weak democratic credentials and stand in an ambiguous relationship to existing systems of national accountability. Under these conditions it is no longer clear, to use Dahl's classic formulation, 'who governs.' For instance, in the midst of the South Korean general election in 1997, just following the East Asian crash, both candidates for the Presidency were requested by the IMF to sign a confidential declaration to abide by the conditions of its proposed financial rescue package, irrespective of the election outcome. In an era in which public and private power is manifested and exercised on a transnational, or even global scale, a serious reappraisal of the prospects for democracy is overdue.

This rethinking of democracy has also been encouraged by the global diffusion of liberal democracy as a system of political rule. In comparison with the early twentieth century, democracy – and liberal representative democracy at that – has emerged as the dominant system of national rule across the globe – at least in a formal sense (Potter *et al.* 1997). Putting aside Fukuyama's misconceived triumphalism, whatever the causes of this Third Wave, democracy has become an almost universal political standard. Of course, for many new democracies the aspiration and political rhetoric far exceed the realization of effective democracy. Public disenchantment with elected politicians and the capacity of democratic governments to deal with many of the enduring problems – from inequality to pollution – confronted by modern societies suggest that all is not well within the old democracies. Despite such failings, both old and new democracies in particular have become increasingly sensitive to the weak democratic credentials of existing structures of global and regional governance, the more so as the actions of such bodies directly impinge on their citizens. As democratic states have come to constitute a majority within global institutions the pressures to make such bodies more transparent and accountable have increased (Commission on Global Governance 1995). Somewhat ironically, many new democracies which have been subject to strictures from the IMF and the World Bank about the requirements of good governance are now campaigning for similar principles and practices to be applied in these citadels of global power. But how to combine effective international institutions with democratic practices remains, according to Keohane (1998), among the most intractable of contemporary international political problems.

One powerful response to this problem has come from the agencies of civil society. The global associational revolution, expressed in the enormous expansion of NGO activity and transnational networks of advocacy groups, business, professionals and associations among others, has created the infrastructure of a transnational civil society (Matthews 1997; Rosenau 1997; Boli and Thomas 1999). Although unrepresentative of the world's peoples, the agencies of transnational civil society have come to be instrumental in representing the concerns of citizens and organized interests in international fora (Boli *et al.* 1999). But the democratic credentials of transnational civil society are ambiguous. Whether transnational civil society is a significant force for the democratization of world order or simply another arena through which the privileged and powerful maintain their global hegemony is a matter of some debate (Wapner 1996; Weiss and Gordenker 1996; Burbach *et al.* 1997; Boli and Thomas 1999).

It is in the context of these developments that the academic discourse about global or transnational democracy finds a certain political resonance. Indeed, the rapidity with which the rhetoric, if not the idea, of democracy has acquired a certain discursive hegemony in current deliberations concerning the reform of global governance is quite remarkable. It is all the more so, given the dogmatic dismissal of early reflections upon democracy and world order. The remainder of the chapter will offer an overview and critique of the debate about transnational democracy elucidating the key normative theories or approaches. Before considering these accounts, the terms of the debate require some clarification.

Is transnational democracy possible?

For the communitarian and realist critics of transnational democracy the answer to the above question is an uncompromising No. Whatever the intellectual merits of any particular design for transnational democracy, those of a sceptical mind question its relevance, desirability and feasibility. They do so on a number of grounds: theoretical, institutional, historical and ethical.

Communitarians take issue with the cosmopolitan premises which inform theories of transnational democracy. Democracy, argues Kymlicka (1999), is rooted in a shared history, language and political culture. These are the defining characteristics of territorial political communities and they are all more or less absent at the transnational level. Despite the way globalization binds the fate of communities together, the reality is that 'the only forum within which genuine democracy occurs is within national boundaries'(ibid.). Even within the European Union transnational democracy is little more than an elite phenomenon (ibid.). If there is no effective moral community beyond the state, there is also no *demos*. Advocates of transnational democracy suggest that political communities are being transformed by globalization such that the idea of the *demos* as a fixed, territorially delimited unit is no longer tenable (Linklater 1998). But in problematizing the *demos*, contest the sceptics, the critical question becomes who, or what authority, decides how the *demos* is to be constituted and upon what basis? In addressing this fundamental theoretical issue, suggest the sceptics, the advocates of transnational democracy almost uniformly fail to establish a rigorous or convincing argument (Gorg and Hirsch 1998; Dahl 1999; Kymlicka 1999; Saward 2000).

For realists, sovereignty and anarchy present the most insuperable barriers to the realization of democracy beyond borders. Even though elements of an international society of states exist, in which there is an acceptance of the rule of law and compliance with international norms, order at the global level, suggest realists, remains contingent rather than institutionalized. Conflict and force are ever present and a daily reality in many regions of the world. These are not the conditions in which any substantive democratic experiment is likely to prosper since a properly functioning democracy requires the absence of political violence and the rule of law. In relations between sovereign states, violence is always a frequent possibility and the rule of law an instrument of *realpolitik*. Given the absence of a democratic world empire or some form of world federation of states in which sovereignty is pooled, the conditions for the possibility of transnational democracy appear theoretically and practically unrealizable. For few sovereign democratic states are likely to trade self-governance for a more democratic world order. Furthermore, there is an irresolvable tension at the heart of theories of transnational democracy between national democracy and democracy above the state. The danger is, as communitarians and realists agree, that the latter has enormous potential to override and undermine the former. A case in point is the EU's recent 'democratically mandated' intervention in Austrian politics, following the electoral success of the far right, when it threatened to withhold official recognition of any coalition government in which Mr Haider, the leader of the main far right party, played a role. This despite the democratically expressed preferences of the Austrian electorate. Whatever the ethics of this particular case, the more general point is that transnational democracy has the potential to extinguish effective self-governance at local or national levels (Hutchings 1999: 166). Finally, the failure of theories of transnational democracy to construct a credible account of how the democratic will of the international community can be enforced against the entrenched interests of the Great Powers of the day raises fundamental questions about the limits to democracy at the international level. Without the capacity to enforce the democratic will on strong and weak states alike, transnational democracy becomes meaningless. But paradoxically the existence of such a capability in itself creates the real possibility of the tyranny of global democracy.

Among many radical critics the very idea of transnational democracy is conceived as harbouring a new instrument of Western hegemony. It is, as with the philosophy of 'good governance' promulgated by G7 governments and multilateral agencies, primarily a Western preoccupation and project. There are, in other words, few constituencies for transnational democracy to be found in Africa, Asia and Latin America. For most of humanity it is a distraction from the most pressing global problem, namely how to ensure that global markets and global capital work in the interests of the majority of the world's peoples and without destroying the natural environment. As the United Nations Development Programme puts it, the most pressing issue for humankind is whether globalization can be given a human face (UNDP 1999). In this context, transnational democracy may be an entirely inappropriate and irrelevant response given that the critical problem is a system of global governance which promotes unfettered global capitalism (Cox 1996; Burbach *et al.* 1997).

Democratizing global governance is much more likely to strengthen and legitimize the hegemony of global capital than it is to challenge its grip on the levers of global power (Burbach *et al.* 1997). The historical record of advanced capitalist societies, argue the critics, illustrates how the imperatives of capitalism take precedence over the workings of democracy (Miliband 1973). Therein lies the fate of transnational democracy. Accelerating global inequality and looming environmental catastrophe will not be resolved by a dose of transnational democracy but, on the contrary, only through powerful global bodies which can override the entrenched interests of Western states and global capital by promoting the common welfare; or alternatively by the deconstruction of global governance and the devolution of power to self-governing, sustainable local communities. Since the former would require the acquiescence of the very geo-political and social forces it is designed to tame, it is nothing but utopian. Thus the ethical and political preference of many radical critics is for forms of direct democracy not transnational democracy: true democracy in this view is therefore always local democracy (Morrison 1995).

These constitute powerful arguments for questioning the relevance and desirability of a more democratic global polity. What they share is a sense that transnational democracy is neither necessarily an appropriate response to globalization nor an ethical possibility to be advocated. On the contrary it is fraught with dangers. Not least among these, suggests Dahl (1999), is the danger of popular control in respect of vital matters of economic and military security. Moreover, historically the development of democracy within most states has been a product of force and violence while the history of national democracy illustrates how enormously difficult it is to nurture and sustain such a fragile system of rule even in the context of shared political culture (ibid.). In a world of cultural diversity and growing inequality the possibility of realizing transnational democracy must therefore be judged to be negligible without its imposition, either by a concert of democratic states or a benign democratic hegemon. For the sceptics, self-governance within states, whether democratic or not, is ethically preferable to the likely tyranny of a more democratic global polity.

Can transnational democracy be dismissed?

In response the advocates of transnational democracy accuse the sceptics of a too hasty dismissal of the theoretical, ethical and empirical arguments which inform designs for democracy beyond borders. More specifically, they argue, that by discounting the significant political transformations being brought about by intensifying globalization and regionalization, the sceptics seriously misread the nature of the contemporary historical conjuncture (Elkins 1995; Castells 1998; Linklater 1998; Clark 1999; Held *et al.* 1999a). These transformations irrevocably alter the conditions which made sovereign, territorial, self-governing political communities possible, for in a world of global flows the local and the global, the domestic and the foreign, are largely indistinguishable. To dismiss such developments is to fall prey to a timeless, essentialist conception of modern statehood and political community which disregards their historically and socially constructed nature (Devetak 1995; Linklater 1998).

Modern political communities are historical and social constructions. Their particular form, coinciding with the territorial reach of the 'imagined community' of the nation, is a product of particular conditions and forces. This form defines the metric by which the unit of modern democracy is calibrated. Historically the state has been the primary incubator of modern democratic life. But, as Linklater (1998) observes, political communities have never been static, fixed creations but have always been in the process of construction and reconstruction. As globalization and regionalization have intensified, modern political communities have begun to experience a significant transformation while new forms of political community are emerging (ibid.). According to Held (2000), national political communities co-exist today alongside 'overlapping communities of fate' defined by the spatial reach of transnational networks, systems, allegiances, and problems. These, in Walker's terms (1991), may be 'thin' communities, as opposed to 'thick' communities of the local and nation-state, nevertheless they constitute necessary ethical and political conditions for the cultivation of transnational democracy. In essence, these overlapping communities of fate define the contours of new articulations of the *demos*.

Critics of transnational democracy, as noted, charge that at the core of such prescriptions is an indeterminate conception of the *demos*. This charge, however, overlooks the indeterminate and constructed nature of the modern (national) *demos* itself. For the constitution of the *demos* within the nation-state has always been the object of contestation – witness the struggle for the female vote and current controversies about citizenship – and has evolved as a product of changing social and political conditions. Thus the contingent nature of the *demos* is not a problem which is specific to the idea of democracy beyond borders, as the sceptics suggest, but, on the contrary, is generic to democracy at all levels (Saward 1998). In the context of transnational democracy the *demos* tends to be conceived not so much in universal terms – a singular global *demos* – but rather as a fluid and complex construction: articulated in a multiplicity of settings in relation to the plurality of sites of power and the architecture of global governance. This complexity, as indicated by the experience of the EU and federal polities, is by no means without historical precedent. In this respect the so-called problem of the *demos* is not as intractable as the sceptics suggest.

In his study of globalization Elazar (1998) points to the growing constitutionalization of world order. What he means by this is that the accumulation of multilateral, regional and transnational arrangements (which have evolved in the past fifty years) has created a tacit constitution for the global polity. In seeking to manage and regulate transborder issues, states have sought to codify through treaties and other arrangements their powers and authority. In so doing they have created an elaborate system of rules, rights and responsibilities for the conduct of their joint affairs. This has gone furthest in the EU where effectively a quasi-federal constitution has emerged. But in other contexts, such as the WTO, the authority of national governments is being redefined as the management of trade disputes becomes subject to a rule of law (Shell 1995). Central to this process has been the elaboration and entrenchment of some significant democratic principles within the society of states (Crawford 1994). Thus the principles of self-determination, popular sovereignty, democratic legitimacy, the legal equality of states, have become the orthodoxies of international society. As Mayall (2000) comments, there has been an 'entrenchment not just of democracy itself, but democratic values, as the standard of legitimacy within international society'. This democratization of international society also appears to have accelerated in recent years in response to processes of globalization, the activities of transnational civil society and the socializing dynamic of an expanding community of democratic states. Despite the unevenness and fragility of this democratization, some argue, in contradistinction to the sceptics, that it forges the nascent conditions – the creation of 'zones of peace' and the rule of law – for the cultivation of transnational democracy (Held 1995).

Further evidence of this process of democratization is to be found in the growing political response to economic globalization among governments and transnational movements. This response is manifest in diverse ways but a common theme among progressive forces is a demand for more accountable, responsive and transparent global governance. With the growing perception that power is leaking away from democratic states and electorates to unelected and effectively unaccountable global bodies, such as the WTO, has come increased political pressure on Western governments especially to bring good governance to global governance (Woods 1999a). But a broader global consensus appears to be emerging on the need for such reform, drawing some political support from across the North–South divide and among diverse constituencies of transnational civil society. Of course, democracy involves more than simply transparent and accountable decision-making and it is interesting to note that the debate about reform draws significantly upon several of the discourses – liberal-internationalism, deliberative, radical and cosmopolitan – of transnational democracy discussed above. In the context of the WTO, for instance, the language of stakeholding has been much in evidence, somewhat curiously in US proposals for its reform (Shell 1995; McGrew 1999). But whatever the immediate outcomes of the current reform process, it has lodged the problem of the democratic credentials of international governance firmly on the global agenda. In doing so it has created a global public space for continual political reflection and debate on this key structural issue.

Of course, for sceptics such as Dahl, these developments do not invalidate the normative argument that international institutions cannot be truly democratic (Dahl 1999). Yet, as advocates of transnational democracy point out, there are numerous examples of international or suprastate bodies, from the EU to the ILO, whose institutional designs reflect novel combinations of traditional inter-governmental and democratic principles (Woods 1999a). While the EU represents a remarkable institutionalization of a distinctive form of democracy beyond borders, it is by no means unique. The International Labour Organization, for instance, has institutionalized a restricted form of 'stakeholding' through a tripartite system of representation corresponding to states, business and labour organizations respectively. Beyond this, newer international functional bodies, such as the International Fund for Agricultural Development and the Global Environmental Facility, embody stakeholding principles as a means to ensure representative decision-making (Woods 1999). Furthermore, virtually all major international institutions have opened themselves up to formal or informal participation by the representatives of civil society (Weiss and Gordenker 1996). Even the WTO has created a civil society forum. The sceptical proposition that effective international governance is simply incompatible with democratic practices appears somewhat dogmatic in the light of the historical record of global governance. On the contrary, in certain respects democratic principles are constitutive of the contemporary global polity.

Finally, in questioning the value of democracy, the sceptics raise the serious issue of whether democracy can deliver greater social justice. In this respect, suggest the critics, the historical record suggests a pessimistic conclusion. By contrast, all but the most radical theorists of transnational democracy build upon a different reading of the relationship between capitalism and democracy. This reading accepts the inevitable contradictions between the logic of capitalism and the logic of democracy. But it departs from the fatalism of the radical critique in arguing, on both theoretical and empirical grounds, that democracy can and does promote social justice – witness the significance of social democracy (Held 1995). Building upon this analysis the argument for transnational democracy therefore also becomes an argument for global social justice. The value of transnational democracy, suggest many of its more passionate advocates, lies precisely in its capacity to provide legitimate mechanisms and grounds for the promotion and realization of global social justice (Held 1995). The fact that existing institutions of global governance fail to do so is no surprise since they are the captives of dominant interests. This, they argue, is not a valid ground for abandoning the project of transnational democracy but on the contrary for advocating it more vigorously. But what meaning(s) can be given to the idea of transnational democracy?

Theorizing transnational democracy

A burgeoning and diverse set of literature exists justifying and elaborating the normative principles of global or transnational democracy. Within this literature, four distinctive normative theories can be discerned, namely: liberal-internationalism; radical pluralist democracy; cosmopolitan democracy and deliberative democracy. Of course, this is a simplistic typology that is open to challenge on a number of grounds. Not least is the danger that it may court caricature for it is evident that individual theorists tend to draw upon a range of democratic traditions. Nevertheless, it provides crude mapping of the intellectual field in so far as it identifies a certain clustering of arguments. In effect these four clusters are ideal types: that is general syntheses of normative arguments and analyses which reflect a shared conception of transnational democracy. As such, this typology provides a framework for a systematic analysis of what is at stake in the debate about the democratization of global governance and the global polity.

Common to each of the above accounts is an attempt to give meaning to the idea of transnational democracy and to clarify the normative principles, ethical ideals and institutional conditions which are necessary for its effective realization. Each account is rooted in a moral cosmopolitanism which issues from a premise that individuals and communities are embedded in a universal moral order (Hutchings 1999: 35, 153). There is also a shared presumption that, under conditions of contemporary globalization, transnational or global democracy is a necessary, desirable and politically feasible project; in other words that democracy is to be valued over alternative systems of rule. Leaving this matter to one side for the moment, how do each of these accounts envisage democracy beyond borders?

Liberal-internationalism

In its earliest manifestations liberal-internationalism presented a radical challenge to the prevailing *realpolitik* vision of world order: that is of might as right. From Kant, through Cobden and Bright, to Woodrow Wilson the essence of the liberal-internationalist project was the construction of a world order based on the rule of law and one in which commerce would generate the conditions of an eventual harmony of interests between states and peoples (Carr 1946; Hinsley 1967). As Long (1995) argues, contemporary variants of liberal-internationalism have lost this radical edge and have settled for the reform, rather than transformation, of world order. Although a radicalism of kinds survives in the orthodoxies of neo-liberalism, paradoxically it is deeply antagonistic to notions of global governance and transnational democracy promoting, instead, a world of unfettered global markets.

Given the intellectual dominance (within international relations) of liberal-internationalism – which is concerned primarily with illuminating the rational basis of international cooperation – the problem of trans-national democracy is defined principally in procedural terms of creating more representative, transparent and accountable international institutions (Commission on Global Governance 1995; Falk 1995). Keohane, for instance, understands democracy at the international level as a form of 'voluntary pluralism under conditions of maximum transparency' (Keohane 1998). A more pluralistic world order, in this view, is also a more democratic world order. Underlying this philosophy is an attachment to the principles of classical pluralism: political and civil rights, the politics of interests, the diffusion of power, the limited state and rule by consensus. It requires, in effect, the reconstruction of liberal-pluralist democracy at the supra-state level but without the complications of electoral politics. Instead a vibrant transnational civil society channels its demands to the decision-makers, while in turn also making them accountable for their actions. Accordingly, 'accountability will be enhanced not only by chains of official responsibility but by the requirement of transparency. Official actions, negotiated among state representatives in international organizations, will be subject to scrutiny by transnational networks' (ibid.). International institutions thus become arenas within which the interests of states and the agencies of civil society are articulated. Furthermore, they are the main political structures through which consensus is negotiated and collective decisions legitimated. This reflects a largely procedural view of democracy as a technique for taking and legitimizing public decisions.

Although other significant articulations of the liberal-internationalist position exist, among the most well known being the report of the Commission on Global Governance, they share with the above a common commitment to more representative, transparent and accountable international governance. Liberal-internationalism is a philosophy whose core principles dominate current thinking about the reform of global institutions, from the IMF to the WTO. It reflects the aspirations and values of the Western states and elites which dominate the institutions of global governance. But, as Falk (1995) identifies, it is a philosophy which offers a restricted and somewhat technocratic view of transnational democracy. As with liberal-pluralism more generally, it fails to acknowledge that inequalities of power tend to make democratic systems the captive of powerful vested interests. For, as Pettit argues, a critical weakness of liberal-pluralism is that by making 'naked preference into the motor of social life' it exposes 'all weakly placed individuals to the naked preferences of the stronger' (1997: 205). Moreover, while transparency and accountability are necessary elements of transnational democracy, they are by no means sufficient in themselves to ensure its substantive realization. The notion that the democratic deficit which afflicts global governance can be resolved through institutional reforms alone issues from an underlying assumption that the existing liberal world order simply requires some institutional tinkering to make it more democratic. Despite its acknowledgement of the significance of transnational civil society the liberal-internationalist account remains singularly state-centric in so far as transnational democracy is conceived effectively in terms of enhancing the accountability of international institutions to national governments.

Radical democratic pluralism

In her overview of political cosmopolitanism Hutchings identifies radical democratic pluralism as a project which rejects the reformism of liberal-internationalism in favour of direct forms of democracy and self-governance alongside the creation of alternative structures of governance from the global through local levels (Hutchings 1999: 166ff.). It rejects vigorously the liberal-reformist position since existing structures of global governance are conceived as privileging the interests of a wealthy and powerful cosmocracy while excluding the possibilities of more humane and democratic forms of governance. Advocates of a radical pluralist democracy are therefore concerned with the normative foundations of a 'new politics' which involves the empowerment of individuals and communities in the context of a globalizing world. It represents a substantive view of democracy in so far as its advocates are concerned with the creation of 'good communities' based upon ideas of equality, active citizenship, the promotion of the public good, humane governance and harmony with the natural environment. This is a normative vision which 'represents something of a cocktail of elements of postmodernist, Marxist and civic republican democratic theory' (ibid.: 166–167). It seeks to adapt notions of direct democracy and self-governance to fit with an epoch in which transnational and global power structures regulate the conditions of daily existence of communities and neighbourhoods across the world.

Radical democratic pluralism is essentially a 'bottom-up' theory of the democratization of world order. The new democratic life politics, as opposed to the old politics of emancipation, is articulated primarily through the multiplicity of critical social movements, such as environmental, women and peace movements, which challenge the authority of states and international structures as well as the hegemony of particular (liberal) conceptions of the 'political'. In 'politicizing' existing global institutions and practices, not to mention challenging the conventional boundaries of the political (the foreign/domestic, public/private, society/nature binary divides), critical social movements are conceived as agents of a 'new progressive politics'. Such a politics builds on the experiences of critical social movements which demonstrate that one of the 'great fallacies of political theory is the assumption that a centralized management of power ... is necessary to assure political order' (Burnheim 1986). Accordingly, democracy and democratic legitimacy do not have to be grounded in territorially delimited units such as nation-states but rather are to be located in a multiplicity of self-governing and self-organizing collectivities constituted on diverse spatial scales – from the local to the global (Connolly 1991). Although the spatial reach of these collectivities is to be defined by the geographical scope of the collective problems or activities they seek to manage, there is a strong presumption in favour of the subsidiarity principle. This is a vision of direct democracy which considers substantive transnational democracy issues from the existence of a plurality of diverse, overlapping and spatially differentiated self-governing 'communities of fate' and multiple sites of power without the need for 'sovereign' or centralized structures of authority of any kind. It identifies, in the political practices of critical social movements, immanent tendencies towards the transcendence of the sovereign territorial state as the fundamental unit of democracy.

Radical democratic pluralism reflects a strong attachment to theories of direct democracy and participatory democracy (Held 1996). It also draws upon neo-Marxist critiques of liberal democracy. For democracy is conceived as inseparable from creating the conditions for effective participation and self-governance including, among other things, the achievement of social and economic equality. Furthermore, it connects to the civic republican tradition in so far as it considers that the realization of individual freedom has to be 'embedded within and sustained by a [strong] sense of political community and of the common good' (Barns 1995).

To the extent that advocates of radical pluralist democracy argue that the effective conditions for the realization of global or transnational democracy require the construction of alternative forms of global governance, it is subversive of the existing world. For its critics it is precisely this rejection of the existing constitution of world order that is problematic

(Held 1995; Hutchings 1999: 178). In resisting the rule of law in global politics and rejecting the idea of sovereignty, the very principles of democracy, argue the critics, are decidedly compromised. Without some notion of popular sovereignty it is difficult to envisage what democracy might mean. While in the absence of the present rather imperfect liberal constitution for world order – embodying (to varying degrees) the principles of the rule of law and constraints on the exercise of force – there would seem to be no institutional foundation for constructing transnational democracy. The theoretical limitations of the radical pluralist argument are therefore to be found in its ambivalence towards the conditions – the rule of law and sovereignty – which make democracy (at whatever level) possible.

Cosmopolitan democracy

By comparison with the radical pluralist account, cosmopolitan democracy pays particular attention to the institutional and political conditions which are necessary to the conduct of effective democratic governance within, between and across states. In its most sophisticated formulation Held (1995) develops an account of cosmopolitan democracy which, building upon the existing principles of the liberal international order, involves the construction of a new global constitutional settlement in which democratic principles are firmly entrenched. Advocating a 'double democratization' of political life, the advocates of cosmopolitan democracy seek to reinvigorate democracy within states by extending democracy to the public realm between and across states. In this respect transnational democracy and territorial democracy are conceived as mutually reinforcing rather than conflicting principles of political rule. Cosmopolitan democracy in effect seeks 'a political order of democratic associations, cities and nations as well as of regions and global networks' (ibid.: 234).

Central to this model is the principle of democratic autonomy, namely the 'entitlement to autonomy within the constraints of community' (ibid.: 156). This is to be assured through the requirements of a cosmopolitan democratic law, that is, law which 'allows international society, including individuals, to interfere in the internal affairs of each state in order to protect certain [democratic] rights' (Archibugi 1995). Accordingly, the principle of democratic autonomy depends upon 'the establishment of an international community of democratic states and societies committed to upholding a democratic public law both within and across their own boundaries: a cosmopolitan democratic community' (Held 1995: 229). This does not presume a requirement for a world government, nor a federal super-state, but rather the establishment of a 'a global and divided authority system – a system of diverse and overlapping power centres shaped and delimited by democratic law' (ibid.: 234). Rather than a hierarchy of political authority, from the local to the global, cosmopolitan democracy involves a heterarchical arrangement. Conceptually this lies between federalism and, the much looser arrangements implied by the notion of, confederalism – what some have referred to as the Philadelphian system (Deudney 1996). For it requires 'the subordination of regional, national and local "sovereignties" to an overarching legal framework, but within this framework associations may be self-governing at diverse levels' (Held 1995: 234). The entrenchment of cosmopolitan democracy therefore involves a process of *reconstructing* the existing framework of global governance.

Essential to the realization of this democratic reconstruction, it is argued, is the requirement that democratic practices be embedded more comprehensively 'within communities and civil associations by elaborating and reinforcing democracy from "outside" through a network of regional and international agencies and assemblies that cut across spatially delimited locales' (ibid.: 237). Only through such mechanisms will those global sites and transnational networks of power which presently escape effective national democratic control be brought to account, thus establishing the political conditions befitting the realization of democratic autonomy.

Cosmopolitan democracy represents an enormously ambitious agenda for reconfiguring the constitution of global governance and world order. Its genealogy is eclectic in so far as it claims significant continuities with a variety of traditions of democratic thought. While it draws considerable inspiration from modern theories of liberal democracy, it is also influenced by critical theory, theories of participatory democracy and civic republicanism. It is distinguished from liberal-internationalism by its radical agenda and scepticism towards state-centric and procedural notions of democracy. While accepting the important role of progressive transnational social forces, it nevertheless differentiates itself from radical pluralist democracy through its attachment to the centrality of the rule of law and constitutionalism as necessary conditions for the establishment of a more democratic world order. But the idea of cosmopolitan democracy is not without its critics.

Sandel argues that 'Despite its merits ... the cosmopolitan ideal is flawed, both as a moral ideal and as a public philosophy for self-government in our time' (1996: 342). This, he argues, is because at the core of cosmopolitanism is a liberal conception of the individual which neglects the ways in which individuals, their interests and values, are 'constructed' by the communities of which they are members. Accordingly, democracy can only thrive by first creating a democratic community with a common civic identity. While globalization does create a sense of universal connectedness, it does not, in Brown's (1995) view, generate an equivalent sense of community based upon shared values and beliefs. Thus cosmopolitan democracy, as transnational democracy, lacks a convincing account of how the ethical resources necessary for its effective realization are to be generated. It is also criticized for its top-down constitutionalism which fails to recognize the inherent tension between the principles of democracy and the logic of constitutional constraints upon what the *demos* may do (Saward 1998). Nor is it clear within an heterarchical system of governance how jurisdictional conflicts between different layers of demo-cratic authority are to be reconciled or adjudicated by democratic means, let alone how accountability in such a system can be made effective. This raises important issues of consent and legitimacy. As Thompson (1999) argues, the problem is one of 'many majorities' such that 'no majority has an exclusive and overarching claim to democratic legitimacy'. Further-more, cosmopolitan democracy will only serve to intensify the enduring tensions between democracy and the protection of individual rights since rights claims may be pursued outside those 'local' or immediate jurisdic-tions whose policies or decisions have been sanctioned by a formal demo-cratic process (ibid.). Finally, some radical critiques reject cosmopolitan democracy since they consider it represents a new mode of imperialism in so far as it presumes the universal validity of Western liberal democracy, thus discounting the legitimacy of alternative or non-Western democratic cultures.

Deliberative democracy

A significant attempt to address some of the problems inherent in the cosmopolitan model of democracy is to be found in the work on delibera-tive democracy and associated varieties of republican or stakeholder democracy (Dryzek 1990a; Deudney 1996; Thompson 1999). Rather than a new constitutional settlement for the global polity, advocates of delibera-tive democracy emphasize its reconstruction to reflect the principles of: non-domination, participation, public deliberation, responsive gover-nance and the right of all affected to contest the decisions or actions of public authorities at all levels of governance (Dryzek 1990b; Pettit 1997; Saward 1998: 64–65). As Dryzek (1999) argues, the realization of trans-national democracy depends upon the recognition that 'the essence of democratic legitimacy is to be found not in voting or representation . . . but rather in deliberation'.

While advocates of deliberative democracy do not discount the value of a liberal attachment to institutional reform of global governance, nor the cosmopolitan requirement for a democratic constitution for world order, these visions are regarded as insufficient in themselves for the grounding of transnational democracy. What is required is the cultivation of trans-national public spheres in which there can be genuine deliberation and dialogue between the agencies of public power and those affected by their decisions and actions. The deliberative ideal looks to the creation of 'an association whose affairs are governed by the public deliberation of its members' (Cohen quoted in Saward 1998: 64). It seeks rational and informed deliberation among all those affected with the object of realizing the common good. This is entirely at odds with a liberal-pluralist conception of democracy in which the expressed interests and preferences of citizens or organized interests predominate (Dryzek 1990a; Pettit 1997; Saward 1998: 64). It requires public authorities to justify their actions and provides for those affected to contest such actions since governance is regarded as democratic 'to the extent that the people individually and collectively enjoy a permanent possibility of contesting what government decides' (Pettit 1997: 185). Accordingly, it requires informed citizens and the promotion of those rights and conditions necessary to empower citizens (ibid.). But in the context of transnational democracy if interests alone are to be paramount, who decides which voices are to be heard?

Crucial to this position is the principle of stakeholding: that all those affected by, or with a stake in, the decisions of public authorities in any domain have the right to a voice in the governance of those matters (Burnheim 1986; Deudney 1998; Eckersley 2000; Saward 2000). Stakeholding, as a principle of transnational democracy, seeks to permit and encourage 'the active participation of people in decision making, sometimes as representatives of specific interests they themselves have, but often too as the trustees of interests that cannot speak for themselves' (Burnheim 1995). Moreover, since the all-affected principle is not defined in territorial terms, the spatial configuration of the relevant deliberative community is entirely contingent on the particular geography of stakeholding on any specific issue or in any domain. In effect, the process of deliberation is itself constitutive of the relevant deliberative community (Thompson 1999). This flexibility makes deliberative democracy admirably suited to a world in which there are overlapping communities of fate and in which the organization and exercise of power no longer coincide with the bounded territorial political community (Dryzek 1999; Eckersley 2000).

Advocates of deliberative democracy argue that it offers a set of principles upon which inclusive, responsive and responsible transnational or global democracy can be constructed. Its more orthodox variants tend to emphasize its reformist ambitions in so far as deliberation is conceived as a mechanism for enhancing the democratic legitimacy of public decision-making at whatever level, from the local to the global (Saward 1998). By contrast, in its more radical manifestation, its transformative potential is highlighted to the extent that it empowers citizens and delivers the possibility of openly contesting global institutional agendas and challenging unaccountable sites of transnational power (Dryzek 1999; Eckersley 2000). This tension within the rather procedural, as opposed to substantive, interpretation of deliberative democracy is primarily a product of its rather eclectic origins. For it draws upon diverse theoretical traditions, including critical theory, discourse analysis, republicanism, participatory and direct democracy.

Critics of deliberative democracy argue that it is not a distinctive model of democracy so much as a mechanism for making and legitimizing public authority. In this respect it only has value in the context of an established system of democracy (Saward 1998). This criticism is valid whether the focus is transnational, local or national democracy. Furthermore, despite its emphasis upon discourse, paradoxically it tends to overlook the problems which language and cultural diversity present to the construction of a genuine transnational deliberative public sphere. This cannot simply be resolved as a technical matter of translation but raises much deeper issues about the role of language and culture in defining the conditions of the possibility of genuine political deliberation (Kymlicka 1999). In arguing too that the deliberative communities are essentially constituted through the all-affected principle, the basis upon which stakeholders are to be incorporated – whether as direct participants or through their representatives – remains largely unspecified. Indeed the emphasis upon self-organization tends to ensure that the procedural requirements and institutional conditions of effective deliberation remain unstipulated. Finally, it remains unclear, in the absence of a general commitment to consensus decision-making, how intractable conflicts of interests or values can be resolved deliberatively without recourse to some authoritatively imposed solution. In this respect deliberative democracy may be of marginal value in dealing with the many global distributional or controversial issues – from debt relief to human rights respectively – which figure on the world political agenda.

Towards a democratic global polity?

For the advocates of transnational democracy there are some grounds for cautious optimism. Globalization and regionalization are stimulating powerful political reactions which in their more progressive manifestations have engendered a serious debate about the democratic credentials of global governance. Furthermore, there is evidence of an emerging global consensus, in the wake of the East Asian crisis and the Battle of Seattle, upon the need for more effective regulation of global financial markets and global capital (UNCTAD 1998; UNDP 1999; Jones 2000). The Washington consensus, championing unfettered global capitalism, no longer appears so secure or hegemonic (McGrew 2000). Regulating globalization is now a paramount political issue and this in turn has provoked much discussion about the precise form which such regulation should take as well as the political values which might inform it. Reform of the major agencies of global economic governance and the UN is now firmly on the global political agenda (Woods 1999b; United Nations 2000). Transparency, accountability, participation and legitimacy are rapidly becoming the values associated with the reform agenda. Progressive elements of transnational civil society too are organizing and mobilizing to maintain the political pressure on governments and institutions to follow through on the reform process. But it is in the historical context of the democratization of the global polity discussed above (and not to be repeated here) that these contingent developments acquire greater political significance. Interpreted in this context, despite the potential for ultimate failure or cosmetic democratic reform, these contemporary developments may yet come to represent the beginnings of a further important political shift towards a more accountable and democratic form of global governance. But in what sense democratic?

Whether any of the above accounts of transnational democracy can be regarded as persuasive or plausible depends upon establishing some criteria of judgement. Plausibility can be understood in terms of political feasibility or alternatively may be defined in terms of an ethical preference. Liberal-internationalism may appear to offer the most convincing account of the trajectory of democratization within the global polity since it is largely compatible with the existing liberal world order and the values of dominant states and elites. But whether its elevation of interest group politics to a principle of global governance can deliver a more substantively democratic global polity is open to question. By comparison radical democratic pluralism has a strong substantive conception of democracy – that is the creation of self-governing communities of active citizens dedicated to the realization of the public good – involving the deconstruction of sovereignty and the construction of an alternative form of world order. But its strong ethical appeal is tarnished by a failure to specify theoretically how, in the absence of any sovereign authority, transnational democracy can be realized or secured.

In considering cosmopolitan and deliberative democracy it is important to recognize that these are not conceived here as mutually exclusive or alternative forms of transnational democracy. Indeed, there are good theoretical and pragmatic reasons for presuming that they can be conceived as complementary. This is particularly so if deliberative democracy is understood in its procedural sense. Both, of course, as the analysis above indicates, can be criticized for idealism and lack of specificity. Nevertheless they offer a credible analysis of the conditions of their own possibility while also being ethically ambitious. Yet this ambition is tempered with an appreciation of the powerful structural and social forces which impede the political prospects for transnational democracy. Finally, by comparison with alternative accounts, cosmopolitan democracy and deliberative democracy explicitly advocate transnational democracy 'not as an alternative to national democracy but in part as its salvation as well' (Clark 1999: 155).

Conclusion

Globalization is generating a political debate about the necessity, desirability and possibility of democratizing the global polity and global governance – i.e. transnational democracy. According to the UNDP, today's political challenge is to 'build a more coherent and more democratic architecture for global governance in the twenty-first century' (UNDP 1999). To meet this challenge requires re-imagining democracy. This chapter has elaborated quite different normative re-imaginings of democracy – liberal-internationalism, radical democratic pluralism, cosmopolitan and deliberative democracy – which in varying degrees find expression in current deliberations concerning the reform of global and regional governance – from the EU to the IMF. These re-imaginings warrant sceptical treatment. But idealistic or utopian as they presently may appear, such scepticism needs to be tempered with E.H. Carr's caution that 'Sound political thought and sound political life will be found only where [utopia and reality] have their place' (Carr 1981: 10).

Bibliography

Abbott, F. (2000) 'NAFTA and the Legalization of World Politics: A Case Study', *International Organization*, 54: 519–548.

Abbott, K., Keohane, R.O., Moravcsik, A., Slaughter, A.M. and Snidal, D. (2000) 'The Concept of Legalization', *International Organization*, 54: 401–420.

Abbott, K. and Snidal, D. (2000) 'Hard and Soft Law in International Governance', *International Organization*, 54: 421–456.

Aggarwal, V.K. (1998) 'Reconciling Multiple Institutions: Bargaining, Linkages, and Nesting', in V.K. Aggarwal (ed.) *Institutional Designs for a Complex World*, Ithaca and London: Cornell University Press.

Agnew, J. and Corbridge, S. (1995) *Mastering Space: Hegemony, Territory and International Political Economy*, London: Routledge.

Akami, T. (1998) 'Post-League Wilsonian Internationalism and the Institute of Pacific Relations, 1925–45', *The Journal of Shibusawa Studies*, 11(October): 3–35.

Albrow, M. (1996) *The Global Age: State and Society Beyond Modernity*, Cambridge: Polity Press.

Allen, D. and Smith, M. (1990) 'Western Europe's Presence in the International Arena', *Review of International Studies*, 16(1): 9–38.

Almond, G.A. and Powell, G.B. (1966) *Comparative Politics: A Developmental Approach*, Boston: Little, Brown.

Alter, K. and Meunier-Aitsahalia, S. (1994) 'Judicial Politics in the European Community: European Integration and the Path Breaking Cassis de Dijon Decision', *Comparative Political Studies*, 24(4): 535–561.

Alter, K.J. (1996) 'The European Court's Political Power', *West European Politics*, 19: 458–487.

—— (1998) 'Who are the "Masters of the Treaty"?: European Governments and the European Court of Justice', *International Organization*, 52: 121–147.

—— (2000) 'The European Union's Legal System and Domestic Policy: Spillover or Backlash', *International Organization*, 54: 489–518.

Amin, S. (1978) *Imperialism and Unequal Development*, Brighton: Harvester Press.

Anderson, B. (1991) *Imagined Communities: Reflections on the Origin and Spread of Nationalism*, London: Verso.

Anderson, J.J. (1995) 'Structural Funds and the Social Dimension of EU Policy: Springboard or Stumbling Bloc', in S. Leibfried and P. Pierson (eds) *European Social Policy: Between Fragmentation and Integration*, Washington, DC: Brookings Institution.

Anheier, H.K. (2001) 'Measuring Global Civil Society', in H.H. Anheier, M. Glasius and M. Kaldor (eds) *Global Civil Society Yearbook 2001*, Oxford: Oxford University Press.

Ansprenger, F. (1989) *The Dissolution of Colonial Empires*, London: Routledge.

Appelbaum, R., Felstiner, W. and Gessner, V. (eds) (2001) *The Legal Culture of Global Business Transactions*, Oxford: Hart Publishing.

Archer, C. (1992) *International Organizations*, 2nd edition, London: Routledge.

Archibugi, D. (1995) 'Immanuel Kant, Cosmopolitan Law and Peace', *European Journal of International Relations*, 1(4): 429–456.

Armstrong, K.A. and Bulmer, S. (1998) *The Governance of the Single European Market*, Manchester: Manchester University Press.

Arthurs, H. (2001) 'The Role of Global Law Firms in Constructing or Obstructing a Transnational Regime of Labour Law', in R. Applebaum, W. Felstiner and V. Gessner (eds) *The Legal Culture of Global Business Transactions*, Oxford: Hart Publishing.

Arzt, D.E. and Lukashuk, I.I. (1998) 'Participants in International Legal Relations', in C. Ku and P.F. Diehl (eds) *International Law: Classic and Contemporary Readings*, Boulder, CO: Westview Press.

Augelli, E. and Murphy, C.N. (1988) *America's Quest for Supremacy and the Third World: A Gramscian Analysis*, London: Pinter Publishers.

—— (1993) 'International Institutions, Decolonization, and Development', *International Political Science Review*, 14: 71–86.

—— (1995) 'La nuova teoria della pace delle Nazioni unite', in G.G. Migone and O. Re (eds) *A cinquant'anni dalla nascita delle Nazioni unite*, a special issue of *Europa/Europe* 4: 97–121.

Austin, J. ([1832] [1863] 1954) *The Principles of Jurisprudence Determined, and the Uses of the Study of Jurisprudence*, London: Weidenfeld and Nicolson.

Bairoch, P. (1993) 'Was There a Large Income Differential Before Modern Development?', in *Economic and World History: Myths and Paradoxes*, Chicago: University of Chicago Press.

Bakvis, H. (1997) 'Advising the Executive: Think Tanks, Consultants, Political Staff and Kitchen Cabinets', in P. Weller, H. Bakvis and R.A.W. Rhodes (eds) *The Hollow Crown: Countervailing Trends in Core Executives*, London: Macmillan.

Balanyá, B., Doherty, A., Hoedean, O., Ma'anit, A. and Wesselius, E. (2000) *Europe Inc.: Regional and Global Restructuring and the Rise of Corporate Power*, London: Pluto Press.

Balbus, I. (1977) 'Commodity Form and Legal Form: An Essay on the Relative Autonomy of the Law', *Law and Society* 11: 571–588.

Barns, I. (1995) 'Environment, Democracy and Community', *Environment and Politics* 4(4): 101–133.

Barry, D. and Keith, R.C. (eds) (1999) *Regionalism, Multilateralism, and the Politics of Global Trade*, Vancouver: UBC Press.

Beck, R., Arend, A. and Vander Lugt, R. (eds) (1996) *International Rules: Approaches from International Law and International Relations*, New York: Oxford University Press.

Beck, U. (1992) *Risk Society: Towards a New Modernity*, London: Sage.

Beck, U., Giddens, A. and Lash, S. (1994) *Reflexive Modernization: Politics, Tradition and Aesthetics in the Modern Social Order*, Cambridge: Polity Press.

Beisheim, M., Dreher, S., Walter, G., Zangl, B. and Zürn, M. (1999) *Im Zeitalter der*

Globalisierung? Thesen und Daten zur gesellschaftlichen und politischen Denational-isierung, Baden-Baden: Nomos.

Berman, H. (1983) *Law and Revolution: The Formation of the Western Legal Tradition*, Cambridge, MA: Harvard University Press.

Bislev, S. (1999) 'New Public Management and Municipal Organization: Danish and German Employment Programmes Employment Policies', in M. Dent, M. O'Neill and C. Bagley (eds) *Professions, New Public Management and the European Welfare State*, Stoke-on-Trent: Staffordshire University Press.

Bislev, S., Hansen, H.K and Salskov-Iversen, D. (2000) 'Transnational Discourse Communities – Globalizing Public Management', paper for 41st Annual Convention, International Studies Association presented at Los Angeles, 14–18 March.

Boli, J., Loya, T.A. and Loftin, T. (1999) 'National Participation in World-Polity Organization', in J. Boli and G.M. Thomas (eds) *Constructing World Culture: International Non-Governmental Organizations since 1875*, Stanford, CA: Stanford University Press.

Boli, J. and Thomas, G.M. (eds) (1999) *Constructing World Culture: International Non-Governmental Organizations since 1875*, Stanford: Stanford University Press.

Börzel, T. (1998) 'Organizing Babylon: On the Different Conceptions of Policy Networks', *Public Administration*, 76: 253–273.

Braithwaite, J. and Drahos, P. (2000) *Global Business Regulation*, Cambridge: Cambridge University Press.

Breckenridge, R.E. (1997) 'Reassessing Regimes: The International Regime Aspects of the European Union', *Journal of Common Market Studies*, 35(2): 173–187.

Breslin, S. and Higgott, R. (2000) 'Studying Regions: Learning from the Old, Constructing the New', *New Political Economy*, 5: 333–352.

Bretherton, C. and Vogler, J. (1999) *The European Union as a Global Actor*, London: Routledge.

Brock, L. and Albert, M. (1995) *Debordering the World of States: New Spaces in International Relations*, Working Paper 2, Frankfurt: World Society Research Group.

Brown, C. (1995) 'International Political Theory and the Idea of World Community', in K. Booth and S. Smith (eds) *International Relations Theory Today*, Cambridge: Polity Press.

Brown, L.D. *et al.* (2001) 'Civil Society Legitimacy: A Discussion Guide', in L.D. Brown (ed.) *Practice-Research Engagement and Civil Society in a Globalizing World*, Cambridge, MA: Hauser Center for Nonprofit Organizations, Harvard University.

Brown, S. (1992) *International Relations in a Changing Global System: Toward a Theory of the World Polity* (2nd edition 1996), Boulder, CO: Westview Press.

Brownlie, I. (1990) *Principles of Public International Law*, 4th edn, Oxford: Clarendon Press.

Bull, H. (1977) *The Anarchical Society: A Study of Order in World Politics*, London: Macmillan.

—— (1984) 'Introduction', in Hedley Bull (ed.) *Intervention in World Politics*, Oxford: Clarendon, pp. 1–7.

Burbach, R., Nunez, O. and Kagarlitsky, B. (eds) (1997) *Globalization and its Discontents*, London: Pluto.

Burnheim, J. (1986) 'Democracy, National-States, and the World System', in D. Held and C. Pollitt (eds) *New Forms of Democracy*, London: Sage.

Burnheim, J. (1995) 'Power-trading and the Environment', *Environmental Politics*, 4(4): 49–65.

Busch, H. (1995) *Grenzenlose Polizei? Neue Grenzen und polizeiliche Zusammenarbeit in Europa*, Münster: Westfälisches Dampfboot.

Buzan, B. (1991) *People, States and Fear. 2nd edn. An Agenda for International Security Studies in the Post-Cold War Era*, Hertfordshire: Harvester Wheatsheaf.

—— (1993) 'From International System to International Society: Structural Realism and Regime Theory Meet the English School', *International Organization*, 47(3): 327–352.

Byrne, A. (1991) 'Women, Feminism and International Human Rights Law, C Methodological Myopia, Fundamental Flaws or Meaningful Marginalisation? Some Current Issues', *Australian Yearbook of International Law*, 12: 205–241.

Caldeira, G.A., Gibson, J.L. and Klein, D.E. (1995) 'The Visibility of the Court of Justice in the European Union', paper for the 1995 APSA Meeting, Chicago.

Camilleri, J.A. and Falk, J. (1992) *The End of Sovereignty*, Aldershot: Edward Elgar.

Campbell, T. (1997) *Innovations and Risk Taking*, World Bank Discussion Paper, No. 357, Washington, DC: The World Bank.

Caporaso, J. (1997) 'Across the Great Divide: Integrating Comparative and International Politics', *International Studies Quarterly*, 41: 563–591.

Carl Bertelsmann Prize (1993) *Democracy and Efficiency in Local Government*, vol. 1 *Documentation of the International Research*, Gütersloh: Bertelsmann Foundation Publishers.

Carr, E.H. (1946 [1981]) *The Twenty Years Crisis: 1919–1939*, 2nd edn, London: Macmillan.

Carty, A. (1991) 'Critical International Law: Recent Trends in the Theory of International Law', *European Journal of International Law*, 2: 66–96.

Castells, M. (1998) *End of the Millennium*, Oxford: Blackwell.

Cerny, P.G. (1995) 'Globalization and the Changing Logic of Collective Action', *International Organization*, 49: 595–625.

Charlesworth, H., Chinkin, C. and Wright, S. (1991) 'Feminist Approaches to International Law', *American Journal of International Law*, 85: 613–645.

Charnovitz, S. (1997) 'Two Centuries of Participation: NGOs and International Governance', *Michigan Journal of International Law*, 18(2): whole issue.

Chayes, A. and Chayes, A. (1995) *The New Sovereignty: Compliance with International Regulatory Agreements*, Cambridge, MA: Harvard University Press.

Chen, M.A. (1995) 'Engendering World Conferences: The International Women's Movement and the United Nations', *Third World Quarterly*, 16: 477–494.

Chibber, A. (1997) 'The State in a Changing World', www.worldbank.org/fandd/english/0997/articles/010997.htm

Chilton, P. (1995) 'Mechanics of Change: Social Movements, Transnational Coalitions, and the Transformation Processes in Eastern Europe', in T. Risse-Kappen (ed.) *Bringing Transnational Relations Back In*, Cambridge: Cambridge University Press.

Chouliaraki, L. and Fairclough, N. (1999) *Discourse in Late Modernity*, Edinburgh: Edinburgh University Press.

Christiansen, T. (1997) 'Reconstructing European Space: from Territorial Politics to Multilevel Governance', in K.E. Jørgensen (ed.) *Reflective Approaches to European Governance*, Basingstoke: Macmillan.

Christiansen, T. and Jørgensen K.E. (1995) 'Towards the "Third Category" of Space: Conceptualizing the Nature of Borders in Western Europe', paper for ECPR meeting, Paris.

Chryssochoou, D. (1994) 'Democracy and Symbiosis in the European Union: Towards a Confederal Consociation', *West European Politics*, 17(4): 1–15.

Citizens Strengthening Global Civil Society (1994), Washington, DC: CIVICUS.

Clapham, C. (1999) 'Sovereignty and the Third World', *Political Studies*, 47: 522–538.

Clark, I. (1999) *Globalization and International Relations Theory*, Oxford: Oxford University Press.

Clark, J. (2002) 'The World Bank and Civil Society: An Evolving Experience', in J.A. Scholte with A. Schnabel (eds) *Civil Society and Global Finance*, London: Routledge.

Clarke, A.M., Friedman, E. and Hochstetler, K. (1998) 'The Sovereign Limits of Global Civil Society: A Comparison of NGO Participation in UN Conferences on the Environment, Human Rights, and Women', *World Politics*, 51: 1–35.

Clegg, S. (1998) 'Foucault, Power and Organizations', in A. McKinlay and K. Starkey (eds) *Foucault: Management and Organization Theory*, London: Sage Publications.

Cohen, J.L. and Arato A. (1992) *Civil Society and Political Theory*, Cambridge, MA: MIT Press.

Cohen, R. and Rai, S.M. (eds) (2000) *Global Social Movements*, London: Athlone Press.

Coleman, W. and Underhill, G.R.D. (1998) *Regionalism and Global Economic Integration: Europe, Asia and the Americas*, London: Routledge.

Commission on Global Governance (1995) *Our Global Neighbourhood*, Oxford: Oxford University Press.

Conca, K., Alberty, M. and Dabelko, G.D. (eds) (1995) *Green Planet Blues: Environmental Politics from Stockholm to Rio*, Boulder, CO: Westview Press.

Connolly, W.E. (1991) 'Democracy and Territoriality', *Millennium*, 20: 463–484.

Corbey, D. (1995) 'Dialectical Functionalism: Stagnation as a Booster of European Integration', *International Organization*, 49: 253–284.

Cox, R.W. (1979) 'Ideologies and the New International Economic Order: Reflections on Some Recent Literature', *International Organisation*, 32: 257–302.

—— (1981) 'Social Forces, States, and World Orders: Beyond International Relations Theory', reproduced in R.W. Cox with T.J. Sinclair (1996) *Approaches to World Order*, Cambridge: Cambridge University Press.

—— (1987) *Production, Power, and World Order: Social Forces in the Making of History*, New York: Columbia University Press.

—— (1992) 'The United Nations, Globalization, and Democracy. The John W. Holmes Memorial Lecture', Providence, RI: The Academic Council on the United Nations System.

—— (1996) 'Globalization, Multilateralism and Democracy', in R. Cox with T. Sinclair *Approaches to World Order*, Cambridge: Cambridge University Press.

Cram, L., Dinan, D. and Nugent, N. (1999) 'The Evolving European Union', in L. Cram, D. Dinan, and N. Nugent (eds) *Developments in the European Union*, Basingstoke: Macmillan.

Crawford, J. (1994) *Democracy in International Law*, Cambridge: Cambridge University Press.

Cutler, A.C. (1991) 'The Grotian Tradition in International Relations', *Review of International Studies* 17: 41–65.

—— (1995) 'Global Capitalism and Liberal Myths: Dispute Settlement in Private International Trade Relations', *Millennium: Journal of International Studies*, 24: 377–397.

—— (1997) 'Artifice, Ideology and Paradox: The Public/Private Distinction in International Law', *Review of International Political Economy*, 4: 261–285.

—— (1999a) 'Locating Authority in the Global Political Economy', *International Studies Quarterly*, 43: 59–81.

—— (1999b) 'Private Authority in International Trade Relations: The Case of Maritime Transport', in A.C. Cutler, V. Haufler and T. Porter (eds) *Private Authority and International Affairs*, New York: State University of New York Press.

—— (1999c) 'Public Meets Private: The International Unification and Harmonization of Private International Trade Law', *Global Society*, 13: 25–48.

—— (2000) 'Globalization, Law, and Transnational Corporations: The Deepening of Market Discipline', in T. Cohn, S. McBride and D. Wiseman (eds) *Power in the Global Era*, London: Macmillan.

—— (2001a) 'Critical Reflections on Westphalian Assumptions of International Law and Organization: A Crisis of Legitimacy', *Review of International Studies*, 27(2): 133–150.

—— (2001b) 'Global Governance and the Modern *Lex Mercatoria*', in T. Sjolander and J.F. Thibault (eds) *On Global Governance*, Ottawa: University of Ottawa Press.

—— (2001c) 'Globalization, the Rule of Law, and the Modern Law Merchant: Medieval or Late Capitalist Associations?' *An International Journal of Critical and Democratic Theory*, 8(4): 480–502.

—— (2002a) 'Historical Materialism, Globalization, and Law: Competing Conceptions of Property', in M. Rupert and H. Smith (eds) *The Point is to Change the World: Socialism through Globalization?*, London: Routledge.

—— (2002b) 'Critical Historical Materialism and International Law: Imagining International Law as Praxis', in S. Hobden and J.M. Hobson (eds) *Historical Sociology of International Relations*, Cambridge: Cambridge University Press.

Cutler, A.C., Haufler, V. and Porter T. (1999) 'Private Authority and International Affairs', in A.C. Cutler, V. Haufler and T. Porter (eds) *Private Authority and International Affairs*, Albany, NY: State University of New York Press.

Dahl, R.A. (1999) 'Can International Organizations Be Democratic?', in I. Shapiro and C. Hacker-Cordon (eds) *Democracy's Edges*, Cambridge: Cambridge University Press.

David, R. (1972) 'The Legal Systems of the World, Their Comparison and Unification', in *International Encyclopedia of Comparative Law*, vol. 11, Chapter 5, The Hague: Mohr, Tubingen: Martinus Nijhoff.

Deacon, B. (1999) 'Towards a Socially Responsible Globalization: International Actors and Discourses', GASPP Occasional Papers, September.

Deacon, B. with Hulse, M. and Stubbs, P. (1997) *Global Social Policy: International Organizations and the Future of Welfare*, London: Sage Publications.

Deetz, S. (1998) 'Discursive Formations, Strategized Subordination and Self-surveillance', in A. McKinlay and K. Starkey (eds) *Foucault: Management and Organization Theory*, London: Sage Publications.

Deibert, R.J. (2000) 'International Plug 'n Play? Citizen Activism, the Internet, and Global Public Policy', *International Studies Perspectives*, 1: 255–272.

den Boer, M. and Wallace, W. (2000) 'Justice and Home Affairs: Integration through Incrementalism?', in H. Wallace and W. Wallace (eds) *Policy-Making in the European Union*, 4th edn, Oxford: Oxford University Press.

Deudney, D. (1996) 'Binding Sovereigns: Authorities, Structures, and Geo-politics in Philadelphian Systems', in T.J. Biersteker and C. Weber (eds) *State Sovereignty as Social Construct*, Cambridge: Cambridge University Press.

—— (1998) 'Global Village Sovereignty', in K.T. Litfin (ed.) *The Greening of Sovereignty*, Boston: MIT Press.

Deutsch, K.W. (1969) *Nationalism and its Alternatives*, New York: Knopf.

Devetak, R. (1995) 'Incomplete States: Theories and Practices of Statecraft', in J. MacMillian and A. Linklater (eds) *Boundaries in Question*, London: Pinter.

Devetak, R. and Higgott, R.A. (1999) 'Justice Unbound? Globalisation, States and the Transformation of the Social Bond', *International Affairs*, 75(3): 483–498.

Dezalay, Y. and Garth, B. (1996) *Dealing in Virtue: International Commercial Arbitration and the Construction of a Transnational Legal Order*, Chicago: University of Chicago Press.

Dieter, H. (2000) *Monetary Regionalism: Regional Integration without Financial Crises?* Warwick Centre for the Study of Globalisation and Regionalisation Working Paper 52/00, University of Warwick.

Dolowitz, D.P. and Marsh, D. (2000) 'Learning from Abroad: The Role of Policy Transfer in Contemporary Policy-Making', *Governance*, 13(1): 5–24.

Drake, W. and Nicolaidis, K. (1992) 'Ideas, Interest and Institutionalization: "Trade in Services" and the Uruguay Round', *International Organization*, 46: 37–100.

Dryzek, J.S. (1990a) 'Transnational Democracy', *The Journal of Political Philosophy*, 7: 30–51.

—— (1990b) *Discursive Democracy*, Cambridge: Cambridge University Press.

—— (1999) 'Transnational Democracy', *The Journal of Political Philosophy*, 7(1): 30–51.

Dyson, K. (1994) *Elusive Union: The Process of Economic and Monetary Union in Europe*, London: Longman.

Dyson, K. and Featherstone, K. (1999) *The Road to Maastricht: Negotiating Economic and Monetary Union*, Oxford: Oxford University Press.

Easton, D. (1990) *The Analysis of Political Structure*, New York: Routledge.

Ebbinghaus, B. (1998) 'Europe Through the Looking Glass: Comparative and Multi-Level Perspectives', *Acta Sociologica*, 41(4): 301–314.

Eckersley, R. (2000) *Deliberative Democracy, Ecological Representation and Risk: Towards a Democracy of the Affected*, Mimeo.

Edwards, G. and Regelsberger, E. (1990) *Europe's Global Links: The European Community and Inter-Regional Cooperation*, London: Pinter.

Edwards, M. and Gaventa, J. (eds) (2001) *Global Citizen Action*, Boulder, CO: Rienner.

Edwards, M. and Hulme, D. (eds) (1996) *Too Close for Comfort? Donors, NGOs and States*, London: Macmillan.

Efinger, M., Mayer, P. and Schwarzer, G. (1993) 'Integrating and Contextualizing Hypotheses. Alternative Paths to Better Explanations of Regime Formation?' in V. Rittberger (ed.) *Regime Theory and International Relations*, Oxford: Oxford University Press.

Eichener, V. (1996) 'Die Rückwirkungen der europäischen Integration auf nationale Politikmuster', in M. Jachtenfuchs and B. Kohler-Koch (eds) *Europäische Integration*, Opladen: Leske und Budrich.

Eichengreen, B. (1989) 'Hegemonic Stability Theories of the International Monetary System', in R.N. Cooper, B. Eichengreen, C.R. Henning, G. Holtham and R.D. Putnam (eds) *Can Nations Agree? Issues in International Economic Cooperation*, Washington, DC: Brookings Institution.

—— (1998) 'Dental Hygiene and Nuclear War: How International Relations Looks from Economics', *International Organization*, 52: 993–1012.

Eichengreen, B., Tobin, J. and Wyplosz, C. (1995) 'Two Cases for Sand in the Wheels of International Finance', *Economic Journal*, 105: 162–172.

Elazar, D.J. (1998) *Constitutionalizing Globalization*, Boston: Rowman & Littlefield.

Eldin, G. (1980) 'Opening Address', in OECD *Strategies for Change and Reform in Public Management*, Paris: OECD.

Elkins, D.J. (1995) *Beyond Sovereignty: Territory and Political Economy in the Twenty-First Century*, Toronto: University of Toronto Press.

Evans, T. (1998) *Bangladesh Country Report*, Santa Fe, NM: Global Health Equity Initiative, Social Determinants Project, October.

Fairclough, N. (1995) *Critical Discourse Analysis: The Critical Study of Language*, London: Longman.

Falk, R. (1995) 'Liberalism at the Global Level: The Last of the Independent Commission?'. *Millennium* 24: 563–578.

—— (1999) *Predatory Globalisation: A Critique*, Cambridge: Polity Press.

Falkner, G. (1999) *Towards a Corporatist Policy Community: EU Social Policy in the 1990s*, London: Routledge.

Featherstone, M., Lash, S. and Robertson, R. (1995) *Global Modernities*, London: Sage.

Ferlie, E., Ashburner, L., Fitzgerald, L. and Pettigrew, A. (1996) *The New Public Management in Action*, Oxford: Oxford University Press.

Fisher, W.F. (ed.) (1995) *Toward Sustainable Development? Struggling over India's Narmada River*, Armonk, NY: Sharpe.

Florini, A.M. (ed.) (2000) *The Third Force: The Rise of Transnational Civil Society*, Tokyo/Washington, DC: Japan Center for International Exchange/Carnegie Endowment for International Peace.

Fomerand, J. (1996) 'UN Conferences: Media Events or Genuine Diplomacy?', *Global Governance*, 2: 361–377.

Foreign Policy (2000) 'Interview: Lori's war', Spring: 28–58.

Forster, A. and Wallace, W. (2000) 'Common Foreign and Security Policy: From Shadow to Substance?', in H. Wallace and W. Wallace (eds) *Policy-Making in the European Union*, 4th edn, Oxford: Oxford University Press.

FORUM 2001: Civil Society, the UN +5s and Beyond (forthcoming), Montreal: Montreal International Forum.

Foucault, M. (1982) 'The Subject and Power', in H. Dreyfus, and P. Rabino (eds) *Beyond Structuralism and Hermeneutics*, Brighton: Harvester.

—— (1991) 'Governmentality', in G. Burchell, C. Gorden, and P. Miller (eds) *The Foucault Effect: Studies in Governmentalities*, Hemel Hempstead: Harvester Wheatsheaf, pp. 87–104.

Fowler, A. (2000) *The Virtuous Spiral: A Guide to Sustainability for Non-governmental Organisations in International Development*, London: Earthscan.

Fox, J.A. (2000) 'The World Bank Inspection Panel: Lessons from the First Five Years', *Global Governance*, 6: 279–318.

Fox, J.A. and Brown, L.D. (eds) (1998) *The Struggle for Accountability: The World Bank, NGOs, and Grassroots Movements*, Cambridge, MA: MIT Press.

Franck, T. (1990) *The Power of Legitimacy Among Nations*, New York: Oxford University Press.

Fried, J. (1997) 'Globalization and International Law – Some Thoughts for States and Citizens', *Queen's Law Journal*, 23: 259–276.

Frieden, J.A. and Rogowski, R. (1996) 'The Impact of the International Economy on National Policies: An Analytical Overview', in R.O. Keohane and H.V. Milner (eds) *Internationalization and Domestic Politics*, Cambridge: Cambridge University Press.

Gaer, F.D. (1995) 'Reality Check: Human Rights Nongovernmental Organizations Confront Governments at the United Nations', *Third World Quarterly*, 16: 389–404.

Gardham, J. (1991) 'A Feminist Analysis of Certain Aspects of International Humanitarian Law', *Australian Yearbook of International Law*, 12: 265–278.

Gemelli, G. (ed.) (1998) *The Ford Foundation and Europe (1950s-1970s): Cross Fertilization of Learning in Social Science and Management*, Brussels: European University Press.

Genschel, P. (1995) *Standards in der Informationstechnik. Institutioneller Wandel in der internationalen Standardisierung*, Frankfurt/M.: Campus.

Genschel, P. and Plümper, T. (1996) 'Wenn Reden Silber und Handeln Gold ist: Kooperation und Kommunikation in der internationalen Bankenregulierung', *Zeitschrift für Internationale Beziehungen* 3: 225–253.

Giddens, A. (1990) *The Consequences of Modernity*, Cambridge: Polity Press.

Gill, S. (1990) *American Hegemony and the Trilateral Commission*, Cambridge: Cambridge University Press.

—— (ed.) (1993) *Gramsci, Historical Materialism and International Relations*, Cambridge: Cambridge University Press.

—— (1995) 'Theorizing the Interregnum: The Double Movement and Global Politics in the 1990s', in B. Hettne (ed.) *International Political Economy: Understanding Global Disorder*, London: Zed Books.

—— (1999) 'The Constitution of Global Capitalism' paper prepared for the British International Studies Association, University of Manchester, 20–22 December.

Gilpin, R. (1981) *War and Change in World Politics*, Cambridge: Cambridge University Press.

—— (1987) *The Political Economy of International Relations*, Princeton, NJ: Princeton University Press.

Goldstein, J. (1996) 'International Law and Domestic Institutions. Reconciling North American "Unfair" Trade Laws', *International Organization*, 50: 541–564.

Goldstein, J., Kahler, M., Keohane, R.O. and Slaughter, A. (2000) 'Introduction: Legalization and World Politics', *International Organization*, 54: 385–399.

Goldstein, J. and Keohane, R.O. (eds) (1993) *The Role of Ideas in Foreign Policy*, Ithaca, NY: Cornell University Press.

Goldstein, J. and Martin, L. (2000) 'Legalization, Trade Liberalization, and Domestic Politics: A Cautionary Note', *International Organization*, 54: 603–632.

Goodman, J. (2000) 'Stopping a Juggernaut: The Anti-MAI Campaign', in J.

Goodman and P. Ranald (eds) *Stopping the Juggernaut,* Annandale, NSW: Pluto Press.

Goodman, P. (1998) *Of One Blood: Abolitionism and the Origin of Racial Equality,* Berkeley, CA: University of California Press.

Gorg, C. and Hirsch, J. (1998) 'Is International Democracy Possible?', *Review of International Political Economy,* (5)4: 585–615.

Gramsci, A. (1988) *An Antonio Gramsci Reader,* ed. D. Forgacs, New York: Schocken Books.

Grieco, J. (1988) 'Anarchy and the Limits of Cooperation: A Realist Critique of the Newest Liberal Institutionalism', *International Organization,* 42: 485–507.

Haas, E.B. (1958) *The Uniting of Europe. Political, Social and Economic Forces, 1950–1957,* Stanford, Stanford University Press.

Haas, P.M. (1992) 'Introduction: Epistemic Communities and International Policy Coordination', *International Organization,* 46(1): 1–35.

Haas, P.M. and Haas, E.B. (1995) 'Learning to Learn: Improving International Governance', *Global Governance,* 1(3): 255–289.

Habermas, J. (1998) 'Die Postnationale Konstellation und die Zukunft der Demokratie', in J. Habermas, *Die Postnationale Konstellation. Politische Essays,* Frankfurt am Main: Suhrkamp Verlag.

Habermas, J., Cronin, C. and de Grieff, P. (eds) (1998) *The Inclusion of the Other: Studies in Political Theory,* Cambridge, MA: MIT Press.

Hajer, M. (1993) 'Discourse Coalitions and the Institutionalization of Practice: The Case of Acid Rain in Great Britain', F. Fischer and J. Forester (eds) *The Argumentative Turn in Policy Analysis and Planning,* London: UCL Press.

Hall, P. (1990) 'Policy Paradigms, Experts and the State: The Case of Macro-economic Policy Making in Britain', in S. Brooks and A.G. Gagnon (eds) *Social Scientists, Policy and the State,* New York: Praeger.

Haltiwanger, J. and Singh, M. (1997) *Cross Country Evidence on Public Sector Retrenchment,* World Bank working paper, Washington, DC: World Bank.

Hann, C. and Dunn, E. (eds) (1996) *Civil Society: Challenging Western Models,* London: Routledge.

Hansen, H.K. (2000) 'Managerialism and Transnational Discourse Communities: The Case of Latin America', paper presented at the 4th International Conference on Organizational Discourse: Word-views, Work-views and World-views, The Management Centre, King's College, University of London, 26–28 July.

Hansen, H.K., Langer, R. and Salskov-Iversen, D. (2001) 'Managing Political Communications', *Corporate Reputation Review,* 4: 167–184.

Harcourt, W. (ed.) (1999) *Women @ Internet: Creating New Cultures in Cyberspace,* London: Zed.

Hart, H.L.A. (1961) *The Concept of Law,* Oxford: Clarendon Press.

Harvey, D. (1990) *The Condition of Postmodernity: An Inquiry into the Origins of Cultural Change,* Cambridge, MA: Blackwell.

—— (1996) *Justice, Nature & the Geography of Difference,* Oxford: Blackwell.

Hasenclever, A., Mayer, P. and Rittberger, V. (1996) 'Interests, Power, Knowledge: The Study of International Regimes', *Mershon International Studies Review* 40(2): 177–228.

—— (1997) *Theories of International Regimes,* New York: Cambridge University Press.

Held, D. (1991) 'Democracy, the Nation-state, and the Global System', in D. Held (ed.) *Political Theory Today*, Cambridge: Polity Press.

—— (1995) *Democracy and the Global Order: From the Modern State to Cosmopolitan Governance*, Cambridge: Polity Press.

—— (1996) *Models of Democracy*, 2nd edition, Cambridge, Polity Press.

—— (1997) 'Democracy and Globalization', *Global Governance*, 3: 251–267.

—— (2000) 'The Changing Contours of Political Community', in B. Holden (ed.) *Global Democracy: Key Debates*, London: Routledge.

Held, D., McGrew, A., Goldblatt, D. and Perraton, J. (1999) *Global Transformations: Politics, Economics and Culture*, Cambridge: Polity Press.

Held, D., McGrew, A. with Goldblatt, D. and Perraton, J. (1999) 'Globalization', *Global Governance*, 5: 483–496.

Helleiner, E. (1994) *States and the Reemergence of Global Finance: From Bretton Woods to the 1990s*, Ithaca, NY: Cornell University Press.

Henderson, D. (1999) *The MAI Affair: A Story and Its Lessons*, London: Royal Institute of International Affairs.

Henley, J. (1992) 'Social Cause and Consequence', Chapter 6 in J.M. Stopford and S. Strange (eds) *Rival States, Rival Firms*, Cambridge: Cambridge University Press, pp. 169–202.

Héritier, A. (1999) *Policy Making and Diversity in Europe: Escape from Deadlock*, Cambridge: Cambridge University Press.

Héritier, A., Knill, C. and Mingers, S. (1996) *Ringing the Changes in Europe: Regulatory Competition and the Transformation of the State*, Berlin: de Gruyter.

Hertz, N. (2001) *The Silent Takeover: Global Capitalism and the Death of Democracy*, London: Heinemann.

Hewett, J. (ed.) (1995) *European Environmental Almanac*, London: Earthscan.

Hewson, M. and Sinclair, T.J. (1999) 'The Emergence of Global Governance Theory', in M. Hewson and T.J. Sinclair (eds) *Global Governance Theory*, Albany, NY: State University of New York Press.

Higer, A. (1997) 'Transnational Movements and World Politics: The International Women's Health Movement and Population Policy', unpublished doctoral dissertation, Brandeis University, Waltham, MA.

Higgins, R. (1985) 'Conceptual Thinking about the Individual under International Law', in R. Falk, F. Kratochwil and S. Mendolvitz (eds) *International Law: A Contemporary Perspective*, Boulder, CO: Westview Press.

—— (1983) *Political Development Theory: The Contemporary Debate*, London: St Martin's Press.

—— (2001) 'Contested Globalisation: New Normative Challenges', *Review of International Studies*, 25(5): 131–153.

Higgott, R., Underhill, G. and Bieler, A. (eds) (1999) *Non-State Actors and Authority in the Global System*, London: Routledge.

Higgott, R.A. and Payne, A.J. (2000) (eds) *The New Political Economy of Globalisation*, Cheltenham: Edward Elgar.

Hill, K.A. and Hughes, J.E. (1998) *Cyberpolitics: Citizen Activism in the Age of the Internet*, Lanham, MD: Rowman & Littlefield.

Hinsley, F.H. (1967) *Power and the Pursuit of Peace*, Cambridge: Cambridge University Press.

Hirschi, C., Serdült, U. and Widmer, T. (1999) 'Schweizerische Außenpolitik im Wandel', *Schweizerische Zeitschrift für Politikwissenschaft*, 5: 31–56.

Hirst, P. and Thompson, G. (1996) *Globalization in Question: The International Economy and the Possibilities of Governance*, Cambridge: Polity Press.

Hix, S. (1994) 'The Study of the European Community: The Challenge to Comparative Politics', *West European Politics*, 17(1): 1–30.

—— (1996) 'CP, IR and the EU! A Rejoinder to Hurrell and Menon', *West European Politics*, 19(4): 802–804.

—— (1998) 'The Study of the European Union II: The New Governance Agenda and its Rival', *Journal of European Public Policy* 5(1): 38–65.

—— (1999) *The Political System of the European Union*, Basingstoke: Macmillan.

Hobsbawm, E.J. (1992) *Nations and Nationalism since 1780: Programme, Myth, Reality*, 2nd edition, Cambridge: Canto.

Holland, M. (1996) 'Foreign Policy Transition in Theory and Practice', *International Relations*, 13(3): 1–18.

Holm, H-H. and Sørensen, G. (1995) *Whose World Order? Uneven Globalization and the End of the Cold War*, Boulder, CO: Westview Press.

Hood, C. (1991) 'A Public Management for All Seasons?', *Public Administration*, 69: 3–19.

—— (1998) *The Art of The State*, Oxford: Clarendon Press.

Hooghe, L. (ed.) (1996) *Cohesion Policy and European Integration: Building Multi-Level Governance*, Oxford: Oxford University Press.

Hornberger, E. and Dombois, R. (1999) 'Auf dem Weg zu "international governance?" Internationale Arbeitsregulierung am Beispiel des NAFTA-Nebenabkommens zum Arbeitsrecht', *Peripherie*, 19: 44–66.

Hurrell, A. (1993) 'International Society and the Study of Regimes: A Reflective Approach', in V. Rittberger (ed.) *Regime Theory and International Relations*, Oxford: Clarendon Press.

Hurrell, A. and Menon, A. (1996) 'Politics Like Any Other? Comparative Politics, International Relations and the Study of the EU', *West European Politics*, 19(2): 386–402.

Hutchings, K. (1999) *International Political Theory*, London: Sage.

Grunberg, I. and Stern, M.A. (eds) (1999) *Global Public Goods: International Cooperation in the 21st Century*, Oxford: Oxford University Press.

IFRC (1997) *World Disasters Report*, Oxford: Oxford University Press.

Ikenberry, J. (1992) 'A World Economy Restored: Expert Consensus and the Anglo-American Post War Consensus', *International Organization*, 46: 289–321.

International Chamber of Commerce (1997) *Business and the Global Economy*, ICC statement on behalf of world business to the Heads of State and Government attending the Denver Summit, 20–22 June 1997.

International Confederation of Free Trade Unions (1996) *Sixteenth World Congress of the ICFTU*, Brussels, June 25–29 Congress Resolutions, http://www.icftu.org/english/congress.html.

Jachtenfuchs, M. and Kohler-Koch, B. (1996) 'Regieren im dynamischen Mehrebenensystem', in M. Jachtenfuchs and B. Kohler-Koch (eds) *Europäische Integration*, Opladen: Leske und Budrich.

Jackson, J.H. (1999) *The World Trade Organization: Constitution and Jurisprudence*, London: Royal Institute of International Affairs.

Jackson, R. (1999) 'Introduction: Sovereignty at the Millennium', *Political Studies* 47: 423–431.

Jackson, R.H. (1993) *Quasi-states*, Cambridge: Cambridge University Press.

Jacobsen, J.K. (1995) 'Much Ado About Ideas: The Cognitive Factor in Economic Policy', *World Politics*, 47: 283–310.

Jacquemin, A. and Pench, L.R. (eds) (1997) *Europe Competing in the Global Economy: Reports of the Competitiveness Advisory Group*, Cheltenham: Edward Elgar.

James, A. (1999) 'The Practice of Sovereign Statehood in Contemporary International Society', *Political Studies*, 47: 457–474.

Janis, M.W. (1984) 'Individuals as Subjects of International Law', *Cornell International Law Journal*, 17: 61–78.

Japan Center for International Exchange (1997) *Global ThinkNet*, Tokyo: Japan Center for International Exchange.

Jessop, B. (1985) *Nicos Poulantzas: Marxist Theory and Political Strategy*, Houndmills: Macmillan.

Joerges, C. (1996) *The Market Without the State? States Without a Market? Two Essays on the Law of the European Economy*, EUI Working Paper Law 2/96, San Domenico.

Johns, F. (1994) 'The Invisibility of the Transnational Corporation: An Analysis of International Law and Legal Theory', *Melbourne University Law Review* 19: 893–923.

Jones, C. (1999) *Global Justice: Defending Cosmopolitanism*, Oxford: Oxford University Press.

Jones, R.J.B. (2000) *The World Turned Upside Down?*, Manchester: Manchester University Press.

Jørgensen, K.E. (1997) 'PoCo: The Diplomatic Republic of Europe', in K.E. Jørgensen (ed.) *Reflective Approaches to European Governance*, Basingstoke: Macmillan.

Joyner, C. (1999) 'The United Nations and Democracy', *Global Governance*, 5: 33–58.

Jupille, J. and Caporaso, J.A. (1996) 'States, Agency, and Rules: The European Union in Global Environmental Politics', in C. Rhodes (ed.) *The European Union in the World Community*, Boulder, CO: Lynne Rienner.

Kahler, M. (1987) 'The Survival of the State in European International Relations', in C. Maier (ed.) *Changing Boundaries of the Political: Essays on the Evolving Balance Between the State and Society, Public and Private in Europe*, Cambridge: Cambridge University Press.

—— (1995) *International Institutions and the Political Economy of Integration*, Washington, DC: Brookings Institution.

—— (1997) 'Inventing International Relations: International Relations Theory After 1945', in M.W. Doyle and G.J. Ikenberry (eds) *New Thinking in International Relations Theory*, Boulder, CO: Westview Press.

Katzenstein, P.J., Keohane, R.O. and Krasner, S.D. (1998) 'International Organization and the Study of World Politics', *International Organization*, 52: 645–685.

Kaul, I., Grunberg, I. and Stern, M.A. (1999) 'Defining Global Public Goods', in I. Kaul, I. Grunberg and M.A. Stern (eds) *Global Public Goods: International Cooperation in the 21st Century*, Oxford: Oxford University Press.

Keck, M.E. and Sikkink, K. (1998) *Activists Beyond Borders: Advocacy Networks in International Politics*, Ithaca, NY: Cornell University Press.

Kelly, C.D. (2000) *The Modern Global Man: The Moderation of the Masculine Model and International Relations*, Wellesley College, Department of Political Science, NSF Aire Student-Faculty Research Collaboration, May.

Kelsen, H. ([1945] 1961) *General Theory of Law and the State,* New York: Russell & Russell.

Kenis, P. (2000) 'Why Do Community-Based AIDS Organizations Co-ordinate at the Global Level?', in K. Ronit and V. Schneider (eds) *Private Organizations in Global Politics,* London: Routledge.

Kennedy, D. (1980) 'Theses about International Law Discourse', *German Yearbook of International Law,* 23: 353–391.

—— (1985/6) 'Critical Theory, Structuralism and Contemporary Legal Scholarship', *New England Law Review* 21: 209–289.

—— (1987) 'The Sources of International Law', *American University Journal of International Law & Policy* 2(1): 1–96.

—— (1988) 'A New Stream in International Law Scholarship', *Wisconsin International Law Journal* 7(1): 1–49.

Keohane, R.O. (1980) 'The Theory of Hegemonic Stability and Changes in International Economic Regimes, 1967–1977', in O.R. Holsti, R.M. Siverson and A.L. George (eds) *Change in the International System,* Boulder, CO: Westview Press, pp. 131–162.

—— (1984) *After Hegemony: Collaboration and Discord in the World Political Economy,* Princeton, NJ: Princeton University Press.

—— (1986) 'Reciprocity in International Relations', *International Organization* 40: 1–27.

—— (1989a) *International Institutions and State Power: Essays in International Relations Theory,* Boulder, CO: Westview Press.

—— (1989b) 'Neoliberal Institutionalism: A Perspective on World Politics', in R.O. Keohane (ed.) *International Institutions and State Power: Essays in International Relations Theory,* Boulder, CO: Westview Press.

—— (1989c) 'International Institutions: Two Approaches', in R.O. Keohane (ed.) *International Institutions and State Power: Essays in International Relations Theory,* Boulder, CO: Westview Press.

—— (1993) 'Institutionalist Theory and the Realist Challenge After the Cold War', in D. Baldwin (ed.) *Neorealism and Neoliberalism. The Contemporary Debate,* New York: Columbia University Press, pp. 269–300.

—— (1995) 'Hobbes's Dilemma and Institutional Change in World Politics: Sovereignty in International Society' in H. Holm and G. Sørensen (eds) *Whose World Order? Uneven Globalization and the End of the Cold War,* Boulder, CO: Westview Press.

—— (1997) 'International Relations and International Law: Two Optics', *Harvard International Law Journal,* 38: 487–502.

—— (1998) 'International Institutions: Can Interdependence Work?', *Foreign Policy* (Spring): 82–96.

Keohane, R.O. and Martin, L. (1995) 'The Promise of Institutionalist Theory', *International Security,* 20: 39–51.

Keohane, R.O. and Nye, J.S. (1989) *Power and Interdependence,* 2nd edn, Glenview, ILL: HarperCollins.

—— (1998) 'Power and Interdependence in the Information Age', *Foreign Affairs,* 77 (Sept./Oct.): 81–93.

Khagram, S. (2000) 'Toward Democratic Governance for Sustainable Development: Transnational Civil Society Organizing around Big Dams', in A.M. Florini (ed.) *The Third Force: The Rise of Transnational Civil Society,* Tokyo/Washington,

DC: Japan Center for International Exchange/Carnegie Endowment for International Peace.

Kim, N. (1993) 'Toward a Feminist Theory of Human Rights: Straddling the Fence Between Western Imperialism and Uncritical Absolutism', *Columbia Human Rights Law Review*, 25: 49–105.

Kindleberger, C.P. (1973) *The World in Depression: 1929–1939*, Berkeley, CA: University of California Press.

Klare, K. (1979) 'Law-Making as Praxis', *Telos*, 40: 123–135.

Klijn, E.H. (1997) 'Policy Networks: An Overview', in W.J.M. Kickert, E-H. Klijn and J.F.M. Koppenjan (eds) *Managing Complex Networks: Strategies for the Public Sector*, London: Sage.

Kline, J. (1988) 'Advantages of International Regulation: The Case for a Flexible, Pluralistic Framework', in C. Adelman (ed.) *International Regulation: New Rules in a Changing World Order*, San Francisco: Institute for Contemporary Studies.

Knight, W.A. (1999) 'Engineering Space in Global Governance: The Emergence of Civil Society in Evolving "New" Multilateralism', in M.G. Schechter (ed.) *Future Multilateralism: The Political and Social Framework*, Tokyo: United Nations University Press.

Kohler-Koch, B. (1993) 'Die Welt regieren ohne Weltregierung', in C. Böhret and G. Wewer (eds) *Regieren im 21. Jahrhundert. Zwischen Globalisierung und Regionalisierung. Festgabe für Hans-Hermann Hartwich zum 65. Geburtstag*, Opladen: Leske und Budrich.

Korten, D.C. (1990) *Getting to the 21st Century: Voluntary Action and the Global Agenda*, West Hartford, CT: Kumarian Press.

Krasner, S.D. (1976) 'State Power and the Structure of International Trade', *World Politics*, 28: 317–347.

—— (1983a) *International Regimes*, Ithaca, NY: University of Cornell Press.

—— (1983b) 'Structural Causes and Regime Consequences: Regimes as Intervening Variables', in S.D. Krasner (ed.) *International Regimes*, Ithaca, NY: Cornell University Press.

—— (1985) *Structural Conflict: The Third World Against Global Liberalism*, Los Angeles: University of California Press.

—— (1993) 'Westphalia and All That', in J. Goldstein and R.O. Keohane (eds) *Ideas and Foreign Policy*, Ithaca, NY: Cornell University Press.

—— (1995) 'Power Politics, Institutions and Transnational Relations', in T. Risse-Kappen (ed.) *Bringing Transnationals Back In: Non-State Actors, Domestic Structures, and International Institutions*, Cambridge: Cambridge University Press.

Krastev, I. (2000) 'Think Tanks: Making and Faking Influence', in D. Stone (ed.) *Banking on Knowledge: The Genesis of the Global Development Network*, London: Routledge.

Kratochwil, F. (1989) *Rules, Norms, and Decisions: On the Conditions of Practical and Legal Reasoning in International Relations and Domestic Affairs*, Cambridge: Cambridge University Press.

—— (1994) 'Preface', in F. Kratochwil, and E.D. Mansfield (eds) *International Organization: A Reader*, New York: HarperCollins.

Krieger, J. and Murphy, C.N. (1998) *Transnational Opportunity Structures and the Evolving Roles of Movements for Women, Human Rights, Labor, Development, and the*

Environment: A Proposal for Research, Department of Political Science: Wellesley College, December.

Kumar, K. (1993) 'Civil Society: An Inquiry into the Usefulness of an Historical Term', *British Journal of Sociology,* 44: 375–395.

Kymlicka, W. (1999) 'Citizenship in an Era of Globalization', in I. Shapiro and C. Hacker-Cordon (eds) *Democracy's Edges,* Cambridge: Cambridge University Press.

Laffan, B. and Shackleton, M. (2000) 'The Budget: Who Gets What, When and How?', in H. Wallace and W. Wallace (eds) *Policy-Making in the European Union,* 4th edition, Oxford: Oxford University Press.

Laïdi, Z. (1998) *A World Without Meaning: The Crisis of Meaning in International Politics,* London: Routledge.

Lange, P. (1992) 'The Politics of the Social Dimension', in A.M. Sbragia (ed.) *Euro-Politics: Institutions and Policymaking in the 'New' European Community,* Washington, DC: Brookings Institution.

Larin, K. and McNichol, E. (1997) *Pulling Apart: A State-by-State Analysis of Income Trends,* Washington, DC: Center on Budget and Policy Priorities.

Lasswell, H. and Reisman, M. (1968) 'Theories About International Law: Prologue to a Configurative Jurisprudence', *Virginia Journal of International Law,* 8: 188–299.

Lauterpacht, H. (1946) 'The Grotian Tradition in International Law', *British Yearbook of International Law,* 23: 1–53.

Lee, E. (1996) *The Labour Movement and the Internet: The New Internationalism,* London: Pluto.

Lee, K. and Zwi, A. (1996) 'A Global Political Economy Approach to AIDS: Ideology, Interests and Implications', *New Political Economy,* 1: 355–373.

Lee, S. (2002) 'Discovering the Frontiers of Regionalism: Fostering Entrepreneurship, Innovation and Competitiveness in the European Union', in S. Breslin, C.W. Hughes, N. Phillips and B. Rosamond (eds) *New Regionalisms in the Global Political Economy: Theories and Cases,* London: Routledge.

Leibfried, S. and Pierson, P. (1995) 'Semisovereign Welfare States: Social Policy in a Multitiered Europe', in S. Leibfried and P. Pierson (eds) *European Social Policy: Between Fragmentation and Integration,* Washington, DC: Brookings Institution.

—— (2000) 'Social Policy', in H. Wallace and W. Wallace (eds) *Policy Making in the European Union,* 4th edition, Oxford: Oxford University Press.

Lerdell, D. and Sahlin-Andersson, K. (1997) *Att lära över gränser – en studie av OECD's förvaltningspolitiska samarbete,* Stockholm SOU 33.

Levy, M.A., Young, O.R. and Zürn, M. (1995) 'The Study of International Regimes', *European Journal of International Relations,* 1: 267–330.

Liebert, U. (1998) 'Gender Politics in the European Union: The Return of the Public', paper prepared for the 1998 Annual Meeting of the American Political Science Association, 3–6 September, Boston.

Lindberg, L.N. (1967) 'The European Community as a Political System: Notes Towards the Construction of a Model', *Journal of Common Market Studies,* 5(4): 344–387.

Lindenberg, M. and Bryant, C. (2001) *Going Global: Transforming Relief and Development NGOs,* Bloomfield, CT: Kumarian Press.

Linklater, A. (1986) 'Realism, Marxism and Critical Theory', *Review of International Studies,* 12: 301–312.

—— (1990) *Beyond Realism and Marxism: Critical Theory and International Relations*, New York: St. Martin's Press.

—— (1998) *The Transformation of Political Community: Ethical Foundations of the Post-Westphalian Era*, Cambridge: Polity Press.

Lipschutz, R.D. (1992) 'Reconstructing World Politics: The Emergence of Global Civil Society', *Millennium: Journal of International Studies*, 21: 389–420.

Long, P. (1995) 'The Harvard School of Liberal International Theory: The Case for Closure', *Millennium: Journal of International Studies*, 24: 489–505.

Luard, E. (1990) *The Globalization of Politics: The Changed Focus of Political Action in the Modern World*, Houndmills: Macmillan.

Luo, Xiawei (2000) 'The Rise of the Social-Development Model: Institutional Construction of International Technology Organizations, 1856–1993', *International Studies Quarterly*, 44: 147–175.

Lutz, E. and Sikkink, K. (2000) 'International Human Rights Law and Practice in Latin America', *International Organization*, 54: 661–684.

Lütz, S. (1997) 'Die Rückkehr des Nationalstaates? Kapitalmarktregulierung im Zeichen der Internationalisierung von Finanzmärkten', *Politische Vierteljahresschrift*, 38: 475–497.

Lynch, C. (1998) 'Social Movements and the Problem of Globalisation', *Alternatives*, 23: 149–173.

—— (1999) 'The Promise and Problems of Internationalism', *Global Governance*, 5: 83–103.

McConnaughay, P. (1999) 'The Risks and Virtues of Lawlessness: A Second Look at International Commercial Arbitration', *Northwestern University Law Review*, 93: 453–523.

McCormick, J. (1999) 'Three Ways of Thinking Critically about the Law', *American Political Science Review*, 93: 413–428.

McDougal, M. and Lasswell, H. (1959) 'The Identification and Appraisal of Diverse Systems of Public Order', *American Journal of International Law*, 53: 1–29.

MacFarlane, S.N. (1985) *Superpower Rivalry and Third World Radicalism: The Idea of National Liberation*, Baltimore: The Johns Hopkins University Press.

McGann, J. and Weaver, R.K. (eds) (2000) *Think Tanks and Civil Societies: Catalysts for Ideas and Action*, London: Transaction Press.

McGrew, A.G. (1992a) 'Conceptualizing Global Politics', in A.G. McGrew and P.G. Lewis (eds) *Global Politics: Globalization and the Nation State*, Cambridge: Polity Press.

—— (1992b) 'Global Politics in a Transitional Era', in A.G. McGrew and P.G. Lewis (eds) *Global Politics: Globalization and the Nation State*, Cambridge: Polity Press.

—— (1997) 'Globalization and Territorial Democracy: An Introduction', in A.G. McGrew (ed.) *The Transformation of Democracy? Globalization and Teorritorial Democracy*, Cambridge: Polity Press.

—— (1999) 'The WTO: Technocracy or Banana Republic?', in A. Taylor and C. Thomas (eds) *Global Trade and Global Social Issues*, London: Routledge.

—— (2000) 'Sustainable Globalization?' in A. Taylor *et al. Poverty and Development in the New Century*, Oxford: Oxford University Press.

McIntosh, M. (ed.) (1998) *Visions of Ethical Business*, London: Financial Times.

Majone, G. (1991) 'Cross-National Sources of Regulatory Policy-Making in Europe and the United States', *Journal of Public Policy*, 11(1).

—— (1994) 'The Rise of the Regulatory State in Europe', *West European Politics* 17(3): 78–102.

—— (1996) 'A European Regulatory State?', in J. Richardson (ed.) *European Union: Power and Policy-Making*, London: Routledge.

Malanczuk, P. (ed.) (1997) *Akehurst's Modern Introduction to International Law*, 7th revised edn, London: Routledge.

Mameli, P. (2000) 'Managing the HIV/AIDS Pandemic: Paving a Path into the Future of International Law and Organization', *Law and Policy*, 22(2): 203–224.

Mann, J., Tarantola, D. and Netter, T.W. (eds) (1992) *AIDS in the World: The Global AIDS Policy Coalition*, Cambridge, MA: Harvard University Press.

Marks, G. (1993) 'Structural Policy and Multilevel Governance in the European Community', in A. Cafruny and G.G. Rosenthal (eds) *The State of the European Community*, Boulder, CO: Lynne Rienner.

Marks, G., Hooghe, L. and Blank, K. (1996) 'European Integration from the 1980s: State–Centric v. Multi-Level Governance', *Journal of Common Market Studies*, 34(3): 341–378.

Marks, G., Nielsen, F., Ray, L. and Salk, J. (1996) 'Competencies, Cracks and Conflicts: Regional Mobilization in the European Union', in G. Marks *et al.* (eds) *Governance in the European Union*, London: Sage.

Marks, G., Scharpf, F.W., Schmitter, P.C. and Streeck, W. (eds) (1996) *Governance in the European Union*, London: Sage.

Martin, L. (1993) 'The Rational State Choice of Multilateralism', in J.G. Ruggie (ed.) *Multilateralism Matters: The Theory and Practice of an International Form*, New York: Columbia University Press.

Martin, L. and Simmons, B. (1998) 'Theories and Empirical Studies of International Institutions', *International Organization*, 52: 729–757.

Marx, K. ([1867] 1996) 'Preface to the First German Edition', in *Capital*, vol. I (*Marx/Engels Collected Works*, vol. 35), London: Lawrence & Wishart.

Marx, K. and Engels, F. (1932/1848) *Manifesto of the Communist Party*, New York: International Publishers.

Matthews, J.T. (1997) 'Power Shift', *Foreign Affairs*, 76: 50–66.

Mattli, W. (1999) *The Logic of Regional Integration: Europe and Beyond*, Cambridge: Cambridge University Press.

Mayall, J. (1999) 'Sovereignty, Nationalism and Self-Determination', *Political Studies*, 47: 474–503.

—— (2000) 'Democracy and International Society', *International Affairs*, 76: 61–75.

Mayer, P., Rittberger, V. and Zürn, M. (1993) 'Regime Theory: State of the Art and Perspectives', in V. Rittberger with P. Mayer (eds) *Regime Theory and International Relations*, Oxford: Clarendon Press.

Mayntz, R. (1996) 'Politische Steuerung: Aufstieg, Niedergang und Transformation einer Theorie', in K. von Beyme and C. Offe (eds) *Politische Theorien in der Ära der Transformation* (PVS-Sonderheft 26/1995), Opladen: Westdeutscher Verlag.

Mayoux, L. (1998) 'From Vicious to Virtuous Circles? Gender and Micro-Enterprise Development', UNRISD UN Fourth World Conference on Women Occasional Paper No. 3, Geneva, May.

Mearsheimer, J. (1994–95) 'The False Promise of International Institutions', *International Security*, 19: 5–49.

Mekata, M. (2000) 'Building Partnerships toward a Common Goal: Experiences of the International Campaign to Ban Landmines', in A.M. Florini (ed.) *The Third Force: The Rise of Transnational Civil Society*, Tokyo/Washington, DC: Japan Center for International Exchange/Carnegie Endowment for International Peace.

Milanovic, B. (1999) *True World Income Distribution, 1988 and 1993: First Calculation Based on Household Surveys Alone*, Washington, DC: World Bank. World Bank Development Research Group Working Paper No. 2244, December.

Miliband, R. (1973) *The State in Capitalist Society*, London: Routledge.

Millennium: Journal of International Studies (1994) 'Special Issue: Social Movements and World Politics', 23(3).

Miller, P. and Rose, N. (1990) 'Governing Economic Life', *Economy and Society*, 19: 1–31.

Milner, H.V. and Keohane, R.O. (1996) 'Internationalization and Domestic Politics: A Conclusion', in R.O. Keohane and H.V. Milner (eds) *Internationalization and Domestic Politics*, Cambridge: Cambridge University Press.

Mitrany, D. (1975) 'A War-time Submission (1941)', in P. Taylor (ed.) *A Functional Theory of Politics*, London: LSE/Martin Robertson.

Modelski, G. (1990) 'Is World Politics Evolutionary Learning?' *International Organization*, 44: 1–24.

Modelski, G. and Thompson, W.R. (1995) *Leading Sectors and World Powers: The Coevolution of Global Economics and Politics*, Columbia, SC: University of South Carolina Press.

Moravcsik, A. (1991) 'Negotiating the Single European Act', in R.O. Keohane and S. Hoffmann (eds) *The New European Community: Decision Making and Institutional Change*, Boulder, CO: Westview Press.

—— (1997) 'Taking Preferences Seriously: A Liberal Theory of International Politics', *International Organization*, 51: 513–553.

—— (1998) *The Choice for Europe: Social Purpose and State Power from Messina to Maastricht*, Ithaca, NY: Cornell University Press.

Morgenthau, H. (1948) *Politics Among Nations: The Struggle for Power and Peace*, New York: Knopf.

Morrison, R. (1995) *Ecological Democracy*, Boston: South End Press.

Murphy, C.N. (1994) *International Organization and Industrial Change: Global Governance since 1850*, Cambridge: Polity Press.

—— (1995) 'Globalization and Governance: "Passive Revolution" and the Earlier Transitions to Larger Scale Industrial Economies in the United Kingdom, Germany, the Northeastern United States, and northeastern Japan', paper prepared for the Annual Meeting of the American Political Science Association, Chicago, September.

—— (1997) 'Leadership and Global Governance in the Early Twenty-First Century', *Journal of International Studies*, 1: 25–49.

—— (1998) 'Globalization and Governance: A Historical Perspective', in R. Axtmann (ed.) *Globalization in Europe*, London: Pinter Publishers.

—— (1999) 'Inequality, Turmoil, and Democracy: Global Political-Economic Visions at the End of the Century', *New Political Economy*, 4: 289–304.

—— (2001a) 'Gender Inequality and the *Realpolitik* of Settled Agricultural Societies', in M.A. Tétreault and R.L. Teske (eds) *Feminist Approaches to Social Movements, Community, and Power*, Columbia, SC: University of South Carolina Press.

—— (ed.) (2001b) *Egalitarian Politics in an Age of Globalization*, London: Palgrave.

Nagel, S. (ed.) (1991) *Global Policy Studies: International Interaction toward Improving Public Policy*, London: Macmillan.

Nardin, T. (1983) *Law, Morality, and the Relations of States*, Princeton, NJ: Princeton University Press.

Naschold, F. (ed.) (1996) *New Frontiers in Public Sector Management*, Berlin: De Gruyter.

Nelson, P.J. (1995) *The World Bank and Non-Governmental Organizations: The Limits of Apolitical Development*, New York: St. Martin's Press.

Nesseth, H. (1999) 'Constructing Authority in the Global Political Economy: Global Consultancy and Financial Liberalization in Indonesia', paper prepared for the Annual Meeting of the International Studies Association, Washington, DC, 16–20 February.

Neufeld, M. (1995) *The Restructuring of International Relations Theory*, Cambridge: Cambridge University Press.

The New Civic Atlas: Profiles of Civil Society in 60 Countries (1997) Washington, DC: CIVICUS.

Newell, P. (2000) *Climate for Change: Non-State Actors and the Global Politics of the Greenhouse*, Cambridge: Cambridge University Press.

North, D.C. (1990) *Institutions, Institutional Change and Economic Performance*, Cambridge: Cambridge University Press.

Nyerere, J. (1980) 'Introduction to Mason Sears', *Years of High Purpose, from Trusteeship to Nationhood*, Washington, DC: University Press of America.

O'Brien, R. (1992) *Global Financial Integration: The End of Geography*, London: Chatham House Papers.

O'Brien, R., Goetz, A.M., Scholte, J.A. and Williams, M. (2000) *Contesting Global Governance: Multilateral Economic Institutions and Global Social Movements*, Cambridge: Cambridge University Press.

OECD (1980) *Strategies for Change and Reform in Public Management*, Paris: OECD.

—— (1993) *Public Management: OECD Country Profiles*, Paris: OECD.

Offe, C. (1998) 'Demokratie und Wohlfahrtsstaat: Eine europäische Regimeform unter dem Streß der europäischen Integration', in W. Streeck (ed.) *Internationale Wirtschaft, nationale Demokratie. Herausforderungen für die Demokratietheorie*, Frankfurt a.M.: Campus.

Ohmae, K. (1990) *The Borderless World: Power and Strategy in the Interlinked Economy*, London: HarperCollins.

—— (1995) *The End of the Nation State: The Rise of Regional Economies*, London: HarperCollins.

Osborne, D. and Gaebler, T. (1992) *Reinventing Government: How the Entrepreneurial Spirit is Transforming the Public Sector*, New York: Plume Books.

Østerud, Ø. (1997) 'The Narrow Gate: Entry to the Club of Sovereign States', *Review of International Studies*, 23: 167–184.

Ostner, I. and Lewis, J. (1995) 'Gender and the Evolution of European Social Policies', in S. Leibfried and P. Pierson (eds) *European Social Policy: Between Fragmentation and Integration*, Washington, DC: Brookings Institution.

Ougaard, M. (1984) 'The Origins of the Second Cold War', *New Left Review*, 147: 61–75.

—— (1995) 'Introduction: Culture and Society – A Perspective on Perspectives', in D. Salskov-Iversen and A.M. Ejdesgaard-Jeppesen (eds) *To Capture the Bird's*

Flight: On the Interface Between Culture and Society, Copenhagen: Copenhagen Business School Press.

—— (1999a) 'NAFTA, the EU, and Deficient Global Institutionality', in K. Appendini and S. Bislev (eds) *Economic Integration in NAFTA and the EU,* London: Macmillan.

—— (1999b) *Approaching the Global Polity.* CSGR Working Paper No. 42, Coventry: University of Warwick.

—— (1999c) 'The OECD in the Global Polity', paper prepared for a workshop in the SSRC Project 'Globalisation, Statehood and World Order', 1–3 October.

Overbeek, H. (1990) *Global Capitalism and National Decline: The Thatcher Decade in Perspective,* London: Unwin Hyman.

Patel, S., Bolnick, J. and Mitlin D. (2001) 'Squatting on the Global Highway: Community Exchanges for Urban Transformation', in M. Edwards and J. Gaventa (eds) *Global Citizen Action,* Boulder, CO: Lynne Rienner.

Patten, C. (1998) *East and West: China, Power, and the Future of Asia,* London: Times Books.

Peterson, J. (1995) 'Decision-Making in the European Union: A Framework for Analysis', *Journal of European Public Policy,* 2(1): 69–94.

Peterson, J. and Bomberg, E. (1999) *Decision-Making in the European Union,* Basingstoke: Macmillan.

Peterson, M.J. (1992) 'Whalers, Cetologists, Environmentalists and the International Management of Whaling', *International Organization,* 46(1): 147–186.

Pettit, P. (1997) *Republicanism: A Theory of Freedom and Government,* Oxford: Oxford University Press.

Philpott, D. (1999) 'Westphalia, Authority, and International Society', *Political Studies,* 47: 566–590.

Piening, C. (1997) *Global Europe: The European Union in World Affairs,* Boulder, CO: Lynne Rienner.

Pierson, P. (1996) 'The Path to European Integration: A Historical Institutionalist Analysis', *Comparative Political Studies,* 29(2): 123–163.

Pieterse, J.N. (1995) 'Globalization as Hybridization', in M. Featherstone, S. Lash and R. Robertson (eds) *Global Modernities,* London: Sage.

Pijl, K. van der (1984) *The Making of an Atlantic Ruling Class,* London: Verso.

—— (1990) 'Socialisation and Social Democracy in the State System', in W. Koole, M. Krätke, H. Overbeek, R. Schildmeijer, and K. van der Pijl (eds) *After the Crisis: Political Regulation and the Capitalist Crisis,* Department of International Relations, Amsterdam: University of Amsterdam.

—— (1998) *Transnational Classes and International Relations,* London: Routledge.

Pinder, J. (1968) 'Positive and Negative Integration. Some Problems of Economic Union in the EEC', *World Today,* 24: 88–110.

Polanyi, K. (1957) *The Great Transformation: The Political and Economic Origins of Our Times,* Boston: Beacon Press.

Pollitt, C. (1993) *Managerialism and the Public Services,* 2nd edn, Oxford: Blackwell.

Potter, D. *et al.* (eds) (1997) *Democratization,* Cambridge: Polity Press.

Poulantzas, N. (1978) *Classes in Contemporary Capitalism,* London: Verso.

Price, R. (1998) 'Reversing the Gun Sights: Transnational Civil Society Targets Land Mines', *International Organization,* 52: 613–644.

Princen, T. and Finger, M. (1994) *Environmental NGOs in World Politics: Linking the Local and the Global,* London: Routledge.

Prodi, R. (2000) 'Europe and Global Governance', speech to the 2nd COMECE Congress, Brussels, 31 March.

Pröhl, M. (ed.) (1997) *International Strategies and Techniques for Future Local Government*, Gütersloh: Bertelsmann Foundation Publishers.

Puchala, D.J. (1972) 'Of Blind Men, Elephants and International Integration', *Journal of Common Market Studies*, 10(3): 267–284.

PUMA (1995) *Governance in Transition: Public Management Reforms in OECD Countries. Conclusions of the Public Management Committee*, Paris: OECD.

Purvis, N. (1991) 'Critical Legal Studies in International Law', *Harvard International Law Journal*, 32: 81–127.

Quigley, K. (1997) *For Democracy's Sake: Foundations and Democracy Assistance in Central Europe*, Washington, DC: The Woodrow Wilson Center.

Radaelli, C. (1999) *Technocracy in the European Union*, London: Longman.

—— (2000) 'Policy Transfer in the European Union: Institutional Isomorphism as a Source of Legitimacy', *Governance*, 13(1) 25–43.

Raffer, K. and Singer, H. (1996) *The Foreign Aid Business*, Cheltenham: Edward Elgar.

Ramamurti, R. (1998) 'Private Sector Development and Public Sector Management', www.worldbank.org/html/rad/evaluation/private.html

Reinicke, W.H. (1998) *Global Public Policy: Governing without Government?*, Washington, DC: Brookings Institution Press.

—— (1999/2000) 'The Other World Wide Web: Global Public Policy Networks', *Foreign Policy* (winter).

Rhodes, R.A.W. and Marsh, D. (1992) 'New Directions in the Study of Policy Networks', *European Journal of Political Research*, 21: 181–205.

Richardson, J. (1996) 'Policy-Making in the EU: Interests, Ideas and Garbage Cans of Primeval Soup', in J. Richardson (ed.) *European Union: Power and Policy-Making*, London: Routledge.

Riedel, M. (1973) 'Geisteswissenschaften – Grundlagenkrise und Grundlagenstreit', in *Meyers Enzyklopädische Lexikon*, vol. 9, Mannheim: Bibliographisches Institut.

Rieger, E. (1995) 'Protective Shelter or Straitjacket: An Institutional Analysis of the Common Agricultural Policy of the European Union', in S. Leibfried and P. Pierson (eds) *European Social Policy: Between Fragmentation and Integration*, Washington, DC: Brookings Institution.

Risse, T. (2000a) ' "Let's Argue!" Communicative Action in World Politics', *International Organization* 54: 1–39.

—— (2000b) 'The Power of Norms versus the Norms of Power: Transnational Civil Society and Human Rights', in A.M. Florini (ed.) *The Third Force: The Rise of Transnational Civil Society*, Tokyo/Washington, DC: Japan Center for International Exchange/Carnegie Endowment for International Peace.

Rittberger, V. (ed.) *Regime Theory and International Relations*, Oxford: Clarendon Press.

Rittberger, V. and Zürn, M. (1990) 'Towards Regulated Anarchy in East–West Relations', in V. Rittberger (ed.) *International Regimes in East–West Politics*, London: Pinter.

Robertson, R. (1992) *Globalization: Social Theory and Global Culture*, London: Sage.

Robinson, W.I. (1996) *Promoting Polyarchy: Globalization, U.S. Intervention, and Hegemony*, Cambridge: Cambridge University Press.

Rosamond, B. (1999a) 'Globalization and the Social Construction of European Identities', *Journal of European Public Policy*, 6(4): 652–668.

—— (1999b) 'Theorizing the European Union: On Disciplines, Knowledge, and Thinking Thoroughly about Integration Theory', *Current Politics and Economics in Europe*, 9(2): 147–163.

—— (2000) *Theories of European Integration*, Basingstoke: Macmillan.

—— (2001a) 'Functions, Levels and European Governance', in H. Wallace (ed.) *One Europe or Several? Interlocking Dimensions of Integration*, Basingstoke: Macmillan.

—— (2001b) 'Constructing Globalisation', in K.M. Fierke and K.E. Jørgensen (eds) *Constructing International Relations: The Next Generation*, New York: M.E. Sharpe.

Rosenau, J.N. (1992) 'Governance, Order, and Change in World Politics', in J.N. Rosenau and E. Czempiel (eds) *Governance without Government: Order and Change in World Politics*, Cambridge: Cambridge University Press.

—— (1997) *Along the Domestic–Foreign Frontier*, Cambridge: Cambridge University Press.

Rosenau, J.N. and Czempiel, E.O. (1992) *Governance Without Government: Order and Change in World Politics*, New York: Cambridge University Press.

Ruggie, J.G. (ed.) (1993) *Multilateralism Matters: The Theory and Praxis of an Institutional Form*, New York: Columbia University Press.

—— (1995) 'The False Premise of Realism', *International Security*, 20: 62–70.

—— (1998) *Constructing the World Polity: Essays on International Institutionalization*, London: Routledge.

Sachs, J. (1998) 'International Economics: Unlocking the Mysteries of Globalization', *Foreign Policy*, 110: 97–111.

Saint-Martin, D. (1998) *How the Reinventing Government Movement in Public Administration was Exported from the United States*, Canadian Political Science Association, University of Ottawa, June.

Salamon, L.M. and Anheier, H.K. (eds) (1997) *Defining the Nonprofit Sector: A Cross-National Analysis*, Manchester: Manchester University Press.

Salskov-Iversen, D. (1999) 'Clients, Consumers or Citizens? Cascading Discourses on the Users of Welfare', in M. Dent, M. O'Neill, and C. Bagley (eds) *Professions, New Public Management and the European Welfare State*, Stoke-on-Trent: Staffordshire University Press.

Salskov-Iversen, D., Hansen, H.K. and Bislev, S. (2000) 'Governmentality, Globalization and Local Practice: Transformation of a Hegemonic Discourse', *Alternatives*, 25: 183–222.

Sand, P.H. (ed.) (1992) *Effectiveness of International Environmental Agreements: A Survey of Existing International Instruments*, Cambridge: Grotius Publications.

Sandel, M. (1996) *Democracy's Discontent*, Cambridge, MA: Harvard University Press.

Sandholz, W. and Stone Sweet A. (eds) (1998) *European Integration and Supranational Governance*, Oxford: Oxford University Press.

Sassen, S. (1998) *Globalization and its Discontents*, New York: Free Press.

Savoie, D.J. (1994) *Thatcher, Reagan, Mulroney: In Search of a New Bureaucracy*, Pittsburgh: Pittsburgh University Press.

Saward, M. (1998) *The Terms of Democracy*, Cambridge: Polity Press.

—— (2000) 'A Crique of Held', in B. Holden (ed.) *Global Democracy: Key Debates*, London: Routledge.

Scharpf, F.W. (1987) *Sozialdemokratische Krisenpolitik in Europa*, Frankfurt/M.: Campus.

—— (1994) 'Community and Autonomy: Multi-level Policy-making in the European Union', *Journal of European Public Policy*, 1: 219–242.

—— (1996a) 'Negative and Positive Integration in the Political Economy of European Welfare States', in G. Marks, F.W. Scharpf, P.C. Schmitter and W. Streeck (eds) *Governance in the European Union*, London: Sage.

—— (1996b) 'Politische Optionen im vollendeten Binnenmarkt', in M. Jachtenfuchs and B. Kohler-Koch (eds) *Europäische Integration*, Opladen: Leske und Budrich.

—— (1999) *Governing in Europe*, Oxford: Oxford University Press.

Scheuerman, W.E. (1999a) 'Economic Globalization and the Rule of Law', *Constellations: An International Journal of Critical and Democratic Theory*, 6: 3–25.

—— (1999b) 'Globalization and the Fate of Law', in D. Dyzenhaus (ed.) *Recrafting the Rule of Law*, Oxford: Hart Publishing.

—— (2000) 'Global Law in Our High-Speed Economy', in V. Gessner (ed.) *The Legal Culture of Global Business Transactions*, Oxford: Hart Publishing.

—— (2001) 'Reflexive Law and the Challenges of Globalization', *Journal of Political Philosophy*, 9(1): 81–102.

Schlotter, P., Ropers, N. and Meyer, B. (1994) *Die neue KSZE: Zukunftsperspektiven einer regionalen Friedensstrategie*, Leverkusen: Leske und Budrich.

Schmitter, P.C. (1996) 'Imagining the Future of the Euro-Polity with the Help of New Concepts', in G. Marks *et al.* (eds) *Governance in the European Union*, London: Sage.

Schmitthoff, C.M. (1968) 'International Business Law: A New Law Merchant', *Current Law and Social Problems*, 2: 129–153.

—— (1982) 'The Nature and Evolution of the Transnational Law of International Commercial Transactions,' in N. Horn and C.M. Schmitthoff (eds) *The Transnational Law of International Commercial Transactions*, Deventer: Kluwer.

Scholte, J.A. (1993) *International Relations of Social Change*, Buckingham: Open University Press.

—— (2000a) *Globalization: A Critical Introduction*, Basingstoke: Macmillan.

—— (2000b) 'Global Civil Society', in N. Woods (ed.) *The Political Economy of Globalization*, Basingstoke: Palgrave.

—— (2002) 'Civil Society and Democracy in Global Governance', *Global Governance*, 8 (forthcoming).

Scholte, J.A. with O'Brien, R. and Williams, M. (1999) 'The WTO and Civil Society', *Journal of World Trade*, 33: 107–124.

Scholte, J.A. with Schnabel, A. (eds) (2002) *Civil Society and Global Finance*, London: Routledge.

Scott, J. and Walters, K.J. (2000) 'Supporting the Wave: Western Political Foundations and the Promotion of a Global Democratic Society', *Global Society*, 14: 237–257.

Searle, J.R. (1995) *The Construction of Social Reality*, London: Penguin.

Sempasa, S. (1992) 'Obstacles to International Commercial Arbitration in African Countries', *International and Comparative Law Quarterly*, 41: 387–413.

Sen, J. (1999) 'A World to Win – But Whose World Is It, Anyway?', in J.W. Foster with A. Anand (eds) *Whose World Is It Anyway?: Civil Society, the United Nations and the Multilateral Future*, Ottawa: United Nations Association in Canada.

Senghaas-Knobloch, E. (1998) *Die internationale Arbeitsorganisation vor neuen Herausforderungen*, artec-paper 61, Bremen.

Senti, M. (1999) 'Globalisierung oder Regionalisierung der internationalen Sozialpolitik? Die Ratifikation der ILO-Konvention im Industrieländervergleich', in A. Busch and T. Plümper (eds) *Nationaler Staat und internationale Wirtschaft: Anmerkungen zum Thema Globalisierung*, Baden-Baden: Nomos.

Shanks, C., Jacobson, H.K. and Kaplan, J.H. (1996) 'Inertia and Change in the Constellation of International Governmental Organizations, 1981–1992', *International Organization* 50: 593–629.

Shapiro, I. (1999) 'Democracy's Edges: Introduction', in I. Shapiro (ed.) *Democracy's Edges*, Cambridge: Cambridge University Press.

Shaw, J. and Wiener, A. (2000) 'The Paradox of the "European Polity", in G. Cowles, M.G. Cowles and M. Smith (eds) *State of the European Union, Vol 5: Risks, Reform, Resistance and Revival*, Oxford: Oxford University Press.

Shaw, M. (2000) *Theory of the Global State: Globality as an Unfinished Revolution*, Cambridge: Cambridge University Press.

Shaw, M.N. (1994) *International Law*, 3rd edn, Cambridge: Cambridge University Press.

Shell, G.R. (1995) 'Trade Legalism and International Relations Theory: An Analysis of the WTO', *Duke Law Journal*, 44: 829–927.

Sherrington, P. (2000a) *The Council of Ministers: Political Authority in the European Union*, London: Pinter.

—— (2000b) 'Shaping the Policy Agenda: Think Tank Activity in the European Union', *Global Society*, 14: 173–189.

Sidenius, N.C. (1999) 'Business, Governance Structures and the EU: The Case of Denmark', in B. Kohler-Koch and R. Eising (eds) *The Transformation of Governance in the European Union*, London: Routledge.

Sieveking, K. (1997) 'Der Europäische Gerichtshof als Motor der sozialen Integration der Gemeinschaft', *Zeitschrift für Sozialreform* 43: 187–207.

Silbey, S. (1997) 'Let Them Eat Cake: Globalization, Postmodern Colonialism, and the Possibilities of Justice', *Law and Society Review*, 31: 207–235.

Sinclair, T. (2000) 'Reinventing Authority: Embedded Knowledge Networks and the New Global Finance', *Environment and Planning C: Government and Policy*, 18: 487–502.

Sklair, L. (2001) *The Transnational Capitalist Class*, Oxford: Blackwell Publishers.

Slaughter, A. (1997) 'The Real New World Order', *Foreign Affairs*, 76(5): 183–198.

Slaughter, A-M., Sweet, A.S. and Weiler, J.H. (1998) *The European Court and National Courts – Doctrine and Jurisprudence: Legal Change in Its Social Context*, Oxford: Hart.

Smart, B. (1999) *Facing Modernity: Ambivalence, Reflexivity and Morality*, London: Sage.

Smillie, I. and Helmich, H. (eds) (1999) *Stakeholders: Government–NGO Partnerships for International Development*, London: Earthscan.

Smith, A. ([1776] 1981) *An Inquiry into the Nature and Causes of the Wealth of Nations*, Oxford: Oxford University Press.

Smith, H. (1996) 'The Silence of the Academics; International Social Theory, Historical Materialism and Political Values', *Review of International Studies* 22: 191–212.

Smith, J., Chatfield, C. and Pagnucco, R. (eds) (1997) *Transnational Social Movements and Global Politics*, Syracuse: Syracuse University Press.

Smith, Martin (1993) *Pressure, Power and Politics: State Autonomy and Policy Networks in Britain and the United States*, Hemel Hempstead: Harvester Wheatsheaf.

Smith, Mike (1996) 'The European Union as an International Actor', in J. Richardson (ed.) *European Union: Power and Policy-Making*, London: Routledge.

Smith, P.J. and Smythe, E. (1999) 'Globalization, Citizenship and Technology: The MAI Meets the Internet', *Canadian Foreign Policy*, 7: 83–105.

Smythe, E. (2000) 'State Authority and Investment Security: Non-State Actors and the Negotiation of the Multilateral Agreement on Investment at the OECD', in R.A. Higgott, G.R.D. Underhill and A. Bieler (eds) *Nonstate Actors and Authority in the Global System*, London: Routledge.

Snidal, D. (1985) 'The Limits of Hegemonic Stability Theory', *International Organization*, 39: 579–614.

Snyder, F. (2001) 'Global Economic Networks and Global Legal Pluralism', in G. Bermann, M. Hedeger and P. Lindseth (eds) *Translantic Regulatory Cooperation*, Oxford: Oxford University Press.

Sørensen, G. (1997) 'An Analysis of Contemporary Statehood: Consequences for Conflict and Cooperation', *Review of International Studies*, 23: 253–269.

—— (1998) 'International Relations Theory After the Cold War', *Review of International Studies*, 24: 83–100.

—— (1999) 'Sovereignty: Change and Continuity in a Fundamental Institution', *Political Studies* 47: 590–604.

Soroos, M.S. (1991) 'A Theoretical Framework for Global Policy Studies', in S.S Nagel (ed.) *Global Policy Studies: International Interaction toward Improving Public Policy*, London: Macmillan.

Sousa Santos B. de (1993) 'The Postmodern Transition: Law and Politics', in A. Sarat and T. Kearns (eds) *The Fate of Law*, Ann Arbor, MI: University of Michigan Press.

Spiro, P.J. (1996) 'New Global Potentates: Nongovernmental Organizations and the "Unregulated" Marketplace', *Cardozo Law Review*, 18: 957–969.

Spruyt, H. (1994) *The Sovereign State and its Competitors. The Analysis of Systems Change*, Princeton, NJ: Princeton University Press.

Stein, A.A. (1983) 'Coordination and Collaboration: Regimes in an Anarchic World', in S.D. Krasner (ed.) *International Regimes*, Ithaca, NY: Cornell University Press.

Sterman, J.D. and Mosekilde, E. (1994) 'Business Cycles and Long Waves: A Behavioral Disequilibrium Perspective', in W. Semmler (ed.) *Business Cycles: Theory and Empirical Methods*, Boston: Kluwer Academic Publishers.

Stienstra, D. (1994) *Women's Movements and International Organizations*, Basingstoke: Macmillan.

Stone, D. (1999) 'Learning Lessons and Transferring Policy Across Time, Space and Disciplines', *Politics*, 19(1): 51–59.

—— (2000) 'Think Tank Transnationalisation and Non Profit Analysis, Advice and Advocacy', *Global Society*, 14: 153–172.

Stopford, J.M. and Strange, S. (1992) *Rival States, Rival Firms: Competition for World Market Shares*, Cambridge: Cambridge University Press.

Strange, S. (1983) '*Cave! hic dragones:* a critique of regimes analysis', in S. Krasner (ed.) *International Regimes*, Ithaca, NY: Cornell University Press.

—— (1988) *States and Markets*, London: Pinter Publishers.

—— (1996) *The Retreat of the State: The Diffusion of Power in the World Economy*, Cambridge: Cambridge University Press.

Streeck, W. (1995) 'Der deutsche Kapitalismus. Gibt es ihn? Kann er überleben?', in IGM-Vorstand (ed.) *Interessenvertretung, Organisationsentwicklung und Gesell-schaftsreform.* Frankfurt a.M.: IGM.

—— (1998) 'Einleitung: Internationale Wirtschaft, nationale Demokratie?', in W. Streeck (ed.) *Internationale Wirtschaft, nationale Demokratie. Herausforderungen für die Demokratietheorie,* Frankfurt a.M.: Campus.

Streeck, W. and Schmitter, P.C. (1991) 'From National Corporatism to Trans-national Pluralism: Organized Interests in the Single European Market', *Politics and Society,* 19: 133–164.

Suganami, H. (1989) *The Domestic Analogy and World Order Proposals,* Cambridge: Cambridge University Press.

Summers, L. (2000) Statement to the International Monetary and Financial Com-mittee, IMF, 16 April 2000.

Swaan, A. de (1992) 'Perspectives for Transnational Social Policy', *Government and Opposition,* 27: 33–52.

Sweet, A.S. and Sandholz, W. (1998) 'Integration, Supranational Governance, and the Institutionalization of the European Polity', in W. Sandholtz and A.S. Sweet (eds) *European Integration and Supranational Governance,* Oxford: Oxford University Press.

Tarrow, S. (1998) *Power in Movement: Social Movements and Contentious Politics,* 2nd edn, Cambridge: Cambridge University Press.

Taylor, C. (1993) *Reconciling the Solitudes: Essays on Canadian Federalism and Nation-alism,* Montreal: McGill-Queen's University Press.

Tesner, S. (2000) *The United Nations and Business,* Basingstoke: Macmillan.

Thompson, D. (1999) 'Democratic Theory and Global Society', *Journal of Political Philosophy,* 7: 111–125.

Thunert, M. (2000) 'Players Beyond Borders? German Think Tanks as Catalysts of Internationalisation', *Global Society,* 14: 191–211.

Tickner, J.A. (1987) *Self-Reliance versus Power Politics: The American and Indian Experience in Building Nation States,* New York: Columbia University Press.

Tilly, C. (1990) *Coercion, Capital and European States: AD 990–1990,* Cambridge: Blackwells.

Tinbergen, J. (1965) *International Economic Integration,* 2nd edn, Amsterdam: Else-vier.

Tomlinson, J. (1999) *Globalization and Culture,* Cambridge: Polity Press.

Trilateral Commission. http://trilateral.org:9999/about.htm. Accessed 5 April 2002.

Trimble, J. (1985) 'International Trade and the Rule of Law', *Michigan Law Review,* 83: 1016–1032.

Twining, W. (1996) 'Globalization and Legal Theory: Some Local Implications', *Current Legal Problems,* 49: 1–42.

UNCTAD (1998) *The Least Developed Countries 1998 Report,* Geneva: UN Conference on Trade and Development.

Underdal, A. (1997) 'Patterns of 'Effectiveness': Examining Evidence from 13 International Regimes', paper presented at the 1997 Annual Meeting of the International Studies Association, Toronto, 19–22 March.

—— (2000) 'One Question, Two Answers', in A. Underdal and K. Hanf (eds) *Inter-national Environmental Agreements and Domestic Politics: The Case of Acid Rain,* Brookfield, VT: Ashgate Publishing Limited.

UNDP (1999) *Globalization with a Human Face: UN Human Development Report 1999*, Oxford: UNDP/OUP.

Union of International Associations (1999) *Yearbook of International Organizations 1999/2000, Vol. 1-B*, Munich: Saur.

United Nations, Secretary General (2000) *Renewing the United Nations*, New York: United Nations.

Valdes, J.G. (1995) *Pinochet's Economists: The Chicago School in Chile*, Cambridge: Cambridge University Press.

Van Rooy, A. (ed.) (1998) *Civil Society and the Aid Industry*, London: Earthscan.

Verdun, A. (1999) 'The Role of the Delors Committee in the Creation of EMU: An Epistemic Community?', *Journal of European Public Policy*, 6(2): 308–328.

Vincent, A. (1993) 'Marx and Law', *Journal of Law and Society*, 20: 371–397.

Vincent, R.J. (1983) 'Change and International Relations', *Review of International Studies*, 9: 63–71.

Viotti, P.R. and Kauppi, M.V. (1993) *International Relations Theory: Realism, Pluralism, Globalism*, New York: Macmillan.

Vogel, D. (1995) *Trading Up: Consumer and Environmental Regulation in a Global Economy*, Cambridge, MA: Harvard University Press.

Walker, R.B.J. (1991) 'On the Spatio-temporal Conditions of Democratic Practice', *Alternatives*, 16: 243–262.

Wallace, H. (1996) 'The Institutions of the EU: Experience and Experiments', in H. Wallace, and W. Wallace (eds) *Policy-Making in the European Union*, 3rd edn, Oxford: Oxford University Press.

—— (2000) 'The Institutional Setting: Five Variations on a Theme', in H. Wallace and W. Wallace (eds) *Policy-Making in the European Union*, 4th edn, Oxford: Oxford University Press.

Wallace, W. (1994) *Regional Integration: The West European Experience*, Washington, DC: Brookings Institution.

—— (2000) 'Europe after the Cold War: Interstate Order or Post-Sovereign Regional System?', in M. Cox, K. Booth, and T. Dunne (eds) *The Interregnum: Controversies in World Politics 1989–1999*, Cambridge: Cambridge University Press.

Wallerstein, I. (1979) *The Capitalist World Economy*, New York: Cambridge University Press.

Walter, G. and Zürn, M. (2001) 'Into the Methodological Void: Drawing Causal Inferences on Systemic Consequences of International Regimes', in A. Underdal and O. Young (eds) *Regime Consequences: Methodological Challenges and Research Strategies* (forthcoming).

Waltz, K. (1979) *Theory of International Politics*, New York: Random House.

Waltz, K.N. (1979) *Theory of International Politics*, Waltham, MA: Addison–Wesley.

Wapner, P. (1996) *Environmental Activism and World Civic Politics*, New York: SUNY Press.

Warleigh, A. (1998) 'Better the Devil You Know? Synthetic and Confederal Understandings of European Unification', *West European Politics*, 21(3) 1–18.

Waterman, P. (1998) *Globalization, Social Movements, and the New Internationalism*, London: Mansell.

Waters, M. (1995) *Globalization*, London: Routledge.

Weber, C. (1995) *Simulating Sovereignty: Intervention, the State and Symbolic Exchange*, Cambridge: Cambridge University Press.

Wedel, J. (1998) *Collision and Collusion: The Strange Case of Western Aid to Eastern Europe*, London: St Martin's Press.

Weiss E.B. (ed.) (1992) *Environmental Change and International Law: New Challenges and Dimensions*, New York: United Nations University Press.

Weiss, T.G. and Gordenker, L. (eds) (1996) *NGOs, The UN, and Global Governance*, London: Lynne Reinner.

Wendt, A. (1995) 'Constructing International Politics', *International Security*, 20: 71–81.

—— (1999) *Social Theory of International Politics*, Cambridge: Cambridge University Press.

White, M. (1977) *Systems of States*, Leicester: Leicester University Press.

Whitman, R. (1997) 'The International Identity of the EU: Identity as Instruments', in A. Landau and R. Whitman (eds) *Rethinking the European Union: Institutions, Interests, Identities*, Basingstoke: Macmillan.

Whitworth, S. (1994) *Feminism and International Relations: Toward a Political Economy of Gender in Interstate and Non-governmental Institutions*, London: Macmillan.

Willetts, P. (ed.) (1996) *'Conscience of the World': The Influence of Non-Governmental Organisations in the UN System*, Washington, DC: Brookings Institution.

Wood, A. and Welch, C. (1998) *Policing the Policemen: The Case for an Independent Evaluation Mechanism for the IMF*, London/Washington, DC: Bretton Woods Project/Friends of the Earth-US.

Woods, N. (1999a) 'Order, Globalisation and Inequality in World Politics', in A. Hurrell and N. Woods (eds) *Inequality, Globalisation and World Politics*, Oxford: Oxford University Press.

—— (1999b) 'Good Governance in International Organization', *Global Governance*, 5: 39–61.

World Bank (1992) *Governance and Development*, Washington, DC: The World Bank.

—— (1997) *World Development Report*, Washington, DC: The World Bank.

World Commission on Environment and Development (1987) *Our Common Future*, Oxford: Oxford University Press.

Wright, E.O. (1997) *Class Counts: Comparative Studies in Class Analysis*, Cambridge: Cambridge University Press.

Wright, S. (1991) 'Economic Rights and Social Justice: A Feminist Analysis of some International Human Rights Conventions', *Australian Yearbook of International Law* 12: 241–264.

Young, O.R. (1979) *Compliance and Public Authority: A Theory with International Implications*, Baltimore: Johns Hopkins University Press.

—— (1994) *International Governance: Protecting the Environment in a Stateless Society*, Ithaca, NY: Cornell University Press.

—— (1997) 'Global Governance: Toward a Theory of Decentralized World Order', in O.R. Young (ed.) *Global Governance: Drawing Insights from the Environmental Experience*, Cambridge, MA: The MIT Press.

Young, O.R. and Osherenko, G. (1993) 'Testing Theories of Regime Formation: Findings from a Large Collaborative Research Project', in V. Rittberger (ed.) *Regime Theory and International Relations*, Oxford: Oxford University Press.

Zacher, M.W. (1992) 'The Decaying Pillars of the Westphalian Temple: Implications for International Order and Governance', in J.N. Rosenau and E. Czempiel (eds) *Governance without Government: Order and Change in World Politics*, Cambridge: Cambridge University Press.

Zacher, M.W. with Sutton, B. (1996) *Governing Global Networks: International Regimes for Transportation and Communications*, Cambridge: Cambridge University Press.

Zangl, B. and Zürn, M. (1999) 'The Effects of Denationalisation on Security in the OECD World', *Global Society*, 13: 139–161.

Zürn, M. (1992) *Interessen und Institutionen in der internationalen Politik: Grundlegung und Anwendungen des situationsstrukturellen Ansatzes*, Opladen: Leske und Budrich.

—— (1997) 'Assessing State Preferences and Explaining Institutional Choice. The Case of Intra-German Trade', *International Studies Quarterly*, 41: 295–320.

—— (1998) *Regieren jenseits des Nationalstaates: Globalisierung und Denationalisierung als Chance*, Frankfurt am Main: Suhrkamp.

—— (1999) *The State in the Post-National Constellation: Societal Denationalization and Multi-level Governance*, University of Bremen: mimeo, draft.

—— (2002) 'The Politics of Denationalization – An Introduction', in M. Zürn (ed.) *The Politics of Denationalization*, forthcoming.

Zürn, M. and Walter, G. (1999) 'Into the Methodological Void. Drawing Causal Inferences on Systemic Consequences of International Regimes', paper prepared for the workshop *The Study of Regime Consequences: Methodological Challenges and Research Strategies*, Oslo, 19–20 November.

Zürn, M., Walter, G., Dreher, S. and Beisheim, M. (2000) 'Postnationale Politik? Über den politischen Umgang mit den Denationalisierungsherausforderungen Internet, Klimawandel und Migration', *Zeitschrift für Internationale Beziehungen*, 7: 297–329.

Index